PROPHETIC DIVERGENCE

Distinguishing Characteristics of the Third Prophetic Dimension

ROBERT G. PAUL

ISBN 978-1-64140-003-9 (paperback)
ISBN 978-1-64140-005-3 (hardcover)
ISBN 978-1-64140-004-6 (digital)

Christian Faith Publishing, Inc.
832 Park Avenue
Meadville, PA 16335
www.christianfaithpublishing.com

Note regarding capitalization: "Church" or "Community" is capitalized when referring to the global or universal, many-membered body of believers or saints in Christ. When these words are not capitalized, they are referring to a localized body of believers or smaller subset of the global whole. The word "Kingdom" is capitalized when referring only to God's Kingdom, as are certain pronouns that refer to any member of the Godhead. The name "satan" and all related forms are not capitalized according to standard grammatical rules because we choose to degrade, diminish, and disregard him in light of Jesus's finished work on the cross.

To the emerging Elijah company of the third prophetic dimension

May you find the strength, courage, and boldness to arise and confront Jezebel and the false prophets of Baal. And may your ascendance serve to accelerate the advancement of the Kingdom of Heaven, hasten the return of Christ, and propel us toward the ultimate finish.

CONTENTS

Chapter 4

Chapter 5

Chapter 6

Chapter 7

INTRODUCTION

THROUGHOUT THE HISTORY of God's Covenant Community (Church), especially during times and seasons of reformation, that which was commonly taught, believed, and practiced would go through a divine process of upgrade, revision, or refinement that usually culminated in a departure or divergence from the old religious order or paradigm. The word *divergence* simply means that there is a distinct separation, departure, or moving away from a set (former) course, convention, or norm. It is normally characterized by a difference of opinion that ultimately results in the newer opinion deviating from the common path established by the old. Of course, any deviation from that which is conventional or common inevitably leads some—if not most—to believe that this new "opinion" or path is in error. Certainly, a look at Scripture and even Church history itself lends credence to the fact that this is very often the case.

For example, the apostle Peter warned that false prophets and teachers would arise that would *bring in destructive heresies*, which they eventually did, probably proclaiming these heresies as "new" revelation or insight from God (2 Pet. 2:1). Jesus and Paul gave similar warnings regarding the proliferation of false prophets, teachers, and teachings during that period just prior to Christ's return (Matt. 24:11; 1 Tim. 4:1–2). Many have arisen in times past who have sought to introduce "new" doctrines into the Body that were really destructive heresies, some quite subtly, making them much harder to detect or discern. The same is true even today. There is so much false teaching flooding the airwaves and media (including print) today that many believers no longer have any capacity to divide truth from error. However, that being said, just as "new" doesn't necessarily mean it's from God, "new" doesn't necessarily mean it is erroneous either. There is undeniable proof found in both history and Scripture that proves that such a divergence can be fueled by the Spirit of God.

The most notable example of this in Scripture was when Jesus emerged on the scene to establish a New Covenant Kingdom Community that was distinct and separate from religious Judaism. Up until that time, the nation of Israel, and Judaism in particular, was the primary focal point of God's Kingdom expression in the earth. The religious rituals, traditions, and practices they had grown accustomed to had been given to their forefathers by the command of God through the prophet Moses, with seemingly no expiration date. It was more than just a religion; it was their identity deeply embedded within the very culture of the nation. But soon, there was a splitting away from the old Judaic forms and practices that once defined their spirituality and religious culture. Through the teachings of first John and then Jesus, a divergent "opinion" was formed. New divine insight and Kingdom technology was thus released in the earth, causing a major shift and separation in what is generally recognized as the first major reformation of God's people.[1]

The early disciples and followers of Jesus in Jerusalem did not cease being Jews. In fact, they continued to maintain many of their old customs as pertaining to the Law (Torah). However, the shift occurred in their mentality. Their spirituality and right standing with God were no longer being defined by the outward observances of the law, the blood sacrifices of animals, or participation in religious holy days. They were more refined and upgraded in their approach to worshiping God. Their standards had been raised in recognition of the fact that what had once been acceptable in the past was now no longer valid in the new. Instead of focusing on outward behavior only or cleaning only the "outside of the cup," there was a new awareness and attention being placed on allowing the Spirit of God to transform the inside, thus making the outside more manageable (Matt. 23:25–28).

The message of the Kingdom Jesus taught differed greatly from the established religious doctrine taught and practiced by the religious leaders of that day. It was not very long before Jesus and His followers were viewed by these religious leaders as not just separate but deviant and destructive. And as is usually the case with all those who radically depart or deviate from that which is religiously common or conventional, they were treated as rebels and as heretics by those who had been entrenched in the old system (Matt. 10:16–26; Acts 4:1–22, 5:22–42).

Approximately, 1,500 years later, we see the same principle of divergence taking place again during the reformation with Martin Luther. After having served faithfully for several years as both a priest as well as a professor of theology within the Roman Catholic Institution—the most dominant and established Christian religious system of that time—Luther began to receive new revelation and understanding of the Scriptures. This new insight and understanding prompted a new spirit of inquiry in the heart of Luther regarding the current teachings and practices of the Roman Catholic Church. Inquiry led to scrutiny, causing Luther to recognize that many of the current beliefs and practices of the Church were inaccurate or false. He began to develop and express a different opinion—an unpopular one!

In an attempt to publicly challenge or correct these false beliefs and practices, Luther wrote and later published his *Ninety-Five Theses*, as well as several other works, which quickly accelerated the divergence from the Roman Catholic Church. Luther began to teach and establish a new and higher standard, which deviated both in theology as well as practice from the old religious order. And once again, a radical break from religious tradition and convention occurred, causing Luther—including all those who ascribed to these new reformation positions and mentalities—to be labeled as heretics rejected by the established religious system and treated as impenitent rebels.

Several important observations can be made from these two major examples of divergence listed above. As alluded to before, divergence does not necessarily mean deviation in error or apostasy. There is a world of difference between *apostasy*—which is a corrupt departure from formerly established religious truth, doctrine, principles, and/or practices—and *apostolic reformation*, which is characterized by new apostolic insight and departure from formerly established and/or deeply entrenched religious error, blindness, or tradition. Apostasy is the "falling away" or downward degradation from God's established truth or pattern, but apostolic reformation or divine divergence is the recognition and elevation of truth previously hidden or concealed for a "finishing" generation. This "new" truth may conflict with popular religious belief, understanding, or practice; nevertheless, it will ALWAYS bring us back to God's original intent and purpose.

Divergence, therefore, can be initiated and driven by heaven itself. This begs the question: How are we able to differentiate between a holy or divine divergence and a heretical or diabolical one? There is a significant common denominator in the examples above that can give us a good clue as to where the divergence originates. When a divergence issues from heaven, God always seeks to challenge the religious status quo in order to raise or elevate the current standards of worship and obedience to a higher level. When a divergence issues out of a carnal or demonic origin, there is always a deterioration or degradation in the standards of worship and obedience. The only exception, which really isn't an exception, is when the new teaching or opinion gives the guise or appearance of elevating the standards of worship and obedience but really does not. In reality, this false teaching distorts sound doctrine in order to bring people into greater religious bondage, most often through various forms of false asceticism, which the teachers themselves fail to thoroughly practice (1 Tim. 4:1–5).

Another significant observation from Jesus and Luther is that *divergence always precedes reformation*. In other words, there can be no reformation without a divergence.

For more than a decade, as far back as the year 2000 or earlier, there have been declarations and demonstrations of reformation among God's Covenant Kingdom People we often refer to as the

Church. Talk about reformation has increased significantly during the last six or seven years. However, in Christian circles, reformation means different things to different people. For some people, reformation must happen primarily in society and effected by the Church. For others, reformation consists solely of changing external structures and patterns in the way we do "church." But true reformation is deeper than that. It requires a change of heart and a change of thinking. It requires a divergence of thought and opinion that causes a head-on collision with commonly accepted and established religious (Christian) thought, values, and practice that are inherently wrong or in need of revision. It requires a distaste for what *is* and a greater preference for what *should be.*

It is my belief, in concert with many others, that we are in a key season of reformation, and it begins with us—His chosen people! Divine insight has led to inquiry, and inquiry has led to deep scrutiny of every facet of our religious existence—from basic and foundational issues such as prayer, to the ministry and function of apostles and prophets today. This book will attempt to identify and articulate the key issues of divergence relative to the prophetic and the new prophetic order that is emerging in the earth as the precursor to what some believe to be the third and final reformation.[2]

Notes

[1]   One can also argue that Moses was the first major reformer and that the law he received and established amongst a newly liberated people constituted the first major reformation.

[2]   The third and final reformation is taught by Dr. Bill Hamon.

1

THE PROPHETIC REDEFINED

THE CHURCH HAS once again entered into a season of major reformation, and God is once again upgrading and refining our current beliefs and practices to a much higher standard than we have known or experienced before. Greater accuracy and Kingdom conformity are being demanded in this hour by the heavenly Architect—the Holy Spirit—and a new divergence is beginning to emerge amongst the prophetic. God's primary agents of reformation are themselves being reformed and personally transformed in obedience to these new heavenly requirements.

The prophetic ministry itself, or what we have usually defined as being *prophetic*, is being radically redefined to accommodate these new standards and requirements, creating a difference of opinion and estrangement from the old prophetic order.

One of the issues that has really grieved my heart of late is the tendency for many to make the word *prophetic* something common and mundane. It is often used trivially, with very little thought given to its true meaning or definition. Like the term *Christian*, it has almost lost its honor and validity in the minds of men. While this "profanation" of the prophetic can be attributed largely to a misapplication of the term by many who have used it ignorantly and erroneously, a lot has to do with poor definition. The former practice or tendency of applying the adjective "prophetic" to those operating or prophesying solely by gifting or to the ability to accurately predict or forecast future events or even to the spectacular ability to disclose detailed or secret information about an individual by word of knowledge is no longer valid. This may come as a shock to many of you, but your ability to prophesy accurate details or foretell future events does not necessarily make you prophetic. Neither does your ability to interpret dreams nor your tendency to experience visions. While these may all be valid aspects of prophetic ministry, neither one of them, in and of themselves, constitutes what it really means to be genuinely prophetic. Instead of misusing the term *prophetic* to describe such people, we should prefer the term *gifted*.

The true prophetic dimension is much deeper than gifting. Some psychics are very gifted, but that doesn't make them prophetic. Judging ministry by gifting or supernatural manifestations alone is a very poor way to determine if someone is genuinely prophetic. For instance, supernatural signs and wonders are stated by Paul as being one of the qualifying or validating marks of an apostle, but almost everyone knows that manifesting signs and wonders does not necessarily mean you're an apostle (2 Cor. 12:12).[1] The same could be said of planting churches or being "sent" as a missionary in global missions. While these are all credible aspects of apostolic ministry, being a church planter does not necessarily make you an apostle or apostolic. Neither does being sent as a missionary. Giftings can be counterfeited, and activities can be copied. Or your gifting may be genuine, but you're still lacking in other more important areas. These are mere surface issues, and there is much more to the apostolic or prophetic than what can be seen on the surface, much like an iceberg.

The Iceberg Principle

Icebergs are very fascinating, at least to me. According to Wikipedia, "An iceberg is a large piece of freshwater ice that has broken off a glacier or an ice shelf and is floating freely in open water."[2] Interesting, right? But hardly fascinating. After all, what can be so fascinating about a floating mass of ice in the ocean? I will tell you.

The fascinating part about icebergs is in how much of their mass is actually exposed above the surface of the water. Because of the density of ice, which is less than that of sea water, typically only a small fraction of the iceberg—less than one-tenth of its total mass or volume—is ever visible above the surface of the water.[3] In other words, there is far greater mass and substance beneath the surface than what is exposed above the surface. This communicates a very profound principle and provides a very powerful and accurate image or example of what it means to be prophetic.

The gifts, manifestations, and activities that are normally ascribed to prophetic ministry such as prophecy, visions, supernatural knowledge, etc., are only the "tip of the iceberg" (pun intended) with regard to what it means to be genuinely prophetic. This is only a small fraction. There is much more to being prophetic than meets the eye. The true identity, reality, character, and substance of the prophetic lie much deeper—hidden from view.

This brings us to another fascinating discovery about icebergs: the true shape or architecture of the underwater portion of an iceberg can be difficult to determine by looking solely at the portion above the surface.[4] An iceberg can take on a completely different shape or form underneath. In other words, you can't define an iceberg based upon what you see on the surface because nine out of ten times, you will be wrong! What you see on the surface usually doesn't provide enough data for you to formulate a clear or accurate picture. Therefore, in order to judge correctly, you must look past the surface. This, again, is a very important principle. If we are to make an accurate judgment on what is truly prophetic, we can't depend on surface manifestations of gifting or accuracy of content. We must go beyond the surface in order to ascertain the true architecture of the ministry. This is called the *iceberg principle*.

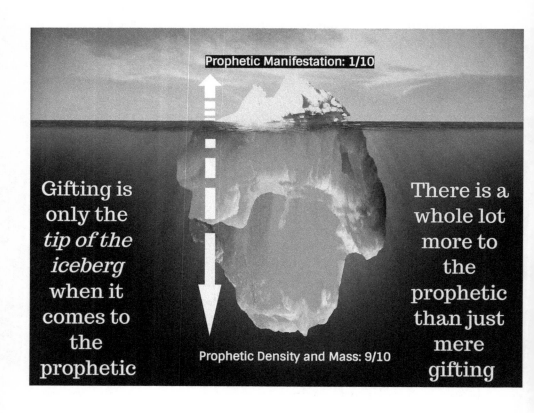

Prophetic Terminology

Depending on the particular version of the Bible you are using, performing a basic word search in order to ascertain how many times the word *prophetic* is used in the Bible would come up empty (e.g. the KJV and CEV) or with varied results (compare NKJV, ESV, and AMP). The reason for this is simple: people choose to translate certain words and phrases differently from others. From a technical standpoint, the adjective *prophetic* is only found twice in Scripture, and only in the New Testament (Rom. 16:26; 2 Pet. 1:19).

> *But now has been made manifest, and by the **prophetic** Scriptures has been made known to all nations, according to the commandment of the everlasting God, for obedience to the faith.* (Emphasis mine)

> *And so we have the **prophetic** word confirmed, which you do well to heed as a light that shines in a dark place, until the day dawns and the morning star rises in your hearts.* (Emphasis mine)

The word translated *prophetic* above is the Greek word **prophētikós**, an adjective formed from another Greek word, *prophḗtēs*, meaning prophet. It is used to describe the ministry of the prophet and, more specifically, their inspired utterance (or writing) of what has since become scripture, as evident from its usage above.[5] You will note that the root of this word is *prophet*, and it is applied narrowly to the prophet and/or his inspired ministry of revealing the divine will and purposes of God. It is never used in a general sense for all prophecy or those who are merely gifted to prophesy.

While the word *prophetic* is used only but a couple of times in Scripture, the terminology most often used is *prophet* (Gen. 20:7), *prophetess* (Ex. 15:20), *company of prophets* (1 Sam. 10:5), *sons of the prophets* (2 Kings 2:3), and those *who prophesy* (Acts 21:9). But there is a significant difference in Scripture between someone who merely prophesies and the ministry of a prophet.

The word *prophetic* in our English usage adds the suffix *ic* to the noun *prophet* (prophet-ic), thus forming an adjective that also carries with it the connotation of having a similar character, form, or manner of a prophet. Note that the operative word here again is **prophet** and not *prophecy* or *prophesy*. This means that to fully understand or comprehend the term *prophetic*, one must first seek to understand the nature and character of a prophet and his ministry. This cannot be accomplished by simply doing a word study. Most biblical lexicons provide a very broad and somewhat obscure definition of what a prophet is, emphasizing mostly their ability to foretell events, speak or teach by inspiration, or bring exhortation and reproof, but there is more to their ministry than this.

Seven Distinct Characteristics of the Prophet's Ministry

There are seven distinct characteristics of the prophet's ministry that can be extrapolated from Scripture. These characteristics clearly distinguish it from one who merely prophesies by gifting or otherwise. This is by no means an exhaustive list, but for the purpose of this writing, we will focus on these seven.

1. *Insight*

One of the most distinguishing characteristics of a prophet is his divine insight. The word *insight* describes the ability to see or comprehend (by the Spirit) that which is otherwise hidden. To have insight means to have spiritual sight. By very definition, a prophet is *one who sees* (Heb. *ro'eh*). They're not blinded by fleshly ambitions, carnal concerns, religious traditions, political or religious allegiances, patriotism, national pride, or popularity of opinion. They don't stumble around in darkness, ignorant of the plans and purposes of God on a personal or corporate level. This type of sightedness does not come by gifting alone; it comes through intimate relationship.

I have known many gifted prophesiers (claiming to be prophets or prophetic) who were able to give impressive words of knowledge and personal prophecies to individuals yet were totally blind and clueless regarding issues in their own lives. I'm not just talking about having blind spots—that can happen to any one of us, including prophets. They were internally blind. There was no capacity to accurately hear and respond to the voice of God in their own personal spheres of existence. These same prophesiers were often in need of prayer and personal prophecy for dealing with issues in their own lives or in making major decisions. When you're operating solely by gifting, it is easy to hear God for others but much harder for yourself. There's a reason for this. The gifts of God were given *to* us but not necessarily *for* us; they were given for the benefit of others (1 Cor. 12:7). The only gift that was given for our own personal benefit is the gift of speaking in tongues (1 Cor. 14:4). Therefore, people prophesying by gifting alone may be able to give incredible prophecies yet in their own personal lives be stumbling along in blindness or be spiritually deficient. I have seen it all too often.

Please don't misunderstand. This doesn't mean that prophets always know everything or are never in need of personal direction or guidance because that simply isn't true. But what it does mean is that true prophets and prophetic people are not shallow one-dimensional prophesiers, able to hear God for others but hardly ever for themselves. Abraham was called a prophet of God before ever uttering one single word of prophecy (Gen. 20:7). It was his ability to accurately hear and respond to the voice of God in his own personal life and sphere of relationships that truly qualified him to be prophetic, not his ability to declare what God was saying to others.

Abraham demonstrated divine insight from the moment he was commanded by God to leave his country and his father's house and migrate to a place that he had never known or seen before (Gen. 12:1). This didn't just require great faith; it required great spiritual sight because the only information he would have to go on would be what God would *show* him.

Abraham expressed insight into the hearts and culture of the Egyptians when he had Sarah (Sarai) pretend to be his sister. By having both insight and foresight, Abraham was able to hatch a plan (even if it was a deceptive one) in order to navigate the life-threatening pitfalls that lay ahead (Gen. 12:10–20). Note that there is no scriptural indication that Abraham warned Sarah to employ the same deceptive tactics in the other places they sojourned or dwelt, except perhaps Gerar with Abimelech (Gen. 20). This suggests that Abraham had specific insight regarding Egypt and the other places they dwelt. This insight served to help tailor his (and Sarah's) approach to the specific region and nation of people with whom they would eventually come into contact.

Abraham also demonstrated insight by having Lot separate from him (Gen. 13). And then again by waging a successful war against four formidable kings and their armies with only 318 men when Lot was captured (Gen. 14). If you think Abraham and his men were able to win that battle with such overwhelming odds against them because they were a bunch of well-armed and well-trained super soldiers, you're greatly mistaken. It took the grace of God and divine insight to strategically wage such a successful warfare.

One could argue that some of the insight Abraham walked in was not purely spiritual. He consciously made himself aware of his surroundings. He wasn't shut up and bent over in prayer all day expecting to receive divine insight by spiritual osmosis, with no practical understanding or common sense relative to everyday life. Having insight, therefore, means that prophets and prophetic people should not be ignorant or stupid. Make yourself aware of what is going on around you. Be in the know! Be in a continual state of spiritual development, not just in prayer but in the study of the Word. Prophets should be great students of the Word, pregnant with great revelation and insight regarding its mysteries, and knowledgeable concerning the divine architecture of God and His Kingdom (Ex. 25–30; Amos 3:7).

It is believed that one of the main components of the prophetic training schools established by Samuel was training in the law or Torah—the literal "bible" of that generation.

> Samuel took measures to make his work of restoration permanent as well as effective for the moment. For this purpose he instituted companies, or colleges, of prophets. One we find in his lifetime at Ramah (1 Sam 19:19–20); others

afterward at Bethel (2 Kings 2:3), Jericho (2:5), Gilgal (4:38), and elsewhere (6:1)… Their chief subject of study was, no doubt, the law and its interpretation-oral, as distinct from symbolical, teaching being henceforward tacitly transferred from the priestly to the prophetical order.[6]

Samuel understood the importance of his young prophets in training both knowing the law (scriptures) as well as being able to accurately interpret them. It was a foundational aspect of their development. The reason for this is simple: if you cannot accurately interpret what is written, there is no way you will ever be able to accurately interpret what is not. Sight begins with understanding. You must first learn to accurately interpret what God has *said* before you can transition to comprehend the deeper things of what God is *saying*. When you neglect to know and understand the Scriptures, you weaken and undermine the integrity of your prophetic revelation. To the degree that there is neglect or error in this regard will be the degree that there is distortion and inaccuracy in your prophetic ministry.

The responsibility to know and handle the Word correctly is a major responsibility of prophets. Most of the Bible was written by prophets (i.e. the Old Testament) and then later interpreted by apostles in the New Testament. Apostles and prophets are uniquely qualified to interpret what was written through the divine insight they possess. They are able to see beyond the dark shroud of religious traditions, deception, man-made doctrines, and error to accurately interpret the divine will of God for their generation. This means that prophets and prophetic people cannot be wishy-washy in their approach to growing in knowledge and understanding of Scripture, as has often been the case among those who often claim to be such.

It is deeply saddening to me to see how biblically ignorant many who claim to be prophets or prophetic people are today. In the New Testament, prophets are closely associated with, and ministering alongside, teachers (Acts 13:1–2); however, today, no two ministries could be further polarized or apart. Many who call themselves prophets today are so reckless and irresponsible with the written Word, seemingly unable to rightly divide or interpret the Word of truth, that they are often at odds with skilled teachers for breaking every hermeneutical and exegetical rule in the book. This is not to say that teachers are always faultless or justified in their criticisms of prophets, because some teachers can often be too rigid, dogmatic and religious in their approach. But prophets in Scripture could teach and minister amicably alongside teachers, with a significant measure of agreement and cohesiveness, because they demonstrated a degree of skill and knowledge in their handling of the Word. Having divine insight does not make you ignorant or reckless. On the contrary, it makes you intelligent and properly grounded when combined with diligent study.

2. Integrity

Integrity is the most important and foundational aspect of every prophet's life and ministry. It is the fundamental standard of everything prophetic. Without integrity, everything falls apart. The word *integrity* means to be whole, complete, and undivided;[7] without hypocrisy or duplicity. This means that the prophet's life, character, and actions are consistent with the word he declares or proclaims. There is no disconnect between his life and his message; no contradiction between what he says and who he is. The prophet literally embodies and becomes the heavenly message. He becomes the "word made flesh," as it were (John 1:14).

This is much more than just strict adherence to a set of moral absolutes or principles. It goes beyond mere good reputation, good deeds, or upright character. You can find both religious as well as nonreligious people who meet these shallow standards, but that doesn't necessarily make them prophets or prophetic. The integrity being described here is best understood by examining a common and consistent theme relative to prophets and their ministry in Scripture. Here are three examples:

> *In the year that Tartan came to Ashdod, when*
> *Sargon the king of Assyria sent him, and he fought*

against Ashdod and took it, at the same time the Lord spoke by Isaiah the son of Amoz, saying, "Go, and remove the sackcloth from your body, and take your sandals off your feet." And he did so, walking naked and barefoot. Then the Lord said, "Just as My servant Isaiah has walked naked and barefoot three years for a sign and a wonder against Egypt and Ethiopia, so shall the king of Assyria lead away the Egyptians as prisoners and the Ethiopians as captives, young and old, naked and barefoot, with their buttocks uncovered, to the shame of Egypt. (Is. 20:1–4)

"You also, son of man, take a clay tablet and lay it before you, and portray on it a city, Jerusalem. Lay siege against it, build a siege wall against it, and heap up a mound against it; set camps against it also, and place battering rams against it all around. Moreover take for yourself an iron plate, and set it as an iron wall between you and the city. Set your face against it, and it shall be besieged, and you shall lay siege against it. This will be a sign to the house of Israel. "Lie also on your left side, and lay the iniquity of the house of Israel upon it. According to the number of the days that you lie on it, you shall bear their iniquity. For I have laid on you the years of their iniquity, according to the number of the days, three hundred and ninety days; so you shall bear the iniquity of the house of Israel. And when you have completed them, lie again on your right side; then you shall bear the iniquity of the house of Judah forty days. I have laid on you a day for each year. Therefore you shall set your face toward the siege of Jerusalem; your arm shall be uncovered, and you shall prophesy against it. And surely I will restrain you so that you cannot turn from one side to another

till you have ended the days of your siege. "Also take for yourself wheat, barley, beans, lentils, millet, and spelt; put them into one vessel, and make bread of them for yourself. During the number of days that you lie on your side, three hundred and ninety days, you shall eat it. And your food which you eat shall be by weight, twenty shekels a day; from time to time you shall eat it. You shall also drink water by measure, one-sixth of a hin; from time to time you shall drink. And you shall eat it as barley cakes; and bake it using fuel of human waste in their sight." Then the Lord said, "So shall the children of Israel eat their defiled bread among the Gentiles, where I will drive them." So I said, "Ah, Lord God! Indeed I have never defiled myself from my youth till now; I have never eaten what died of itself or was torn by beasts, nor has abominable flesh ever come into my mouth." Then He said to me, "See, I am giving you cow dung instead of human waste, and you shall prepare your bread over it." Moreover He said to me, "Son of man, surely I will cut off the supply of bread in Jerusalem; they shall eat bread by weight and with anxiety, and shall drink water by measure and with dread, that they may lack bread and water, and be dismayed with one another, and waste away because of their iniquity. (Ezek. 4:1–17)

The word of the Lord that came to Hosea the son of Beeri, in the days of Uzziah, Jotham, Ahaz, and Hezekiah, kings of Judah, and in the days of Jeroboam the son of Joash, king of Israel. When the Lord began to speak by Hosea, the Lord said to Hosea: "Go, take yourself a wife of harlotry And children of harlotry, For the land has committed great harlotry By departing from the Lord." So he went and took Gomer the daughter of Diblaim, and she conceived and bore him a son. Then the Lord said to him: "Call his name Jezreel, For in a little while I will avenge the bloodshed of Jezreel on the house of Jehu, And bring an end to the kingdom of the house of Israel. It shall come to pass in that day That I will break the bow of Israel in the Valley of Jezreel." And she conceived again and bore a daughter. Then God said to him: "Call her name Lo-Ruhamah, For I will no longer have mercy on the house of Israel, But I will utterly take them away. Yet I will have mercy on the house of Judah, Will save them by the Lord their God, And will not save them by bow, Nor by sword or battle, By horses or horsemen." Now when she had weaned Lo-Ruhamah, she conceived and bore a son. Then God said: "Call his name Lo-Ammi, For you are not My people, And I will not be your God. (Hosea 1:1–9)

In the biblical accounts or examples listed above, and despite the diversity in each of these individual prophets and their experiences, there is one common denominator that ties them all together and becomes the basis for defining authentic prophetic ministry—God demands more than just the prophet's words or voice; God requires that their very lives and actions become His message! Isaiah had to be willing to surrender his pride and divest himself of human glory and dignity to walk "naked and barefoot" in public for three years as a prophetic sign to the nation.

Some scholars and Bible interpreters argue that the word *naked* in this context does not necessarily imply complete and utter nakedness or being "absolutely without any clothing" (A person was called naked, they say, whose outer garments were thrown aside, leaving nothing but the tunic and girdle. Thus, in their interpretation, Isaiah was naked by simply removing his sackcloth mantle.)[8] However, this is an inaccurate interpretation considering the fact that God clearly identifies complete nakedness (*with their buttocks uncovered*) as the coming reality that Isaiah's prophetic symbolism was meant to represent. The sign was meant to mirror the substance of the coming reality in detail. Therefore, what was being demanded of Isaiah in this instance was no less degrading and shameful than what the prisoners experienced as they were led away naked and captive. Can you even begin to imagine the great price of discomfort and humiliation Isaiah endured in order to accurately express the heart and mind of God to His people? Think of what this would have done to his reputation, family, and circle of friends.

Ezekiel was commanded to enact a siege, lay on his left side for 390 days (almost 13 months), lay on his right side for 40 days, and then eat the meager, lowly rations of someone starving (about 8 ounces of bread baked over cow's dung and a little more than a half liter of water per day).[9] Even though we are not told how long the periods were that he had to lay on his side, we know it must have become extremely uncomfortable if the prophet needed restraints to keep from turning over before completion (Ezek. 4:8). This translates into a little over fourteen months of not only great inconvenience and discomfort but intense suffering and deprivation as well. How would you like to be a prophet now?

Then we have Hosea, who was basically commanded to marry a whore—meaning an unfaithful woman who consistently indulges in sexual sin and violates the marriage covenant—and raise her bastard children. It is believed that only the first child this woman bore to Hosea was his (Jezreel) and that the other two (Lo-Ruhamah and Lo-Ammi) were fathered through adulterous relationships. The hurt, betrayal, and emotional distress that Hosea must have endured are incomprehensible, at least to me, yet not only his life but that of his family became a prophetic message.

It is important that you don't become distracted by the bizarre actions or activities listed in these accounts and lose sight of the underlying principle of integrity they communicate. The principle here is that the prophetic is not shallow or one-dimensional but multidimensional and comprehensively holistic. It is not merely about having a word from God or hearing His voice; it is about *becoming* God's "word made flesh" and *being* God's voice. To put it succinctly, the prophetic is a lifestyle.

Whenever I am given the opportunity to teach at a "prophetic" training seminar, I usually take the time to emphasize this point to the students. Attending a training seminar or taking a course is not going to make anyone prophetic.[10] Most of the time, the emphasis is placed on teaching others how to prophesy or hear God's voice, but as we have said before, there is more to being prophetic than that. Generally, it takes less than twenty minutes to teach someone the basics of how to prophesy (that's the easy part); but it can take a lifetime to train someone to be truly prophetic. You won't find any prophet in Scripture who was trained and ready for public ministry in a matter of weeks or months. This type of integrity and prophetic lifestyle doesn't come out of reading books or attending training seminars. It requires faith, maturity, and absolute surrender. Before you can become God's voice, every other voice in your life has to die. Every dimension of your earthly existence must be subject to God's divine influence. This has both practical as well as internal ramifications.

On a practical level, God's voice can be demonstrated in what we wear (or don't wear) as it pertains to clothing (e.g. Isaiah); by what (and how) we eat or choose to allow our flesh to consume, as well as how we posture ourselves during times of offense and opposition (e.g. Ezekiel); or through our marriage and family relationships or willingness to forgive and keep covenant with those who have betrayed and hurt us at the deepest level (e.g. Hosea).

From an internal point of view, becoming God's voice means transparency; humility; rejection of pride, human reasoning or wisdom, and fleshly effort; not fearing rejection and not valuing your own earthly rank or reputation (Isaiah). It means being willing to accept suffering, inconvenience, or discomfort; being willing to "bear the iniquity" of God's people (not as their messiah, but as an intercessor); and being willing to deny yourself (Ezekiel). It also means being married and committed to an unfaithful and adulterous spiritual people (the Church), serving and loving her despite her unfaithfulness, rejection, and betrayal; laying aside your own personal interests and desires; and being willing to endure great hurt and emotional distress (Hosea). Being prophetic with this kind of integrity costs you everything!

Unfortunately, we live in a day and age when this type of prophetic integrity is sorely lacking. The current Prophetic Movement itself is suffering from a pandemic of what has been called spiritual "AIDS" (Acute Integrity Deficiency Syndrome), tainted by the spirit of the age where narcissism, self-interest, the love of money, and the pursuit of personal pleasure is the norm (2 Tim. 3:1–9). It will take much more than eloquent words and great skill in prophesying to be a prophetic ambassador of heaven. It will require complete death to self and a level of integrity that follows closely after the pattern left for us by our prophetic forefathers.

3. Integrated

The word *integrated* has a number of very interesting definitions, two of which accurately suit the context of that which we are trying to describe. It can mean being incorporated or brought together as part of a whole, or "having, including, or serving members of different racial, religious, and ethnic groups as equals."[11] The first definition has to do primarily with *connectivity*, while the second definition deals primarily with *nonexclusivity* or *partiality*. Prophets generally function and operate as an integrated part of a local Kingdom community and are not isolated, detached, or independent. Before you get the wrong idea by thinking that prophets are always connected or committed to formal or established religious structures, it is important that we clarify the term *Kingdom community*. This term is used in preference of "church" to identify God's *ekklēsía* (Greek)—a word used in Scripture to describe the entire community of God's people regardless of whether or not they were formally gathered together.[12] In other words, when you see *Kingdom community* (ekklēsía), think *people* rather than church building or church service. A prophet may choose to totally reject the corrupt formal or established religious (including Christian) structures of his day yet still be totally committed and connected to God's covenant people, as we will see later on in this study. Conversely, there may be "prophets" who are resident, faithful, and active within a community of believers or established religious structure and yet be isolated, excluded, and rejected as true members of God's Covenant community (Ezek. 13:1–9).

Prophetic integration must transcend mere physical presence or religious activity. It is being committed to God and being His voice to His people, and this does not require familiarity, conformity or false unity within the context of religious fellowship. As a matter of fact, most of the prophetic ministry performed in Scripture was performed outside of formal or traditional religious settings like a temple, synagogue, or corporate worship gathering, thus negating the need for traditional religious participation in order to fulfill their prophetic assignments. A careful examination of Scripture in its entirety will support this statement, revealing far lesser instances when this was otherwise, especially in the Old Testament where a far greater number of prophetic examples are found.

Nevertheless, prophets are deeply invested in, and committed to, God's people, whether within or without formal or established religious structures. They accurately represent the heart of God by loving and keeping covenant with His bride. They are intimately connected to the Head (Jesus) which, by extension, makes them intimately connected to His Body. Therefore, they continue to remain connected and serve despite the hurt, rejection, persecution, exclusion, dishonor, or humiliation they receive from an adulterous people such as we saw earlier with Hosea. Many of the prophets in Scripture served under these conditions, yet they continued to remain faithful and connected. They may have never joined or participated with the people in their sin, idolatry, or false worship, but they continued to express the heart of God by sounding warnings and calling them to repentance while maintaining a certain level of proximity and relationship. It must be the same with prophetic people, refusing to participate in false or corrupt religious systems or activities yet maintaining healthy relationship and proximity.

This provides a wonderful segue into the next part of the definition; however, I need to interject with another important point before we do so. Prophets must recognize and understand their place among other ministers, ministries, and members of the body (Acts 13:1; Eph. 4:11). To be *integrated* implies that prophets are only *part* of a whole. This means that prophets are not complete in themselves; they only form one part. The ministry of Jesus was broken into five equal parts—apostles, prophets, evangelists, pastors, and teachers (Eph. 4:11)—and it takes all five parts working in concert together to provide a complete and accurate picture of who Jesus is. When any part is missing, the image becomes deficient or distorted. Therefore, when prophets operate from a place of isolation, independence, or individuality—refusing to properly honor, value, or acknowledge the divine grace and spiritual resource given through the other ministries—what was once prophetic becomes frustratingly *pathetic* and serves to misrepresent Christ and His Kingdom.

I have seen this happen very often in so-called "prophetic" churches where great emphasis is placed on prophecy and hearing God's voice with little to no allowance for true apostolic government or wisdom, purposeful evangelism, authentic pastoral oversight, or structured expository teaching. The result was a very immature and deformed expression of Christ through an immature and deficient company of believers who claimed to "hear from God." But a true prophetic people will remain integrated, submitted, and connected to the other four ministries. The only accurate context for prophetic ministry is in concert with the other four.

The second part of the definition we have yet to discuss is the issue of being non-exclusive and impartial. We briefly mentioned before that prophets and prophetic people should be proximate and relational. Being prophetic shouldn't make anyone spooky or unapproachable, and it definitely shouldn't make anyone a bigot. True prophets are without prejudice. They have no special allegiance to any man, ministry, denomination, network, race, or religion; and they are never exclusive. Paul was willing to affirm a foreign prophet based on his accurate critical testimony regarding the corrupt moral character of people from his own nation (Tit.1:12–13). This prophet, who many believe to be a Cretan poet, proved a level of authenticity not just by his valid testimony but his willingness to show impartiality rather than prejudice in favor of his own people.

The prophet Elisha is probably the best example of this principle. Rather than make his gifting and ministry the exclusive opportunity of his cultural and religious people or ethnic circle, Elisha showed impartiality and provided open access to nations and leaders who considered Israel (including Judah) and its people to be their mortal enemies (2 Kings 5:1–19, 8:7–15). But providing open access to these foreign nations was only one part; he also had to make sure that his ministry or revelation was not tainted with prejudice in favor of his own people, which he did. This impartiality is especially notable in Elisha's ministry to Hazael, the Syrian, who was a high ranking officer serving under the king (2 Kings 8:7–15). By prophesying the termination of Syria's current executive leadership (Benhadad), Elisha served to empower and accelerate Hazael's destiny to the throne. It broke Elisha's heart to do so, knowing by divine insight the horrible atrocities this man would later perform against his people, yet it did not prevent him from proclaiming the truth. There was no prejudice at all in his ministry. Most people who consider themselves patriots and deeply love their country would rather die than help facilitate the destruction of their own nation or people, but Elisha was more than a patriot; he was a prophet. He represented God, not the nation of Judah or Israel. This proved that his ministry was accurate and authentic, free from blindness and distortion. It also demonstrated that God was not a bigot.

When the prophet Ahijah prophesied Jeroboam's succession to the throne during the reign of Solomon, as well as the fracture or splintering of the nation into two distinct kingdoms (the northern kingdom of Israel and the southern kingdom of Judah), this required the same lack of prejudice and impartiality but on a political level. Considering the fact that David's dynasty was expected to last "forever" and had been permanently established by God (2 Sam. 7:11–17), prophesying Jeroboam's ascension in this regard would have not only been unpopular (remember, this word was given while Solomon still reigned) but would have appeared politically foolhardy and in opposition to God's clearly revealed will (1 Kings 11:26–40). Furthermore, prophesying the fracturing and division of the nation would definitely not have been in either the nation's or the prophet's interest. There was no political or religious motivation involved; no carnal commitment to any political party or leader. Therefore, when the time came for God to judge Jeroboam for his sins and condemn his legacy, Ahijah could also do so without any internal restraint (1 Kings 14:5–17). Ahijah proved beyond a doubt that he was impartial and without any political or religious prejudice. He was not blinded by his own personal, political, or national self-interests.

The moment we open up our hearts to entertain any form of prejudice, for or against, any race, religion, nationality, political persuasion, etc., we compromise and corrupt the prophetic ministry and distort the public's view of God and His Kingdom. Unfortunately, this type of prejudice is seen all too often among those who claim to be prophets, especially here in America, where much of their so-called "revelation" and pronouncements are tainted by religious or political persuasion, race, or nationalism.

4. *Industrious*

The word *industrious* means to be diligently active and skillful.[13] This begs the question: Exactly what type of activity are prophets and prophetic people supposed to be diligently involved in? And what type of skill is needed to effectively engage in such activity? Most people reading this statement would naturally assume that the skill or activity is prophecy, but that would not be entirely correct. Prophets are called to be much more than just able prophesiers, and their activity encompasses much more than just personal prophecy. This core understanding will be reemphasized throughout this book and will be addressed in greater detail in a subsequent chapter.

The prophet Jeremiah is an excellent example. When God first called and commissioned Jeremiah, embedded within the Father's prophetic charge to this prophet are very clear and precise instructions that serve to define the core parameters of a prophet's calling and activity. These instructions are universal in nature and apply to every prophet of every age or era. Every revelation a prophet receives is toward this end.

> *Then the Lord put forth His hand and touched my mouth, and the Lord said to me: "Behold, I have put My words in your mouth. See, I have this day set you*

*over the nations and over the kingdoms, To **root out** and to **pull down**, To **destroy** and to **throw down**, To **build** and to **plant**."* (Jer. 1:9–10, emphasis mine)

At first glance, these may appear to be very negative instructions, portraying the prophet as being overly critical and negative in his assignment. After all, the negatives outnumber the positives by a ratio of two to one. But what many people fail to understand is that the ultimate objective is entirely positive. Each of these four negative verbs are working in anticipation and preparation of the two positive ones that follow at the end. In other words, the *rooting out, pulling down, throwing down,* and *destruction* are in preparation for *building* and *planting* (which can also be translated *establishing*). Demolition and destruction are often an important prerequisite to construction. What is being described here is powerful building activity and architecture.

There are an abundance of principles we can glean from this passage. The activity being described here is primarily an internal and spiritual process rather than physical. The prophet's assignment is not to try to change or alter earthly structures. He is attempting to *uproot* deeply embedded but false religious mind-sets, *pull down* corrupt mental strongholds, and totally demolish or violently overthrow belief and value systems that are in opposition to the architecture of God's Kingdom. Again, this is an internal process, which is why God has the prophet employ the same terminology again later on in the context of a potter and his clay.

> *The word which came to Jeremiah from the Lord, saying: "Arise and go down to the potter's house, and there I will cause you to hear My words." Then I went down to the potter's house, and there he was, making something at the wheel. And the vessel that he made of clay was marred in the hand of the potter; so he made it again into another vessel, as it seemed good to the potter to make. Then*

*the word of the Lord came to me, saying: "O house of Israel, can I not do with you as this potter?" says the Lord. "Look, as the clay is in the potter's hand, so are you in My hand, O house of Israel! The instant I speak concerning a nation and concerning a kingdom, to **pluck up**, to **pull down**, and to **destroy it**, if that nation against whom I have spoken turns from its evil, I will relent of the disaster that I thought to bring upon it. And the instant I speak concerning a nation and concerning a kingdom, to **build** and to **plant** it, if it does evil in My sight so that it does not obey My voice, then I will relent concerning the good with which I said I would benefit it. (Jer. 18:1–10)*

Jeremiah was commanded to go to *the potter's house* so that he could receive new insight and revelation from God. While there, he was able to observe the activity of the potter working on his clay. The potter was taking a marred vessel—which in the Hebrew carries the connotation of being morally ruined, worthless, or corrupt—and was remolding, reshaping, or *reforming* it into another vessel *as it seemed good to the potter* (not the clay). Believers should know that this refers to much more than just an alteration of human behavior but an alteration of the heart and internal architecture. This is reformation technology. It is not about what the people desire; it is about what God demands!

The prophet's assignment is to reproduce God's Kingdom architecture in the earth through a deliberate and powerful building initiative. And this building activity requires the prophet to operate from a higher and more elevated dimension of sight, spiritual rank, and authority to uproot and destroy every false nation (value, culture, and belief system) and every false kingdom (dominating principle, principality, or power). This is where the skill comes in. It takes apostolic wisdom and prophetic skill to be able to tear down these false or corrupt internal structures and systems without tearing down the people who support and uphold them due to internal blindness or deception. Prophets must be able to hate the sin but still love the people. People will resist, but the prophet must be a tireless builder.

The Jeremiah principle (Jer. 1:10) dictates that it will take twice as much effort to uproot and overthrow the false than it will take to actually build and establish the accurate architecture of truth in people's hearts. But the negative must precede the positive; there is simply no other way. You cannot build new Kingdom architecture upon an existing foundation of error. The Kingdom of God cannot be built upon human or false religious structures. You have to tear up the old inaccurate foundation and demolish everything that man has built, which does not conform to Christ.

In short, you cannot ignore this powerful building ethic and still consider yourself to be prophetic. In fact, this building activity must first be accomplished in the prophet's own heart and life before any accurate building can be effected in others. This principle is again demonstrated through the integrity of Jeremiah's own life and ministry.

> For behold, I have made you this day A **fortified city** and an **iron pillar**, And **bronze walls** against the whole land-- Against the kings of Judah, Against its princes, Against its priests, And against the people of the land. (Jer. 1:18, emphasis mine)

Notice the terminology being used in the text above—*fortified city...iron pillar...bronze walls*. Each of these concepts describe powerful, mature, and enduring building architecture that has been developed in Jeremiah's own personal life (compare to Prov. 25:28). He is not internally deficient but strong and impregnable to the corrupt issues that God has called him to address in the nation. God could now trust him with His message; and he is only authorized to speak because he has allowed God to mature and perfect the building process in his own life first (Jer. 1:17). If you want to be truly prophetic, you will have to allow God to do the same in you. You have no authority to speak or build into the lives of others what has not already been firmly built or established into your own personal life and internal architecture. You can't address issues in others when you're still privately dealing with the same issues. This powerful building activity must first be activated *in* you before it can be demonstrated *through* you.

5. *Inspired*

The prophet, by definition, is *a person **inspired** to proclaim or reveal divine will or purpose.*[14] This means that inspiration is the very heartbeat and lifeblood of the prophetic. It is what fuels and propels all prophetic activity. The word *inspired* means to be guided, affected, or aroused by divine influence.[15] Pay special attention to the words *divine influence* in this definition because "inspiration" can come from many different sources. For example, we may say to a person who has accomplished great success or notoriety despite their adverse situations or challenges that "you inspire me…" Or we may read a book about someone's biography and feel very "inspired." But a prophet's inspiration comes from God. It is not a soulish or emotional phenomenon.[16] The prophet's inspiration is *divine* in nature—meaning it originates from heaven and not from any natural, human, earthly, or fleshly occurrence. It has nothing to do with your body's natural chemistry and very little to do with your psychological state of mind.

There are many self-proclaimed "prophets" and "prophetic" people today who claim to be inspired, but their unction and influence does not originate from heaven. It is often soulish and even demonic (Acts 16:16–18). Proclaiming accurate personal information or details doesn't mean you were divinely inspired because if that was the case, many psychics, soothsayers, and clairvoyants would be divinely inspired also. Additionally, operating from a place of divine influence should not be confused with being overly mystical, esoteric, or flaky. People who act in such a way are either immature or emotionally imbalanced, but divine influence is not the cause for such behavior.

So the real question that should be confronting us at this point is how do we tell the difference between divine influence and every other base form of inspiration? The quickest way is through Holy

Spirit discernment, but there are other—more practical—ways. Inspiration, as we stated before, is the very lifeblood of the prophetic and, as such, carries a very distinct and unique DNA (Divine Nature and Attributes). When a prophet is operating or functioning by divine influence, his ministry carries and manifests within it this divine DNA, generating a divine or heavenly "footprint" within the hearts of men that points them to the Father in heaven and never to the prophet or themselves. It is as if a piece of heaven is released on the inside of you. On the other hand, when the inspiration is not divine in nature, it leaves a fleshly, human, carnal, or even demonic deposit—appealing to your emotions and natural senses, catering to your fleshly concerns or desires, and indulging your human ambitions or pride. Instead of magnifying the Father in heaven, this type of base inspiration often magnifies the "prophet" and his ministry.

Let's briefly examine a biblical example:

> *Now an old prophet dwelt in Bethel, and his sons came and told him all the works that the man of God had done that day in Bethel; they also told their father the words which he had spoken to the king. And their father said to them, "Which way did he go?" For his sons had seen which way the man of God went who came from Judah. Then he said to his sons, "Saddle the donkey for me." So they saddled the donkey for him; and he rode on it, and went after the man of God, and found him sitting under an oak. Then he said to him, "Are you the man of God who came from Judah?" And he said, "I am." Then he said to him, "Come home with me and eat bread." And he said, "I cannot return with you nor go in with you; neither can I eat bread nor drink water with you in this place. For I have been told by the word of the Lord, 'You shall not eat bread nor drink water there, nor return by going the way you came.'" He said to him, "I too am a prophet as you are, and an angel spoke to me by the word of the Lord, say-*

ing, 'Bring him back with you to your house, that he may eat bread and drink water.'" (He was lying to him.) So he went back with him, and ate bread in his house, and drank water. (1 Kings 13:11–19)

I would encourage you to read the entire chapter of this account since it contains so many great points and principles that time and space will not allow us to get into in great detail. The story begins with a *man of God*—a term used several times in Scripture as a synonym for prophet—being sent from Judah to Bethel by *the word of the Lord* (divine influence or inspiration) for the purpose of confronting and dismantling (Jeremiah 1:10 principle) a false and idolatrous system of worship (1 Kings 13:1–3). This false system, by the way, was established by the newly appointed king of Israel, Jeroboam, for the purpose of securing and establishing *his* (personal) kingdom.[17] In addition, it was a new "seeker friendly," comfortable, and convenient system of worship that demanded less from the people with no personal migration (1 Kings 12:28).

The man of God does well by being obedient to God and acting as an agent of destruction against the idolatrous altars, even demonstrating prophetic authenticity and skill by his merciful and loving treatment of Jeroboam despite his resistance and intended persecution (1 Kings 13:4–6). He gives one of the most detailed prophecies recorded in Scripture, and God validates his ministry with supernatural signs and wonders. Heaven's (supernatural) DNA is all over this prophet's ministry, leaving no doubt in the people's minds that this was a true prophet of God operating by divine influence. By the time the prophet's ministry is over, Jeroboam has experienced a divine encounter with God through His divine mercy and healing. In testament to this fact, Jeroboam invites the prophet to his home for refreshment and reward—which in that culture was a display of recognition, gratitude, and honor to a prophet of God (1 Sam. 9:6–8; 2 Kings 4:8–10; 5:3–5; 8:7–9).[18]

The man of God, however, refuses the king's hospitality and honor, not out of arrogance or disrespect, but because it violated the divine command given to him by God (1 Kings 13:8–10). By the man of God refusing to participate in "brotherly" hospitality among those who followed and/or practiced a corrupt and idolatrous form of worship, God was setting a clear line of demarcation, separation and division.[19] Whereas eating and drinking together was a sign of fellowship and communion, the man of God was saying that he refused to associate, fellowship, participate, or keep covenant with those who had ascribed to such error. It was a total rejection of the system. This parallels Paul's command to believers later on in the New Testament (1 Cor. 5:9–11; 2 Tim. 3:1–5).

This brings us to our current text. There is an *old prophet* who dwells in Bethel, and his sons—not necessarily biological offspring but apprentice prophets or prophets in training (*sons of the prophets*)—were apparently present at this idolatrous worship event before they rushed home to tell the old prophet all that had transpired with the man of God from Judah. Note that the word *old* here represents more than just age. It is a word often associated in Scripture with blindness (Gen. 27:1, 48:10; 1 Sam. 4:15) and employed somewhat as a euphemism for foolishness, corruption, or error (1 Kings 11:4; Eccles. 4:13; 1 Tim. 4:7). To put it simply, this was a false prophet. His habitation is in the center of corruption. He literally functions and dwells in the midst of apostasy, perversity, and error without protest. He has set down his roots and established permanent structures in the midst of idolatrous systems and architecture. This false prophet's error is compounded even further by the fact that his "sons" are all present during this idolatrous event, either functioning as a corrupt prophetic order in favor of the system, idolatrous priests serving within the system, or, at the very least, worshipping participators supporting the system. In effect, this false prophet and his sons represent an adulterated and corrupt prophetic order.[20]

After getting all the information he needed from his sons, the false prophet pursues after the man of God on his donkey and invites him home, knowing the entire conversation that had already taken place between the man of God and the king (v. 11). When the man of God basically repeats the same words he told the king, the false prophet responds that he is "a prophet" also. Note that you won't find anywhere in Scripture where a prophet of God makes this kind of self-declaration because they don't. The only other time this type of self-declaration/affirmation is made is by the *woman Jezebel, who* **calls herself** *a prophetess* (Rev. 2:20). The first key point here is that divine inspiration never emanates from a place of self-validation (John 7:18). When you are truly inspired by God, people will know it. If you have to publicly announce yourself as being a "prophet" of God before people will recognize your ministry as such, you're no prophet—at least not of God. Divine inspiration is divinely validated. Also, divine inspiration is never motivated by self-interest. Although the text does not explicitly state the reasons for the false prophet wanting to have the man of God at his home, we can clearly surmise that it was for his own self-interest, whatever that may have been. Whenever someone's prophecy or revelation serves to benefit them—whether directly or indirectly—you can be sure it was not inspired by God.

The next thing this false prophet says is that "an angel spoke to me." Here is an insightful comment regarding this false claim:

> A communication through a celestial messenger would seem to have been regarded as a higher form of revelation than a subjective communication to the mind of the prophet. Cf. Acts 7:53; Heb. 2:2; Luke 1:13, 29; Acts 27:23.[21]

In other words, this false prophet was claiming to have a higher form of revelation, which made him superior to the man of God. This, of course, was not true. However, the principle here is that false prophets usually portray themselves as having superior insight, details, and revelation. People usually tend to buy into the deception that they're divinely inspired due to the hype they create regarding details, angelic visitations, or divine encounters. Most true apostles and prophets who have these encounters don't go around harping about them for greater fame or recognition, no matter how pious they may sound while doing so.[22] When you're divinely inspired you don't need hype, and you don't employ it either. The fruit of divine inspiration speaks much louder and clearer than the emotional enthusiasm often stirred up by that which originates from the flesh or devil.

There are several other principles we can glean from this false prophet's ministry. We know that he wasn't divinely inspired because he clearly contradicted what God had already spoken to the man of God. Divine inspiration never contradicts God's inspired Word. God is not fickle or schizophrenic, so He will never contradict Himself.[23] Also, you will notice that this false prophecy appealed to the man of God's natural needs, human senses, and fleshly desires—all sure signs of base and fleshly inspiration. Divine inspiration magnifies the Father and leaves an imprint of heaven within you; it does not magnify your human or fleshly desires to make you the center of your own universe. Bear in mind also that the distance between Jerusalem (in Judah) and Bethel was approximately twelve miles "as the crow flies" and could have been a much longer distance depending on the route the man of God had taken along those dry dusty roads. He is also on foot. This means that by the time he has arrived at Bethel and executed his ministry, he is tired, hungry, and thirsty (which is probably why the false prophet found him resting under an oak when he met him). This type of suffering and self-denial was necessary for the man of God to accurately complete his assignment. However, by the false prophet appealing to his base (human) appetites and temporal needs, he was seeking to lessen or diminish the man of God's God-ordained suffering. The principle here is that divine inspiration never provides false comfort (this is a major principle that will be elaborated on more fully later on). Any revelation that seeks to lessen or diminish the Kingdom principles of suffering and self-denial in favor of making you happy, content, or comfortable is not divinely inspired (Matt. 10:38–39; Mark 8:31–35).

Unfortunately, the man of God ends up being deceived by this false prophet, disobeys God's original commands, and goes back to the false prophet's home to accommodate his fleshly appetites. This shows the powerful seduction false inspiration can have even on people versed in hearing the voice of God.

The rest of the story doesn't bode well for the man of God, but even worse is what his disobedience does to undermine his ministry.

At the end of the entire account are these words, "After this event Jeroboam did not turn from his evil way" (1 Kings 13:33). What happened to Jeroboam's heart after the divine encounter he had with God and his desire to honor the man of God as a true prophet? It's difficult to prove for certain, but it is quite obvious to me that word would have gotten back to the king regarding the man of God's whereabouts and that he was being entertained at the old prophet's house. To the king (and many others), this would have meant that the man of God's credibility was lost. In their minds, only an impostor operating by a spirit of divination would contradict his own statements by doing what he claimed God had clearly commanded him not to do. And how do you explain his untimely end if it was not God's judgment on him for having defiled the altar of "god?" At any rate, having close fellowship at the home of the old prophet who served within this idolatrous system meant that the man of God accepted and validated it. These are some of the thought processes that the king would have entertained and may have led to his outright rejection of his prior message, encounter, and experience. The principle here is that false revelation or inspiration ultimately creates or fosters rebellion against God and hinders Kingdom advance. It also ends in spiritual death, which means that it ultimately separates you from God instead of draw you closer to Him (1 Kings 13:24).

When divine inspiration is present, it becomes *profitable*—not to the flesh but to the spirit—bringing instruction, correction, and reproof; all in righteousness (2 Tim. 3:16). It doesn't emanate from the prophet's own heart, mind, or vision but from a much higher and elevated source (2 Pet. 1:20). Scripture says that *holy men of God spoke as they were moved (or inspired) by the Holy Spirit*, which means that divine inspiration requires holiness of life (2 Pet. 1:21). It also brings with it doctrinal clarity and understanding (2 Tim. 3:16). I have often said that if the Scriptures were *written* by divine inspiration, they can only be accurately *interpreted* by the same means. As we stated before, prophets are especially qualified in this regard.

You can't be prophetic without divine inspiration. Prophets and prophetic people are inspired preachers, teachers, heralds, messengers, ambassadors, and reformers.

6. *Intercessor*

The word *intercessor* has very often been relegated and restricted—especially in Christian or religious circles—to the very narrow and limited definition of "one who prays and petitions God on behalf of another." There is no argument that this partial definition is true of prophets. From the very beginning, when the concepts of prayer and the prophetic are first formally introduced in Scripture, they are introduced together—as two mutually inclusive parts forming one complete whole. The prophetic doesn't function merely by gifts; it functions through an intimate relationship with the Father through prayer. Prophets carry the burden of the Lord in this regard, often functioning in a priestly capacity between man and God (Ex. 32:30–35; Num. 27:5; Deut. 9:18; Jer. 15:1; Ezek. 4:5). However, you're mistaken if you believe that being prophetic and an intercessor entails a preoccupation with personal or corporate prayer requests and petitions. Leading a prayer group or participating in "intercessory" prayer teams doesn't necessarily make you prophetic or an intercessor. More accurately, the word *intercessor* describes someone who attempts to bring mediation or reconciliation between parties during a dispute. You can pray and fast all day long and still do very little in regard to accomplishing this end purpose—*reconciliation*! Intercessory prayer alone can only plead for mercy or delayed judgment from the *offended* (wronged) party (God), but it takes additional action to convince the *offending* party (man) of their sin and transgression that created the breach. Since this topic is covered more fully in our book, *The Technology of Prayer: Reexamining the Biblical Purpose, Power, and Principles of Prayer from a Kingdom Perspective*, it will not be discussed any further here.

Sufficed to say, prophets are ministers of reconciliation who are called to turn the hearts of people—including Covenant communities (churches) and nations—back to God by boldly confronting, criticizing, and condemning their complacency, corruption, subtle forms of syncretism, and prevailing wayward culture. The burden of the Lord in intercession is equally divided and expressed through prayer and petition, as well as bold declaration and confrontation. Even though the prophet may often appear to be critical, his ultimate purpose and objective is to bring reconciliation and restoration. Remember the Jeremiah 1:10 principle that while there may be a higher ratio of negatives, the ultimate destination is a positive one. This means that prophets are not ministers of condemnation. They are not sent to damn you to hell; they are sent to reconnect you to God and His divine purpose. They are skilled spiritual surgeons, not malevolent murderers. Surgeons wound to heal, but murderers wound to kill.

Prophets and prophetic people, therefore, should be kind and caring and merciful and compassionate. There is no place for being rude, obnoxious, or abrasive nor any justification for being intentionally harsh, overly critical, overbearing, or unbiblically judgmental. No true prophet of God delights in calling down judgment or issuing words of correction, but neither should they shy away from it when called upon to do so either. Beware of any "prophet" with an "itchy trigger finger," always ready and willing to blast away at every conceivable infraction they encounter. God has not appointed anyone to be a spiritual sheriff in His Kingdom, and no prophet has the right to take the place of the Holy Spirit in people's individual lives (John 16:8–11).[24]

7. Influence

The word *influence* describes the ability or power to sway, affect, shift, or change things. In this particular context, the influence occurs primarily in the realm of the spirit and then extends outward into physical reality. In other words, it is divine influence. True prophets are endued with the divine power and authority to shift things in the realm of the spirit as well as effect visible changes in the heavens and the earth. This type of influence doesn't come by earthly position, power, popularity, or prestige. Ordination papers or religious credentials do not give you this type of spiritual rank. Your title or position within ecclesiastical circles does not give you the authority to shift the heavens or effect change in the spirit. The size of your network or large number of followers does not provide you with this supernatural ability. And neither does your high-level contacts or recognition in Washington DC, the White House, or UN. You may be able to effect temporal, insignificant, and superficial human changes through these means, but nothing that penetrates beyond the shallow barriers and limitations of the flesh.

There are many who claim to be prophets and prophetic people today whose words carry no weight in the spirit. At the beginning of every year here in America, there are an abundance of prophecies and declarations made by several recognized and unrecognized "prophets" regarding the new calendar year. Unfortunately, what I have discovered about many of them is that after the hype is over and the dust has all settled, nothing has truly changed or shifted in the realm of heaven or earth. Often all we are left with by the end of the year are empty words and/or promises. By the time the new year rolls over again, most of the susceptible—or rather gullible—people who follow after these prophecies have forgotten that the previous words have all fallen flat and are eagerly anticipating the next one. A prophet's words are not empty or filled with fluff but carry the creative force necessary for fulfillment.

> *So Samuel grew, and the Lord was with him and let none of his words fall to the ground. And all Israel from Dan to Beersheba knew that Samuel had been established as a prophet of the Lord.* (1 Sam. 3:19–20)

Samuel was recognized as *a prophet of the Lord* because the people realized that he had divine influence. *The Lord was with him,* supernaturally backing up every word he said. There was a recognition by all of the people that when Samuel spoke, something shifted, something changed, and things didn't continue as normal (1 Sam. 12:16–18). There was a weight, potency, and creative power that made Samuel's words effectual and unfailing. It wasn't just that his words came to pass (Deut. 18:22). Even a broken clock can be right twice a day! It was the divine creative force pulsating through every prophetic proclamation so that there was no doubt in people's minds that God was involved. The union between God and Samuel—the Sender and the sent—was so profound and complete that it was virtually impossible to distinguish whether or not the prophet was responding to God, or God was responding to the prophet. While the text would seem to imply the latter, the principle of the prophetic more fully supports the former, thus the reason why I suggest it is virtually impossible to distinguish between the two. Whichever way you choose to slice it, the fact remains that when Samuel spoke, heaven responded (Ps. 99:6–8). This is the potency of the prophetic.

> *And I will give power (authority) to my two witnesses, and they will prophesy one thousand two hundred and sixty days, clothed in sackcloth." These have power to shut heaven, so that no rain falls in the days of their prophecy; and they have power over waters to turn them to blood, and to strike the earth with all plagues, as often as they desire.* (Rev. 11:3, 6, parenthesis mine).

Notice again the divine influence of authentic prophetic ministry. Scripture describes *two witnesses*—an end-time apostolic-prophetic company—who have been divinely authorized and supernaturally empowered to *prophesy*. Their prophetic ministry is not weak or anemic but powerful and effectual in its operation. When they speak, things are shifted in the heavens, and when they prophesy, things are changed in the earth. But notice the last part of the final clause—*as often as they desire.* As in the case of Samuel, it is virtually impossible to distinguish exactly who is really initiating the action by the way the text is worded. Are these prophets responding to God's intent or is God responding to theirs? Once again, the text seems to imply the latter. The principle here is that a prophet can be so fused—so intimately connected, united, and synchronized with heaven—that the will of God and the will of the prophet are literally one. There is no discernible difference, diversity, divergence, or dissimilarity between them. When the prophet speaks, it is as if the Lord Himself is speaking. Heaven's architecture is embedded so deeply and thoroughly within them that when they speak, the hosts of heaven respond as if God had thundered from heaven with His own lips. That, my friend, is a powerful prophetic dimension that has been virtually unseen in our present day.

You can't shift heaven by your earthly or carnal decrees, no matter how much you preface them with the words "prophetic" or "apostolic." I hear people speak and pray this way all the time as if these words, or the use of the word "decree," make it so. There is no magic in these words. Heaven will only respond to you to the degree and dimension that you have first responded to heaven by allowing God to uproot and dismantle every carnal, ungodly, or religious belief system within you and replace it with heaven's architecture. Heaven is trained to respond to the voice of God, not the voice of man or religion. When we allow the voice of God to be developed *within* us, we will experience the voice of God working powerfully *through* us.

A More Accurate Definition

The prophetic, therefore, can more accurately be defined as the ability to consistently access hidden wisdom and divine architecture from heaven for the purpose of executing skillful, authentic building activity in the earth while being modeled through an accurate character and lifestyle that functions within the context of connectedness and community and is infused with spiritual energy to turn the hearts of men back to God as well as shift things in the spiritual and earthly realms so that there is greater Kingdom alignment.

Based upon this definition, most of the activity, as well as the people, that we have commonly ascribed this terminology to are, in fact, not prophetic at all. This new understanding or "difference of opinion" is at the heart of this new prophetic divergence. It is a significant redefinition for the simple fact that we live in a day and age where *prophetic* terminology is being thrown around quite loosely and indiscriminately to the point of causing mass confusion. There are now numerous churches, ministries, and schools offering "prophetic" training seminars and classes that are based upon little more than teaching people how to prophesy. Please don't misunderstand me; I am in no way attempting to condemn this practice because there is nothing necessarily wrong with teaching people to prophesy.

The author himself was taught, and has taught, in such seminars. And who can deny the fact that the Bible clearly teaches that we "may all prophesy" (1 Cor. 14:1, 31)? People should be trained on how to do so effectively. However, we need to begin to distinguish between being gifted or able to prophesy and being genuinely prophetic. It is erroneous to believe or teach that the frequent discharge of personal prophecies alone—regardless of how accurate or specific—constitutes a complete or accurate representation of valid prophetic activity.

There is more! There is a higher (and deeper) dimension of the prophetic that we have yet to attain. There is another nine-tenth of the iceberg we have yet to discover. Please allow me to introduce you to the *third prophetic dimension.*

Notes

[1] According to Jesus, manifesting miraculous signs should be a standard occurrence for *all* believers that have been obedient to His command to *go* and preach the gospel (Mark 16:17).

[2] Wikipedia contributors, "Iceberg," *Wikipedia, The Free Encyclopedia,* http://en.wikipedia.org/w/index.php?title=Iceberg&oldid=593911909 (accessed February 12, 2014).

[3] Ibid.

[4] Ibid.

[5] *The Complete Word Study Dictionary: New Testament,* ed. Spiros Zodhiates Th.D. (Chattanooga, TN: AMG International, 1993), 4397.

[6] "Prophet." *The New Unger's Bible Dictionary.* Originally published by Moody Press of Chicago, Illinois. Copyright © 1988 [PC Study Bible © 2008, Biblesoft, Inc].

[7] "Integrity." *Webster's II New Riverside University Dictionary* (Boston, MA: Houghton Mifflin Company, 1994).

[8] James M. Freeman and Harold J. Chadwick, *Manners & Customs of the Bible* (North Brunswick, NJ: Bridge-Logos Publishers, 1998), 216.

[9] ESV Study Bible notes on Ezekiel 4:10–11.

[10] Please note that the author is in no way implying that prophetic training seminars or events are without merit or that there is no significant profit or benefit in attending these events for training and development in prophetic ministry. However, the type of integrity needed in order to authenticate and sustain genuine prophetic function requires a far greater level of time, impartation through association, and mentoring. In other words, there is no "fast track" to being prophetic.

[11] Integrated. Dictionary.com. *Dictionary.com Unabridged.* Random House, Inc. http://dictionary.reference.com/browse/integrated (accessed: February 20, 2014).

[12] For more information on this subject, please refer to the series of articles on our website entitled *Ekklesia Redefined.* http://www.kaiembassy.com/index.php/blog-articles/86-articles.html.

13   "Industrious." *Webster's II New Riverside University Dictionary* (Boston, MA: Houghton Mifflin Company, 1994).

14   William Arndt, Frederick W. Danker, and Walter Bauer, *A Greek-English Lexicon of the New Testament and Other Early Christian Literature* (Chicago: University of Chicago Press, 2000), 890.

15   "Inspired." *Webster's II New Riverside University Dictionary* (Boston, MA: Houghton Mifflin Company, 1994).

16   Note that you can be soulish or emotional without being truly inspired, but you can never be truly inspired without this divine influence having an effect on the emotions and soul.

17   Every false kingdom or corrupt system of worship (religion) is based upon the principles of self-interest and personal advancement.

18   Some Bible commentators incorrectly misconstrue Jeroboam's invitation as emanating from selfish or diabolical motives in an attempt to try to sway or "bribe" the prophet. Since the text is silent on Jeroboam's true motives, and in the absence of any evidence to the contrary, the only accurate way to interpret his actions in light of biblical or historical culture.

19   Note the principle of being *integrated* coming into play. While the prophet or "man of God" was *proximate*, he continued to be *separate*.

20   Note that Bethel was a recognized location for a company or community of prophets (2 Kings 2:3).

21   H. D. M. Spence-Jones, ed., *1 Kings*, The Pulpit Commentary (London; New York: Funk & Wagnalls Company, 1909), 296.

22   Note that of the few instances in Scripture where prophets did describe their personal supernatural experiences or calling, it was never for the purpose of gaining credibility or stirring up fleshly hype; and it was almost certainly not a part of their public messages or preaching. Their public messages are clearly identified by what the Lord commanded them to *go* and *speak* and is usually recorded sometime after the prophet's short personal bio describing their personal calling and encounter with God. God had these prophets write or document their supernatural calling and/or experiences for the benefit of present and future gener-

ations, not for the benefit of the prophets themselves. In other words, they never tried to use these experiences as leverage to try to sway or convince the people of their authenticity (Is. 6–7:4; Jer. 1:4–2:1; Ezek. 1–3).

23 Note that this is only a general principle and that there are biblical exceptions, however seldom, to this rule that can be occasioned by prayer, sin, or repentance (Ex. 32:9–14; 2 Kings 20:1–7; Jer. 18:7–10; Jon. 3:1–10).

24 Note that the issue being addressed here is excess. God may at times reveal sinful issues in people's lives that need to be confronted and addressed; however, a prophet doesn't make this his focus by going out and looking for them. He doesn't scrutinize the lives of everyone he meets to find sin because that's not his job—that's the Holy Spirit's job to convict and convince of sin.

2

THE THIRD PROPHETIC DIMENSION

EVER SINCE THE prophetic was first introduced and established in the earth, it has gone through significant seasons or stages of development. It is an immutable principle that nothing begins in the earth fully matured or developed. Even the Son of God, when He walked the earth, was subjected to a personal process of physical and spiritual development toward maturation in manhood and ministry (Luke 2:51–52). When God's Covenant Kingdom Community was first birthed and introduced into the earth in the book of Acts in mighty power and miracles, that was only the beginning—an infancy stage, as it were—though in many respects it was also the development and maturation of a much earlier principle or concept in existence since the exodus from Egypt, extending as far back as Abraham (Acts 3:12–26; 7:38).

The prophetic dimension is no different. It operates according to a Kingdom dynamic, meaning it is never static or stagnant but vigorously progressive by nature. Though gradual, there is continual forward motion and advancement to a higher place or dimension. This prophetic development can be identified and tracked through three—the biblical number of completion—distinct stages in Scripture, ranging from inception to complete maturation.

Stage One: Inception

From a technical standpoint, the prophetic dimension can be traced from as early as Adam. However, from an official standpoint, the ministry of *prophet* is first introduced and identified in Scripture through the life of Abraham (Gen. 20:7). As we alluded to in the previous chapter, when the prophetic dimension was first introduced through Abraham and the other patriarchs (Ps. 105:9–10, 14–15), it was not on account of any prophetic proclamation or prophecy they had given, even though their patriarchal blessings to their sons often carried a strong element of such (Gen. 49). It was the insight and intimacy displayed through covenant relationship that became the primary identifiable characteristics of the first prophetic dimension (2 Chron. 20:7; Is. 41:8; Jam. 2:23).

Since we have already briefly discussed the subject of *insight* in the previous chapter, in the context of Abraham's life, we will not attempt to repeat the same points here. Instead, we will attempt to briefly address the subject of *intimacy* since it was excluded from the list of *seven distinct characteristics of the prophet's ministry* by reason of it being foundational to them all.

Intimacy

The word *intimacy* describes *a close, familiar, and usually affectionate or loving personal relationship with another person.*[1] Scripture records that the prophet Abraham was called *the friend of God* (Jam. 2:23). The word *friend* in this context has been translated from the Greek word, **phílos**, and is describing someone *who is on intimate terms or in close association with another.*[2] The original Hebrew word used in the Old Testament to describe Abraham's intimate relationship with God and translated *friend* is **âhêb**, which means to have *an affection based on a close relationship, sometimes in comparison to other persons with a lesser relationship.*[3] You can see how both the Greek and Hebrew definitions of *friend* align very closely with our English definition of *intimacy*. What Scripture is describing of Abraham here is not just a casual friendship with God but a close, intimate relationship that stands above and beyond what most religious people would consider "normal" or regular.

This is how the prophetic dimension was first birthed and recognized—through an undeniably, yet uncommonly, high degree of personal intimacy with God. The prophetic dimension is first and foremost about intimacy with the Father and transferring that intimacy, passion, and hunger for God to others. It is not performance driven. It is not based upon how well you pray, prophesy, preach, teach, minister or work miracles. It is about how well you reflect, communicate and impart the presence of God to others.

This is the true core architecture of the prophetic that can't be humanly replicated or demonically counterfeited. When someone has been in the presence of God you will know it. There is tangible evidence. Something changes that separates you from everyone else. For Jacob, it was a limp—indicating a change in his walk (Gen. 32:22–32). For Moses, it was his countenance—radiating the splendor of God's glory (Ex. 34:29–35). For Jesus, it was His words, deeply penetrating the hearts of men despite His changed appearance or their lack of earthly recognition for who He really was—a tangible anointing (Luke 24:15–32).

It is worth noting that despite all of the complaining, rejection, and rebellion that took place with the children of Israel against Moses in the wilderness, there was NEVER any debate as to him having been in the presence of God or having direct communication with Him. That fact was undeniable, even to his worse critics. They could deny his leadership, but they could never deny his close, intimate relationship with the Father (Num. 12:1–2; 16:1–3).

You may be very gifted, but you will never be genuinely prophetic without having developed a close, intimate relationship with the Father also. And without this type of intimacy, you have no real access to insight. The relationship between these two spiritual principles is clearly expressed in Jesus' message to His disciples.

> *You are My friends if you do whatever I command*
> *you. No longer do I call you servants, for a servant*
> *does not know what his master is doing; but I have*

called you friends, for all things that I heard from My
Father I have made known to you. (John 15:14–15)

One of the first things you may have noticed in this passage is that Jesus is discussing the principle of friendship. In case you were wondering, it is the same Greek word— *phílos*—that we examined earlier in reference to Abraham. However, what many people miss is the important clause or condition that is issued at the beginning as a prerequisite for this type of intimate relationship—*You are My friends if you do whatever I command you.* This is very important because the usual tendency is to assume that true intimacy with God is determined by time spent in prayer, hours spent in worship, church attendance, or perhaps some other spiritual discipline or exercise. While these can all be good and beneficial toward that end, they do not determine genuine intimacy. You can be faithful in doing all of these things and still be a servant. Genuine intimacy with God is determined solely by our obedience to what He commands, not just in a moral or doctrinal sense, but by our receptivity and response to His voice in matters of everyday life. In other words, you may read your Bible and pray for seven hours a day, faithfully and frequently participating in "church" religious activities, and be quite passionate in your singing or worshipping to the hit song, "I Am a Friend of God," yet never be His true friend. He creates the terms, not you. It is based upon His initiative, not yours. He sanctions the friendship and chooses you, and it is always based upon meeting His condition of obedience (John 15:16).

As Jesus proceeds to redefine the nature of His relationship to His disciples—based, of course, upon their faithful obedience to His commands—He reveals a profound connection between intimacy and insight. Intimacy creates access to secret information that even faithful servants are not privileged to. A *servant does not know what his master is doing,* but an intimate friend does. Note the similarity and contrast here to the words of the prophet Amos.

Surely the Lord God does nothing, Unless He reveals
His secret to His servants the prophets (Amos 3:7).

Even though the prophets are being described as *servants* in this context—designated as such because they never spoke their own message or of their own accord, only the words of their Master as He commanded them to—they are clearly being depicted as friends. They have been given access to privileged information from the Lord God that others do not have. They are intimately aware of what their *Master is doing*. God does absolutely *nothing* without their knowledge. They are given incredible insight on account of their intimate friendship and relationship with God, thus expressing once again the core architecture of the first prophetic dimension.

Stage Two: Recognition and Expansion

The second distinct and official stage of the prophetic ministry's development occurs centuries (just around 1,000 years) later, during the days of Samuel.

> *And all the prophets who have spoken, from Samuel and those who came after him, also proclaimed these days.* (Acts 3:24, ESV, emphasis mine)

You will notice in the text above that Peter—who is the one speaking—identifies Samuel as marking a clear and distinct period in the prophetic movement. Earlier in his message, relative to Jesus Christ, Peter stated that *God has spoken by the mouth of all His holy prophets **since the world began*** (v. 21). He then goes on to quote from Moses as one of the prophets from this earlier era [*since the world began*] (vs. 22–23). However, when he gets to verse 24, which is the text quoted above, he makes a distinction, separating Samuel and those after him from Moses and the earlier prophets *since the world began*. So now we have two distinct eras: The era represented by *all of His holy prophets since the world began*, and the era represented by *all the prophets who have spoken, from Samuel and those who came after him*.

The significance of this distinction between the two eras is further emphasized by the author of one of the books attributed to the prophet Samuel.

> *[Formerly in Israel, when a man went to inquire of God, he spoke thus: "Come, let us go to the seer"; for he who is now called a prophet was formerly called a seer.]* (1 Sam. 9:9)

In this particular text, which is a parenthetical insertion by the author, there is a clear distinction and contrast being made between the period before Samuel and the current one. Whenever there is a major spiritual shift, reformation, development or upgrade in the Kingdom of God, it is usually accompanied by a change of vocabulary, terminology, or definition of spiritual principles. For example, in the first major upgrade or reformation of God's Covenant People, initiated by Jesus, new vocabulary was introduced (e.g. "apostles," "Christians," etc.). In addition to this, there was also new terminology (e.g. "kingdom of heaven," "kingdom of God," etc.) and a redefinition of spiritual principles (e.g. prayer, priesthood, etc.) A similar pattern is quite evident in the present context where there is a change in terminology from *seer* to *prophet*.

While it may be quite obvious to some of us that the term *seer* has never been used in Scripture before now, and that the word *prophet*, till now, has been the near exclusive designation for the prophetic function, it is important that we understand that the context is referring to what was popular among the people, especially during that period just prior to Samuel. It is also important that we recognize that these two distinct—but synonymous—terms are being applied to the same ministry function.

Prophets versus Seers: Debunking the Myths

The only thing worse than having no information is having wrong or false information. Misinformation can be much more destructive than ignorance. For decades, it has been commonly taught and believed, especially in certain religious circles, that prophets and seers represented two distinct but similar ministries. The seer was often viewed as the visionary—seeing mostly visions and pictures—while the prophet was viewed as an ecstatic who would prophesy from an unction "bubbling up" from within him. The seers "saw" and the prophets "heard" or "felt." Books have been written by some very well-meaning, though sadly misinformed, individuals seeking to explain the differences between these two ministries and how they function. Some prophetic training seminars have even been tailored to separate the "seers" from the "hearers" or "feelers," often encouraging the participants to choose the category they best fit into. As plausible as this position may sound—its plausibility demonstrated by the number of scholars who once accepted it—this type of dichotomy is simply untrue and cannot be adequately supported in Scripture. On the contrary, new scholarly evidence now disproves this theory, as does practical wisdom and experience.

At the risk of getting too technical, here are some interesting scholarly insights regarding the use of these two prophetic terms:

> The concept of prophecy is connected with three Hebrew roots:
>
> *R'h, hzh,* and *nb'*. These three roots and their derivatives were sometimes used synonymously, but each had its own semantic field and history of application. The verb *rā'â* has the basic meaning "see, perceive, understand." When it refers to a prophet, the participle *rō'eh* has traditionally been translated "seer." 1 Sam 9:9 indicates that the *rō'eh* was a person who revealed secrets by inquiring of God for an answer. Some have concluded on the basis of etymology that the seer's revelation always came in visual form. But in the twelve places where *rō'eh* occurs (most referring to Samuel), there is little or no indication that the seer's answer came in the form of a dream or vision. The verb *rā'â* is used in numerous cases to

describe the visual part of a theophany, dream, or vision (e.g., Gen 16:13; 1 Sam 28:13; 1 Kings 22:17,19; 1 Chron 21:16,20; Isa 6:1,5; Jer 1:11–13; Ezek 1:1,27 f; Dan 8:2–7,15,20; Amos 7:8; 8:2; Zech 1:8,18), but these occurrences do not coincide with the use of the participle rŏ'eh. The derived nouns *mar'eh* and *mar'â*, appearing predominantly in the late books of Ezekiel and Daniel, describe the "visions" that these prophets saw. This evidence does not, however, support the view that the seer was primarily a visionary or a dreamer of dreams. The essence of the idea is that God allowed certain people to "see" (i.e., understand)—or receive a divine communication that contained insight into—past, present, or future events...

The main term used in the OT to refer to a prophet is *nābî'* (or fem. *Nēbî'â*). Various theories concerning its etymology have been proposed. Gesenius, Kuenen (p. 42), and von Orelli (pp. 11 f) connected it with *nābā'* ("bubble forth"), thus understanding the prophets as ecstatics who bubbled forth words with great fervor. Arnold (p. 93) and Pfeiffer (p. 83) regarded the term as a passive (niphal) participle from bô' ("enter"), describing one who was entered by a spirit. Cornill (pp. 9 f), Eiselen (p. 23), and Konig (p. 260) traced the term to an Arabic root meaning "announce"; thus the prophet was an announcer or spokesman of God's words. Meek (pp. 150 f), Johnson (pp. 24 f), Haldar (p. 109), and Scott (p.45) favored an Akkadian etymology meaning "speaking or proclaiming." Albright (p. 303), Rowley (pp. 103–05), and Lindblom (p. 102) preferred a passive interpretation, "the one who is called by God." These differences of interpretation indicate the necessity of caution in using an etymological approach to determine the meaning of *nābî'*. The exact historical origin of the root may remain uncertain, but a careful study of the usage of its verbal and noun forms can reveal its semantic range...

The role of the *nābî'* is clarified in the relationship between Moses and Aaron. Because Moses refused to speak to Pharaoh, Yahweh appointed Aaron to be his *nābî'* (Ex 6:28–7:2). Moses himself is called a *nābî'* because God spoke through him (cf. Num 12:1, 6–8). The prophets were persons who spoke the words that God put in their mouths (Deut 18:18–22); they were messengers... The complexity and dynamic development of the prophetic movement argue against any clearcut distinction between the inspiration and central function of the *nābî'* and that of the *rō'eh* or hōzeh. Rō'eh was a more popular title during the early history of Israel while *nābî'* became the preferred title at a later date (1 Sam 9:9).[4]

In Saul's day a **prophet** was known primarily as a **seer** (*rō'eh*) undoubtedly because the major thrust of his ministry was associated with receiving divine revelation, even in matters as mundane as finding lost animals. Later prophets served more as proclaimers of revelation, spokesmen for God (*nāḇî'*), though of course all prophets were both seers and proclaimers. Samuel, for example, was expressly described by both terms (9:11; 3:20).[5]

For those of you who may have been lost by some of the technical jargon or Greek and Hebrew words, let me summarize. The

Hebrew word translated as *seer* in our English Bibles is derived from another Hebrew word describing sight, perception, or understanding. This "seeing," by the way, covers every sensory and supersensory (or extrasensory) dimension of perception and comprehension, including hearing and feeling.[6] In the same way that we use the words "**I see** what you mean" when having a conversation with someone to denote comprehension (when there's nothing actually being *seen* but *heard*), is a similar way to how the word is used in Scripture. The word *seer*, therefore, is not limited to someone who receives revelation solely or primarily through visions or pictures but describes the process of *reception* and the powers of *perception* granted to the prophet.[7] In other words, what is being described here is the prophet's *insight*. Thus, when the author of the first book of Samuel says that *formerly*—indicative of the previous era—prophets were called seers, he is stating that prophets of the former era were recognized primarily by their ability to receive divine revelation or insight, which attests to what we have already established from the first prophetic dimension (Stage One).

In the second prophetic dimension, however, the preferred terminology is *prophet* because it represents and highlights a different facet or aspect of their ministry. The emphasis is shifted from what is *seen* to what is *said*.

Furthermore, the Hebrew word translated as *prophet* in Scripture has often been wrongly defined due to it being traced to inaccurate etymological sources. Because of relying too heavily on etymology and not on usage and context, the erroneous interpretation of a prophet being someone who ecstatically "bubbles forth words with great fervor"—pouring forth words automatically while under divine influence—was the accepted definition among many scholars. However, this definition is now being widely rejected, and for good reason.[8] When God applied the term *prophet* to Aaron (as being Moses' prophet), it was clearly in the context of Aaron speaking on Moses' behalf, with absolutely no connotation whatsoever of ecstatic behavior or "bubbling forth" (Ex. 4:14–17; 7:1–2). This idea of speaking or proclamation is consistent with the general usage of the word *prophet* in Scripture. Therefore, we can conclusively say that while *seer* is indicative of revelatory *perception* or *reception*, the term *prophet* is indicative of *proclamation* or *declaration*, thus its preferred usage in the current era of Samuel. It represents the natural transition from just having or receiving divine insight to boldly communicating this divine insight to others. Incidentally, if you refer again to the text from Acts 3:24 (ESV) that was quoted when we first started this section (Stage Two), you will notice the word *proclamation* employed as an important defining characteristic of that prophetic dimension closely identified with Samuel.

A Formally Established Movement

The prophet Samuel played a major role in redefining and upgrading the prophetic movement in his era. Through his efforts, the prophetic was taken out of the shadows and brought from a place of obscurity to public recognition. Effectively, Samuel was able to expand the prophetic dimension beyond its previous borders and boundaries.

> Samuel, of the Levite family of Kohath (1 Chron 6:28; 9:22), not only reformed the priests but gave the prophets a new standing... Prophets existed before: Abraham, and the patriarchs as recipients of God's revelations, are so designated (Ps 105:15; Gen 15:12; 20:7); but Samuel constituted them into a permanent order. He instituted theological colleges of prophets; one at Ramah where he lived (1 Sam 19:12,20), another was at Bethel (2 Kings 2:3), another at Jericho (2 Kings 2:5), another at Gilgal (2 Kings 4:38, also 2 Kings 6:1)... Official prophets seem to have continued to the close of the Old Testament, though the direct mention of "the sons of the prophets" occurs only in Samuel's, Elijah's, and Elisha's time.[9]

63

As you can see from above, Samuel brought the movement into a place of "official" standing.[10] One could even say he solidified the movement. Prophets became a formally recognized ministry operating from an "official" capacity within the nation. From this point on, prophets are ranked in a similar capacity as priests, with a succession continued by formal training and impartation instead of bloodline or birthright. Being both priest and prophet himself, Samuel essentially created an overlapping and assimilation in these two areas, demonstrated by the fact that *prophet* and *priest* are mentioned together about thirty times in Scripture, especially in the late monarchic period.[11]

Parallels and Principles

There are several significant similarities between the prophetic movement pioneered by Samuel during his era and the fairly recent prophetic movement that rose into prominence during the late '80s.

Firstly, before the prophetic movement was elevated to the next dimension during the days of Samuel, it was preceded by a period of darkness where insight and revelation was rare (1 Sam. 3:1). This is not to imply that there were no functional prophets during this "dark" period because that would be inaccurate (Judg. 4:4, 6:8; 1 Sam. 2:27). However, such ministry was infrequent and uncommon. Similar conditions existed in the '80s where there was hardly any open vision (insight) or prophetic revelation. Some would argue that conditions still haven't changed much today despite the thousands of people prophesying who claim to have the "word of the Lord" (Jer. 14:14, 23:16, 26; Ezek. 13:2–3, 17).

Secondly, just as prophets took on formal recognition and acceptance (alongside priests) during Samuel's era, prophets were formally recognized and accepted within certain Christian religious structures as being a valid ministry function in operation today that did not cease after God's Covenant Kingdom Community was birthed on Pentecost and the canon of Scripture was deemed completed centuries later. Like in Samuel's era, it was not that prophets never existed or functioned prior to that time, just that they were never formally accepted and recognized as such, especially within the formal religious structures. Recognition and acceptance gradually grew to the point that they were formally institutionalized, just like pastors or evangelists (priests). People were being "ordained" as prophets and wearing the title proudly. Many of us can distinctly remember that season when it seemed like almost every minister you met was carrying the title of "prophet." Yet as is often the case when spiritual principles and functions are relegated to formal religious practice and professional service, error crept in. Authenticity gave place to illegitimacy, corruption, and excess.

Scripture furnishes us with ample historical evidence testifying to this error. Less than three or four generations later—after Samuel has pioneered this new prophetic movement—we find an apostate prophetic order functioning at Bethel—one of the main recognized sites where the *sons of the prophets* were gathered and trained (1 Kings 13; 2 Kings 2:3). God had to send a prophet all the way from Judah to condemn the error because there was apparently no other prophet present there who was accurate enough to do it (1 Kings 13:1). Soon after that, we find even more inaccuracy with an established prophetic order being loyal and favorable to corrupt kings (leaders) and operating according to the power and influence of Baal and Asherah [false gods] (1 Kings 18:19). By the time Jeremiah and Ezekiel emerge generations later, the established prophetic order is so corrupt that it appears that almost every formally recognized prophet functioning within the established religious system is perverse (Jer. 13:13, 23:14–15, 32:32; Ezek. 13:2–4, 16: 22:25–28).

This pattern of degradation has proven true—albeit at a much faster rate—in our generation. Twenty-nine years into what has been widely recognized to be a prophetic movement, we see the same aspects of corruption permeating the current movement. Many proudly wear a title with no authenticity. Many promote and endorse a system of worship that is in clear violation of the Kingdom of God. Many are more concerned about gaining favor with leaders than accurately communicating the heart and mind of God. And many have ascribed to a mantic—not prophetic—pattern that conforms more closely to divination and the spirit of Baal. If these statements appear to be a little vague, fear not. These issues will be addressed in greater detail as we go along.

Thirdly, one of the most outstanding characteristics of the prophetic movement of Samuel's day was the establishment of prophetic companies—regarded by various scholars and commentators as prophetic schools, prophetic guilds, prophetic communities, prophetic bands, or theological colleges—for teaching, training, and equipping in prophetic ministry. These prophetic training centers were apparently established by Samuel for much more than just providing training, community, mature leadership, and sound structure in the development of young budding and immature prophets. Samuel sought to ensure that the prophetic dimension was not monopolized or exercised as the exclusive possession of a select few but was more widely distributed and reproduced in others.

Proof that the prophetic dimension is both transferrable as well as reproducible is evident by the several biblical accounts where either Saul or his "messengers"—most likely trained soldiers—were subjected to the same prophetic spirit, behavior, and mentality as the prophetic company (1 Sam. 10:5–13, 19:18–24).[12] This was not just a shallow manifestation of prophesying, which is always the first, quickest, and easiest manifestation of the prophetic that can take place within minutes. After he prophesied, the text states that he would *be turned into another man* (internal transformation)—which is the true breadth and measure of the prophetic dimension (1 Sam. 10:6). Even though Saul's transformation was only temporary and evanescent—due to his very brief proximity and association with the prophetic company and Samuel's leadership—the results are very telling. When one of the accounts of this experience records of Saul that *he also stripped off his clothes and prophesied before Samuel in like manner...naked*—with the words *he also* (which is repeated in the text) and *in like manner* indicative of the fact that Saul's behavior followed the pattern of what was being expressed through the entire prophetic company, including the servants who were sent before him[13]—we are being informed of the depth of internal transformation that is initiated through close proximity and submission to an accurate prophetic dimension.

The stripping off of their clothes and lying down *naked* before Samuel is not the same as we examined in the previous chapter with Isaiah. This time, it really does not imply total nakedness. It is referring to their outer garments, including the soldiers' (messengers) uniforms or armor and Saul's kingly robes of regality.[14] Beyond the external stripping and divestment is a much deeper and profound spiritual principle. It represents a deep spiritual humility where there is no longer any recognition of earthly rank, human ability, or accomplishment. It represents a heart and life that is completely surrendered to God, allowing Him full access because we are no longer "guarded" or "protected" as a result of our past hurts, wounds, fears, or disappointments. To be stripped of outer garments is to be stripped of selfishness, pride, and human ambition. It is to be divested of ulterior motives and carnal intent. This represents a powerful internal transformation. Unfortunately, Saul never remained in that prophetic environment long enough for the process to be completed. Had he continued indefinitely, he would never have reverted to his old ways.

Similar to the prophetic movement of Samuel's day, the prophetic movement of the late '80s spawned what is now rapidly becoming a massive thrust in providing prophetic training and activation in spiritual gifts to desirous believers. One particular camp boasts of having trained over 250,000 in this regard. There are now numerous prophetic training seminars being held by various individuals, ministries, churches, and camps all over the United States and across the world. However, even in this major similarity, there are several key or significant differences. Most of the prophetic training camps or seminars I know of place an inordinate amount of attention on the simplest and shallowest aspect of the prophetic—prophesying. Learning to prophesy correctly is important, but Samuel clearly placed the emphasis on more important areas in order to produce such a powerfully accurate prophetic dimension during his time.

In addition, most of the prophetic training offered today can be completed in a matter of hours or days, but this was not the case in Samuel's era. Prophetic companies didn't just meet for a couple of hours a day or a few times per week. They lived together, worshipped together, and shared meals together—both single and married—under the leadership of Samuel as a corporate prophetic community,[15] similar to the way the apostles (or disciples) of Jesus were called to be with their Master on a seemingly continuous or permanent basis. The reason for this is simple: It takes time and the right cultivated environment to thoroughly and effectively reproduce a true prophetic dimension. There must be mentoring involved because true impartation follows close association. Even Jesus understood this principle in preparing His disciples. Are we greater than Jesus? The account of Saul and his servants in 1 Samuel 19:18–24 is proof that the ability to prophesy can come in minutes, but if we are not continually exposed and subjected to an accurate prophetic environment indefinitely, we abort the process and revert to simply being people who can prophesy. In an era when we pride ourselves on doing almost everything more quickly and efficiently, it is important that we understand that there is no fast-track to the things of the Spirit.

Fourthly, the prophetic movement of Samuel's day brought a new dimension to the corporate worship expression of that era. This should not be surprising since, scripturally, there has always been a close link or connection between music (as an expression of worship to God) and the prophetic (Ex. 15:20–21; 2 Kings 3:15). As a matter of fact, the first time the concept of a "company of prophets" is introduced in Scripture, it is in the context of powerful prophetic worship with the accompaniment of stringed (harp), percussion (tambourine), and wind (flute) instruments (1 Sam. 10:5). Eventually, prophets (or seers)—Asaph, Heman (Samuel's grandson) and Jeduthun—are recognized as the established leading participants in Israel's corporate worship activities under David, able to *prophesy* skillfully with their instruments (1 Chron. 25:1–6; 2 Chron. 29:30). This prophetic dimension inevitably brought a new dynamic to their corporate worship experience. There would have been greater vitality and spontaneity in their worship. There would have been a new prophetic *sound* and a new prophetic *song* released from the Lord (Ex. 15:1; Judg. 5:1). This prophetic element wasn't just an insignificant appendage to their corporate worship routines; it was the primary component and central aspect of their expression.

This prophetic integration into the worship dynamic of Samuel's era—especially under David's leadership—finds a similar parallel in the current worship practices of many churches today. With the prophetic movement of the late '80s came a new recognition and release of prophetic psalmists and musicians. A new emphasis and expectation was placed on cultivating a spiritual climate through worship where the song of the Lord—*the voice of the bridegroom and the voice of the bride* (Jer. 33:11)—was heard in the midst of the congregation. A new *sound* and a new *song* were heard in the midst of corporate praise and worship. Militant warfare praise became the staple of the early movement, tapering off later on to various other forms of expression, including "harp and bowl."[16] Some have even attempted to replicate David's 24-7 worship pattern in this context.

Nevertheless, this aspect of the prophetic movement has not been without its share of error, excess, and imbalance. I have been in some "prophetic" churches where it was almost impossible to enter into deep corporate communion with God through worship due to the fact that there were often numerous distractions from people breaking the flow of worship to give prophecies or words of exhortation.[17] This is often perpetuated by the immature and insecure who feel the need to prophesy during almost every service in order to cement their legacy as the recognized "house prophet."[18] There is nothing wrong with having *occasional* prophecies during the course of worship when the occasion demands or encourages it, but when prophecy becomes the focus of your worship, that is when the tail is wagging the dog! The prophetic was intended to enhance our worship, not distract from it. When anything or anyone serves to distract from Jesus or the Father, it/he/she ceases to be prophetic. When a true prophetic word, note, rhythm, melody, or song is issued from heaven, it will take the corporate worship experience to a higher level; when it emanates from the flesh, the opposite occurs. The really sad part about it is after the service was over—and I inquired of several people about the various words that were given during the course of the praise and worship—nobody could recall what was said, not that I was in any way surprised. Like a puff of smoke or the vapor of steam from a hot cup or plate, these words quickly evaporate and disappear from remembrance because they do not carry the weight or force of heaven.

One of the other hindrances I have experienced with regard to so-called "prophetic" praise and worship has been the misdirected focus upon ourselves. The overemphasis on "spiritual warfare"[19]—which some could argue was another aspect or parallel of the prophetic movement pioneered by Samuel and then brought into fruition under David as the warrior king—and the desire for personal or corporate "breakthrough" has created a subtle opening for the enemy to exploit. When the focus of our worship is shifted from honoring and magnifying the Lord for who He is to magnifying our personal or corporate needs and desires for blessing or breakthrough, we are no longer engaging in true prophetic worship. As a matter of fact, we are no longer engaging in true worship—period! The prophetic dimension was always intended to point to Him, not to ourselves.

Finally, another significant aspect of similarity that can be found between the prophetic movement of Samuel's era and the one in our current era is the fact that they were both precipitated by deep internal deficiency, dysfunctionality, and degeneracy in the priesthood of their time. A new prophetic dimension usually precedes a season of divine reformation. In many respects, the prophetic movement of Samuel's day was necessitated by ecclesiastical corruption.[20]

When Samuel was still a young boy serving under Eli with no prophetic experience, he received divine insight from the Lord informing him of the corruption that existed within the priesthood and God's unrelenting intent to dispense certain judgment upon Eli's household according to a previous prophecy that was yet unfulfilled (1 Sam. 2:22–3:18). In other words, God informed Samuel very early in his ministry that he was serving under a rejected and corrupt priesthood that was shortly going to be judged. Samuel understood from this message that there was a dire need for reformation within the priesthood; however, he continued to faithfully serve as priest under Eli—within the corrupt system—until the word of the Lord was fulfilled and Eli's priestly heritage was destroyed. With the fulfillment of this word came the temporary loss of the Ark of the Covenant (symbolizing the presence and glory of God) and a shift from Shiloh—being formerly the center for all spiritual activity under the charge of the priests—to Samuel and his company of prophets (1 Sam. 4–7). The prophetic movement, therefore, was largely birthed and assimilated into the priesthood through Samuel.

Here is the problem: By Samuel choosing to remain submitted to a deficient and dysfunctional spiritual leader in Eli, while faithfully serving within a corrupt priestly system, he exposed himself to the defilement of similar error. The issue here isn't whether or not Samuel should have remained submitted to Eli and continued serving among a defiled priesthood. As far as we can tell from the text, God never gave Samuel any explicit instructions to leave Eli's side. As a matter of fact, Samuel was dedicated to this service even before birth, so one could argue that he may not have had much of a choice but to remain under Eli (1 Sam. 1:11, 20–28, 2:11). And who can forget the account years afterward of David being placed under the demented leadership of rejected Saul (1 Sam. 17:19–21)? There are times when God places us under corrupt leaders in order to expose the corruption within us and teach us what *not to do*! No doubt Samuel learned quite a lot from his experience under Eli. Nevertheless, it is impossible to argue with the scriptural and historical evidence that Samuel repeated the same fundamental error as his predecessor and mentor Eli.

> *Now it came to pass when Samuel was old that he made his sons judges over Israel. But his sons did not walk in his ways; they turned aside after dishonest gain, took bribes, and perverted justice. Then all the elders of Israel gathered together and came to Samuel at Ramah, and said to him, "Look, you are old, and your sons do not walk in your ways. Now make us a king to judge us like all the nations."* (1 Sam. 8:1, 3–5)

Samuel's unwillingness to restrain or rebuke his immoral sons is indicative of an internal deficiency, defilement, or weakness inherited from Eli (1 Sam. 3:13). And it was on account of this paternal deficiency and corruption of his sons, whom he had appointed as judges, that the people chose to reject God's government, whether through prophet, priest, or judge. In other words, they were directly—or indirectly—rejecting Samuel and his new prophetic order when they demanded a king (1 Sam. 8:7). The people had a valid argument, but what displeased God about this request was that the people chose to *reject* rather than *correct* what was wrong. They chose to throw the proverbial "baby out with the bathwater" instead of address what was wrong in the current movement. And what was wrong was Samuel was repeating the same error of the priesthood he was called to reform and correct—by failing to confront error in those closest to him and seeking to establish a permanent personal legacy through hereditary judges like the formal priesthood, an idea that Gideon had totally rejected before (Judg. 8:22–23).

Fast-forward once again to the current prophetic movement today and we are confronted with the same issues. God birthed the prophetic movement of the late '80s to begin a reformation within the hearts of His people. To my knowledge, it was after the prophetic movement was birthed that the first and earliest rumblings of reformation occurred during the post-protestant era. The movement was largely birthed and integrated into the existing and prevailing religious "church" culture and environment. It was developed under a system and philosophy of ministry that God has rejected and is prepared to judge. The founding "Samuels" had been previously mentored, pastored, and instructed by deficient "Elis," serving loyally and faithfully within a system of "church" and ministry that was predominantly dysfunctional and corrupt. They may have learned to avoid many of the pitfalls and errors of their predecessors, but they were still subjected to the limitations of an eternal principle: Everything produces (or reproduces) after its own kind. In other words, like begets like (Gen. 1:11, 24–25). As such, the prophetic movement was subject to defilement from the beginning, inheriting the same weaknesses and error as the religious system it was called to reform. The overwhelming emphasis of the movement today is on making people feel good with promises of peace, blessing, or breakthrough instead of confronting the greed, self-indulgence, and corruption that takes place within the priesthood [including pastors, ministers, leaders and pulpits] (1 Sam. 2:12–17, 22). The main motivating factor for most public speaking ministry today is not to speak the truth but to be invited back. How sad that for most today, these do not imply the same thing. When a prophet is invited to speak, the expectation on both sides is that he affirms and blesses what the pastor or senior leader is doing rather than confront any error or bring adjustment so that there is correct alignment with heaven.

And then there is the issue of legacy to consider. Ministry—including "prophetic" ministry—today is driven by a desire to be remembered and immortalized by a lasting legacy. Most ministers are too preoccupied with trying to make a name for themselves than establishing God's Kingdom. Furthermore, many ministries and churches today are run like a family business or a formal priesthood, completely hereditary and passed on from father to son. There is nothing necessarily wrong with having family members or relatives share in the work of the ministry or be appointed to key positions of leadership as long as they are qualified and deserving of it. James—the brother of Jesus—was not appointed to apostolic leadership simply on account of him being Jesus's brother but on account of the grace of God that was clearly demonstrated in his life (Acts 15:13–21; Gal. 1:19; see also the epistle of James). But in Samuel's case, his sons were definitely not deserving of such authority or responsibility. Many sons, daughters, nieces, nephews, etc., are not deserving of such today. When people are appointed or promoted to key positions based solely upon familial or hereditary ties, that is a sure indication of error. This type of nepotism, cronyism, favoritism, narcissism, greed, and just blatant error is rampant in the current movement, leaving no doubt as to why some have chosen to reject the movement in its current state. While the people today may not have demanded a "king," God has graciously sent us one in the form of the apostle or apostolic dimension, sent to establish accuracy and order in a defiled and corrupted movement.

Stage Three: Maturation

The final major shift or upgrade to the prophetic movement recorded in Scripture occurs a little over 1,000 years later, following what has been traditionally recognized as a roughly 400-year period of "silence" or dormancy in the movement. Like the period preceding the movement in Samuel's day, there was apparently a scarcity or absence of any genuinely significant prophetic ministry or revelation during that time (1 Sam. 3:1). This does not imply total silence or that there were not those who called themselves prophets who presumed to speak for God during this period, only that there was a lack of valid, God-breathed revelation. It would seem, then, that since these periods of "silence" just prior to every major upgrade in the prophetic movement are so common, it must be God's way of hitting the "reset" button or "rebooting" the spiritual operating system in order to install a new upgrade. Whatever the case, this time, it is John the Baptist who marks the beginning of a new prophetic dimension.

> But what did you go out to see? A prophet? Yes, I say to you, and more than a prophet. For this is he of whom it is written: "Behold, I send My messenger before Your face, Who will prepare Your way before You." Assuredly, I say to you, among those born of women there has not risen one greater than John the Baptist; but he who is least in the kingdom of heaven is greater than he. And **from** the days of John the Baptist until now the kingdom of heaven suffers violence, and the violent take it by force. For all the prophets and the law prophesied **until** John. (Matt. 11:9–13, emphasis mine)

Once again, we find a clear distinction being made in the prophetic movement, this time with reference to John. Jesus states very clearly that *all the prophets prophesied **until** John* (v. 13). And just in case you still needed help being convinced, Jesus draws a clear separator or dividing line in the previous verse with the words, ***from** the days of John* (v. 12). Regardless of whatever prophetic dimension or ministry occurred in the past, Jesus is saying that what is being birthed at present through John the Baptist is something completely new! In fact, it is so new that it requires new vocabulary and new terminology. You will recall the principle we mentioned earlier that with every major spiritual shift, reformation, development, or upgrade in the Kingdom of God, it is usually accompanied by a change of vocabulary, terminology, or definition of spiritual principles. This very same principle is established in this third prophetic dimension; the only difference being that this new vocabulary is not clearly defined. When Jesus questions the multitudes on what they went out into the wilderness to see, He responds by affirming that they went out to see a *prophet*. However, this was not a totally accurate definition because, according to Jesus, he was *more than a prophet* (v. 9).

In support of His statement that John was *more than a prophet*, Jesus begins to quote from the prophet Malachi about the *messenger* who would be sent as a precursor or forerunner to prepare the way for the heavenly *Messenger*—Jesus the Messiah (Mal. 3:1; Matt. 11:10). In other words, Jesus was saying that the prophetic dimension being introduced through John would find the fullness of its expression through the Messiah Himself. Jesus—the Messiah—would be the ultimate expression of this new prophetic dimension. As far as I can tell from Scripture, Jesus is identified with the ministry of the prophet above all other ministries (Deut. 18:15–19; Matt. 16:14; Mark 6:4, 15; Luke 7:16, 24:19; John 4:19, 5:46–47, 6:14). But who would argue that Jesus wasn't *more than a prophet* (Heb. 3:1)? John, therefore, is *more than a prophet* because he represents—through Jesus—the ultimate prophetic dimension—the most concentrated, accurate, and fully matured prophetic dimension that ever existed on earth. No other human being—representative of all past prophetic dimensions or movements—was greater than John [or the prophetic dimension now being introduced through him] (v.11).

Apostolic Integration

Interestingly, the word *messenger* in the above passage (v. 10) is translated from the Greek word, **aggelos**, describing a *human messenger serving as an envoy* or *one who is sent*.[21] In the original Malachi passage, the Hebrew word employed is **mal'ākh**, also used to describe *one sent*, or *a prophet*,[22] with the general sense of *an ambassador repre-*

senting someone who sent him.[23] This emphasis on being a "sent one" and functioning as an ambassador (or envoy) that is charged with representing the interests of a person, entity, or government higher than himself highlights a new aspect of this new prophetic dimension. In other words, what is being described here is a powerful apostolic dimension being integrated into the prophetic. It is one of the reasons why John was *more than a prophet* and the new prophetic dimension he ushered in was greater than all others. He was an apostolic prophet. This is not to say that this apostolic "sent" dimension wasn't already present in the prophetic movements of the past to a certain degree, but in John's era, it takes on a new emphasis. In the first prophetic dimension, the emphasis was on what was *seen* (revelation); in the second prophetic dimension, the emphasis was on what was *spoken* or *said* (proclamation); but in the third prophetic dimension, the emphasis is clearly on being *sent* (authorization).

Divine Authorization

Authorization is representative of rank and authority, and the extent or degree of this rank and authority is determined solely by the sender. Like an earthly ambassador, the power and authority he walks in is determined by the nation or government he represents. When an earthly ambassador speaks, he speaks on the sole authority of his nation or government that he has been officially deputized to represent. It doesn't matter if the people he is sent to are more qualified, educated, or successful than he is personally; it does not diminish his authority or rank. Similarly, the apostolic prophet's rank and authority comes solely from the Father in heaven—not from any man, minister, church, denomination, or network. It doesn't come from any earthly credentials, accomplishments, or degrees. When the prophet speaks, it is as if the Father Himself is speaking, and all the power and authority of the Kingdom of Heaven is at his disposal. In other words, he is divinely authorized, and regardless of the fact that the people he is sent to may be more humanly or religiously qualified, accomplished, or successful than he is personally, his true rank and authority does not diminish as a cause of it.

It is important to interject here that being recognized and authorized by your ministry, church, or network does not necessarily imply being divinely authorized by God. I know many prophets and ministers who are authorized in such a religious fashion and who are expected to properly represent the ecclesiastical or religious entity that sent them. There is nothing necessarily wrong with having ecclesiastical or religious authorization so long as you understand their limitations. It is one thing to have an organization backing you, but it is quite another thing to have heaven's regard or approval. Divine authorization speaks of spiritual rank, not religious rank; and contrary to popular opinion, these two terms are not synonymous or interchangeable. In other words, one does not imply the other. In the same way that one could have religious rank and authorization and yet never gain heaven's backing or approval, one could have heaven's rank and authorization and yet never be recognized or approved within earthly religious structures. This principle will be explored more fully shortly when we take a closer look and examination of the life and ministry of John.

Preparing the Way

This new authorization from heaven is not just given for the validation or endorsement of the apostolic prophet's ministry or this new prophetic dimension; it is given for the purpose of "preparing the way" for the King and His Kingdom (v. 10). We get a much clearer picture of this concept, as well as the true mission and mandate of this third prophetic dimension by examining the original prophetic text in the book of Malachi.

> "Behold, I send My messenger, And he will prepare the way before Me. And the Lord, whom you seek, Will suddenly come to His temple, Even the Messenger of the covenant, In whom you delight. Behold, He is coming," Says the Lord of hosts. "But who can endure the day of His coming? And who can stand when He appears? For He is like a refiner's fire

> *And like launderer's soap. He will sit as a refiner and*
> *a purifier of silver; He will purify the sons of Levi,*
> *And purge them as gold and silver, That they may*
> *offer to the Lord An offering in righteousness. "Then*
> *the offering of Judah and Jerusalem Will be pleasant*
> *to the Lord, As in the days of old, As in former years.*
> *And I will come near you for judgment; I will be a*
> *swift witness Against sorcerers, Against adulterers,*
> *Against perjurers, Against those who exploit wage*
> *earners and widows and orphans, And against those*
> *who turn away an alien—Because they do not fear*
> *Me," Says the Lord of hosts.* (Mal. 3:1–5)

As alluded to before, there are two messengers in this passage. The first is the human *messenger*, pointing forward to John the Baptist. The second, but most important, is the heavenly *Messenger*, pointing forward to Jesus Christ. John is the precursor, forerunner, or foretaste of a powerful apostolic-prophetic dimension that Jesus would personify in its fullness. As *messengers*, they both point to and represent the same thing. They both function as ambassadors of the Father and His Kingdom. Therefore, any principle that can be ascribed to either one as *messenger* can be ascribed to the prophetic dimension they represent as a whole.

The first aspect of the mission is applied to the human *messenger*, which is to *prepare the way*. The Hebrew verb translated *prepare* (*pānâ*) can be rendered a number of different ways in English, but in its current form and context, it means *to clear away* or *remove*.[24] From the way that this term ("prepare the way") has been employed in various other parts of Scripture, it is clear that the main emphasis is not only the removal of every obstacle or impediment that detracts or hinders access or view of the Father and His Kingdom but establishing accurate or correct building architecture as well (Is. 40:3–4, 57:14, 62:10). It echoes the Jeremiah 1:10 prophetic principle where there must first be a deliberate removal or clearing away of that which is incorrect or corrupt (negatives) before accurate building and establishing can take place (positives). In other words, the third prophetic dimension is concerned specifically with the correct architecture of building, and this building initiative is focused solely upon the Father and His Kingdom, not on personal blessing or comfort. It is authorized and deputized by the Father in Heaven to boldly *clear away* or *remove* anything—including that which may be religiously acceptable or popular—that hinders or obstructs in this regard. To resist or reject this spiritual process is to resist and reject the Lord Himself. He will not return to *His temple* (His People) without it (v. 1). The sad thing is many won't care since we have largely grown accustomed to having "church" without His divine presence anyway.

The second aspect of this third prophetic dimension mandate is applied in the text to the heavenly *Messenger*, who is like a *refiner's fire and like launderers' soap* (v. 2). Lest your Western mind-set causes you to miss the intended concept of what these two word-pictures were meant to convey, let me point out that the *fire* here is not the kind for making you comfortable or cozy. This is the type of fire that exposes and consumes defilement. Similarly, the *soap* here is not the gentle fragranced or refreshing kind like Dove that you shower with in your bathroom. Neither is it the gentle form of detergent that many people use in their washing machines. This *soap* (or lye) is a powerful chemical agent with a strong and deeply penetrating cleansing effect. In everyday terms, it may be more like modern bleach than modern soap.[25] The imagery used in this context is very aggressive and strong, indicating what the ESV Study Bible describes as a sense of *thoroughness and severity* in the purification or cleansing principle they convey.[26] It then goes on to describe just how harsh this process was:

> The heat of the refiner's fire was intense in order to separate the dross from the molten pure metal. Similarly, the fuller [launderer] washed clothes using strong lye soap, after which the clothes would be placed on rocks and beaten with sticks.[27]

From the process described above, it is fitting that the Lord asks, *But who can endure the day of His coming? And who can stand when He appears?* This is not the type of *Messenger* that most people look forward to seeing. As a matter of fact, this is exactly the type of *Messenger* that most religious people reject. He is not coming to make you feel good. This is not a "bless me" prophet that most churches open their doors to in order to have their ears tickled. The process described above doesn't appear at all to bring any "comfort." He is not interested in your personal or corporate "blessing" or "break-through." He comes to initiate an intense purification process that is deep and penetrating rather than shallow or religiously externalized. He comes to expose error and separate the holy from the profane. His ministry may burn and you may feel like you're being "beaten with sticks," but the end process is a people prepared for God. This is what the third prophetic dimension is all about. It is established by God for bringing purification and judgment.

The focal point of this deeply profound purification process and divine initiative of judgment isn't something generalized or random; it is targeted specifically to the *sons of Levi…that they may offer to the Lord an offering in righteousness.* In other words, the people being targeted here are those functioning within the established "priest-hood" of public ministry. Today, such people may be referred to by a number of different titles, such as apostle, prophet, evangelist, pastor, teacher, elder, deacon, reverend, bishop, etc. Regardless of whichever "priestly" term they may choose to ascribe to, the text suggests that what is currently being done or *offered* in service or ministry by them is comprehensively unrighteous or defiled, thus the need for them to be comprehensively purified and refined. God is, therefore, sending His *Messenger*—representing the third prophetic dimension—to set His house in order by focusing primarily on its stewards (priests and ministers). Interestingly, the word *prepare* ascribed to the human *messenger* (v. 1), also carries a similar connotation in the original Hebrew, meaning *to put* [set] *a house in order.*[28] Both messengers are charged with clearing away the obstacles of religious defilement. And it is clear from the text that these obstacles of defilement are most present and prevalent in the priesthood of public or established ministry.

Some of us may recall that when Jesus walked the earth, He reserved His harshest criticism and judgment for the religious leaders—*the sons of Levi*—of His day (Matt. 23). However, He was also known for being *a friend of sinners* (Matt. 11:19). There isn't one instance in Scripture where you will find Jesus harshly rebuking a common sinner, but there are numerous occasions in these same scriptures where you will find Jesus harshly rebuking or condemning the Scribes and Pharisees. As a matter of fact, the people Jesus identified as being *of your* [their] *father the devil* were not "regular" sinners but religious Jews who thought they were in right standing with God—an assumption that many "Christians," ministers, and religious leaders incorrectly make today (John 8:44). What characterized these religious leaders as having the devil's DNA (Diabolical Nature and Attributes) was not their immoral lifestyles as pertaining to the outward requirements of the law but the defilement of their hearts and their rejection of truth. Based upon these requirements, there are many "children of the devil" operating in pulpits and churches today (2 Tim. 3:1–8).

One of the problems I have often encountered with our current generation of religious leaders is that we often tend to exclude ourselves from the error recorded in Scripture as if we are somehow immune to these things by virtue of Christ's advent or our perceived knowledge of God. But what we fail to understand is that this same self-righteous attitude is what led to the demise of the religious leaders of Jesus's day. We view the Scribes and Pharisees as blind, self-righteous followers of religious tradition when we are just as entrenched in our religious beliefs and practices. Put yourself in their shoes. They were doing everything they knew to do according to the scriptural revelation they had. There wasn't any New Testament scripture written yet, and there was never any indication that such should be expected. As far as they knew, they had the complete canon of Scripture. They were jealous after God and the keeping of the law, and there was nothing explicitly stated therein that God intended to change what He Himself had commanded them to practice for centuries. Then some "unrecognized" (by religious standards) and "unqualified" (by religious standards) prophet comes along acting like the Son of God when He hasn't even been formally trained or educated in Scripture (from an established theological institute or Bible college), telling them that they were in error and that God was establishing a new way of doing things. What would you have done? Most likely, the same as they did being jealous for the preservation of truth. Many today would have said, "If God wanted to change anything, which we doubt, wouldn't God have informed His duly appointed leaders first?"

The point here is that if the religious leaders of Jesus's day could resist the truth and reject the powerful prophetic dimension that Jesus personified because it wasn't "pulpit friendly" or desirable, what makes us think that we cannot succumb to the same error in judgment today with the emergence of this third prophetic dimension (Is. 53:2–3)? Will your religious self-righteousness and spiritual pride keep you from submitting to this penetrating and comprehensive spiritual cleansing that God is bringing to His spiritual priesthood? Will you, therefore, reject this powerful prophetic dimension as false and as having "a demon" because it doesn't fit into your religious paradigm (John 8:48)? I sure hope not. But if you do, it will be to your demise as well.

It is important to interject here that pharisaism is the counterfeit expression of this apostolic prophetic dimension. They can appear almost identical at times in their desire for truth, purity, and judgment, but the Pharisee dimension is concerned with maintaining religious tradition, not magnifying the current voice and speaking of God or returning to the Father's original intent. The Pharisee dimension is concerned with purity but from a shallow external or behavioral dimension. Therefore, they are quick to judge moral or behavioral infractions, focusing on cleaning and purifying the *outside of the cup* only (Matt. 23:25). The true apostolic-prophetic dimension is rarely ever focused on externals but is deep and penetrating. It sees into the hearts of man to determine the governing internal principle that influences his life, behavior, decisions, and ministry. In other words, the emphasis is on cleaning *the inside of the cup*, and its judgment is concerning internal architecture and matters of the heart (Matt. 23:26). It is not that external behavior is ignored; just that it is addressed from a much deeper and internal dimension.

Key Areas of Judgment

According to the text, there are four key areas of corruption—all attributed to the notable absence of the fear of God—that this third prophetic dimension is intended to *witness* (or testify) *against* in judgment (v. 5). Before we identify these four key areas, it is important that we first recognize the implication here. Since it is a lack of the fear of God that is identified as the cause of this evil, it will require the increase and restoration of the fear of God to correct or contain it. Therefore, it is safe to assume that this third prophetic dimension will bring an increase of the fear of God to the hearts of God's people once again. It is a dimension that is characterized by the fear of God rather than the fear (or praise) of man, which is something that is noticeably absent in the current movement.

As we proceed to identify the four key areas of corruption outlined in the text, keep in mind that the entire book of Malachi was written on the premise that the apostasy of the nation was rooted in an apostate priesthood. As such, even though these infringements may seem to be directed against the nation as a whole, the priesthood should still be kept in view as the major sect responsible for the proliferation of this error. When applied today, I view these infractions as specifically applicable to the current prophetic movement. These four key areas are:

1. *Sorcery.* This word is associated with every form of divination or witchcraft in Scripture. While this may be bewildering or confusing to some, the fact that this form of corruption is listed first testifies to the fact of just how deeply embedded and accepted it had become as part of their religious culture (Acts 8:9; 13:6). Overt forms of divination or witchcraft (like child sacrifice) were easy to distinguish and condemn, but it was the subtle forms of syncretism that integrated divination into their "prophetic" ministry practices—something Moses had warned about centuries earlier (Deut. 18:9–14)—that remained hidden, unchecked, and unchallenged until the emergence

of this new prophetic dimension (Acts 13:6). Thus, you can expect this third prophetic dimension to bring a high degree of scrutiny and judgment to the corrupt architecture of men's hearts that would seek to control or manipulate heaven or earth for their own selfish desires. It will boldly challenge and confront the movement's current corrupt practices of integrating divination with the divine, and it will expose every form of sorcery currently accepted today within established religion (especially Christianity).

2. *Adultery.* Closely connected to sorcery in principle, this word is often employed metaphorically rather than literally in Scripture, usually in reference to Israel's (or Judah's) unfaithfulness to God and their worship of idols (Jer. 3:9, 5:7, 9:2). Many aspects of the idolatrous worship practices of the heathen involved a degree of sorcery, thus the connection with adultery in its metaphorical usage. The principle here is not only departure from God or the breaking of a spiritual marriage covenant but a defilement of heart that causes one's love to be divided as a result of competing interests. Adultery occurs when our own interests take precedence over God's, or when our worship is motivated more by what *we* want rather than what *He* wants. It occurs when our hearts have become narcissistically divided and we are *lovers of pleasure rather than lovers of God* (2 Tim. 3:1–5; Jam. 4:1–4). And it occurs when a prophetic movement has become corrupted by the dangerous influences of Baal, which will be discussed later (Jer. 23:13–14). But God is raising up this third prophetic dimension to expose and judge this error, and this judgment will begin first with the corrupt prophets who have helped to perpetuate it (Jer. 29:21–23).

3. *Perjury.* The original term in the Hebrew is used to describe every form of *lie, falsehood,* or *deception,*[29] especially while invoking the name of the Lord as its authority. This Hebrew term is especially employed by Jeremiah in his prophetic pronouncements against the false prophets

of his era and is translated as *lies* (Jer. 23:14). What is even more interesting is the fact that Jeremiah also uses this term in close relationship or association to both divination (sorcery) and adultery, and connects it specifically once again to the false prophets (Jer. 14:14, 23:14). In other words, what is being described here is not only the presumptuous act of speaking for God without having received any genuinely divine revelation or authorization but the practice of engaging in "prophetic" activity from an idolatrous or adulterous position through a process of divination. The end result of such corrupt activity is widespread spiritual deception, such as exists today. But thank God that He is raising up a new prophetic dimension to expose these lies, falsehood, and deception in the midst of a people who do not yet recognize that they are already deceived. The question is, will we have ears to hear, or will we continue with our wrong assumption that "everything is okay"?

4.   *Tyranny*. While this word is not officially used in the text, the concept is. Those *who exploit wage earners and widows and orphans and...who turn away an alien* are representative of spiritual tyrants that exploit and oppress the weak or perpetuate a system of injustice. They have no mercy or compassion on those who most need it. Instead, they are motivated and hardened by their own greed and self-interest, desiring only to get ahead, even if it is upon the backs of the less fortunate. It describes a religious system *whose god is their* [its] *belly* and is built upon the principle of exaction (Phil. 3:18–19). Ministry becomes a business and the church becomes an avenue for personal wealth and increase while the spiritual and physical needs of the people are neglected. The tithes and offerings we manipulate the people to give for their "breakthrough" accrue for our benefit. Networks are built as "pyramids" for financial gain. High-profit margins are attached to the products or services that are sold. And those who are not from our "camp" or too poor to afford it are denied access to the

resources they need. Then, of course, there are the other forms of religious injustice, including nepotism, cronyism, favoritism, racism, etc., that are rampant in churches today. This religious corruption and injustice is reinforced by a perverse prophetic order that not only encourages and supports it but which itself is known to *divine for money* while viciously and ferociously devouring their prey (Jer. 23:14; Ezek. 22; Mic. 3:11). God is going to judge this error and confront this injustice through this third prophetic dimension.

Kingdom Pursuit

As Jesus continues His remarkable testimony concerning John and this new prophetic dimension he was ushering in, He makes a statement that has Bible scholars and interpreters divided regarding its interpretation:

> *And from the days of John the Baptist until now the kingdom of heaven suffers violence, and the violent take it by force.* (Matt. 11:12)

The coming of John marks a distinct change or acceleration in spiritual activity relating to the Kingdom. The question is, was Jesus communicating a negative change or a positive change? Because of the construction and verbiage used in the original Greek, there are valid arguments to support either position. Those who choose to interpret this text in a negative fashion view John's ministry as the beginning of violent opposition against Kingdom advance. Thus, John is seen as marking the beginning of persecution and suffering against the agents or ambassadors of God's Kingdom. This interpretation is highly plausible considering the fact that John was in prison at the time (John 11:2).

The second position, which is positive, is clearly underscored in translations like the Amplified, which renders the text in this way:

*And from the days of John the Baptist until the pres-
ent time, the kingdom of heaven has endured violent assault, and violent men seize it by force [as a
precious prize—a share in the heavenly kingdom is
sought with most ardent zeal and intense exertion].*
(Matt. 11:12, AMP)

Even Greek scholars like Kenneth Wuest favor this positive
interpretation:

Indeed, from the days of John the Baptizer until
this moment, the kingdom of heaven is being
taken by storm, and the strong and forceful ones
claim it for themselves eagerly.[30]

Taken in a positive light, John and the new prophetic dimension he represents mark the beginning of *aggressive* Kingdom pursuit!
This third prophetic dimension is characterized by a *violent* opposition to every religious hindrance or distraction that would seek to
deter or separate from God's Kingdom. It is intense and relentless in
its zeal for the Father and His Kingdom. There is no tolerance for any
religious, carnal, or demonic substitutes. It has no mercy on man-
made or counterfeit kingdoms. And just in case you have bought
into the popular religious lie that the Kingdom of God is about you
or your church or ministry, let me make it emphatically clear that
the Kingdom of God is about the King! It is about what the King
demands, not what we desire. It is about the establishment of His
throne, not the erection of ours. Our human needs, our carnal goals,
our earthly ambitions, and our personal "breakthroughs" are irrelevant, insignificant, and inconsequential in light of the Father and
His Kingdom.

Whichever position we choose to take regarding this text—
whether positive or negative—the emphasis clearly and irrefutably
remains on the Kingdom of God. Whether John is identified with
aggressive pursuit or aggressive persecution, the Kingdom of God
is still the primary principle. I personally ascribe to both positions

since they represent cause and effect. In other words, it is on account of John's aggressive Kingdom pursuit that he encountered aggressive religious and political persecution. Therefore, expect the Kingdom of God to be the primary principle and emphasis that characterizes this third prophetic dimension.

Notes

1   Intimacy. Dictionary.com. *Dictionary.com Unabridged*. Random House, Inc. http://dictionary.reference.com/browse/intimacy (accessed: March 13, 2014).

2   William Arndt, Frederick W. Danker, and Walter Bauer, *A Greek-English Lexicon of the New Testament and Other Early Christian Literature* (Chicago: University of Chicago Press, 2000), 1059.

3   James Swanson, *Dictionary of Biblical Languages with Semantic Domains: Hebrew (Old Testament)* (Oak Harbor: Logos Research Systems, Inc., 1997).

4   "Prophet." *International Standard Bible Encyclopedia, revised edition*, Copyright © 1979 by Wm. B. Eerdmans Publishing Co. All rights reserved [PC Study Bible © 2008, Biblesoft, Inc.].

5   Eugene H. Merrill, "1 Samuel," in *The Bible Knowledge Commentary: An Exposition of the Scriptures*, ed. J. F. Walvoord and R. B. Zuck, vol. 1 (Wheaton, IL: Victor Books, 1985), 440–441.

6   Ernst Jenni and Claus Westermann, *Theological Lexicon of the Old Testament* (Peabody, MA: Hendrickson Publishers, 1997), 1178.

7   Walter A. Elwell and Barry J. Beitzel, *Baker Encyclopedia of the Bible* (Grand Rapids, MI: Baker Book House, 1988), 1781.

8   Walter C. Kaiser, Jr., "Prophet, Prophetess, Prophecy," in *Baker Theological Dictionary of the Bible*, ed. Walter A. Elwell (Grand Rapids, MI: Baker Books, 2000), 641.

9   "Prophet," from *Fausset's Bible Dictionary*, Electronic Database Copyright © 1998, 2003, 2006 by Biblesoft, Inc. All rights reserved [PC Study Bible © 2008, Biblesoft, Inc.].

10 The word *official* here is parenthesized because it is being used in an "unofficial" sense. Technically speaking, the prophetic ministry was never institutionalized into an office by law like the priesthood was. Even though Moses clearly spoke about the function and prophesied of a prophet eventually emerging like unto himself, there is no official sanction for the establishment of any such office by law (Deut. 13:1–5; 18:9–22).

11 Ernst Jenni and Claus Westermann, *Theological Lexicon of the Old Testament* (Peabody, MA: Hendrickson Publishers, 1997), 699.

12 See also Numbers 11:16–18, 25–29 and 2 Kings 2:9–15 for further evidence of this spiritual principle.

13 Carl Friedrich Keil and Franz Delitzsch, *Commentary on the Old Testament*, vol. 2 (Peabody, MA: Hendrickson, 1996), 497.

14 James M. Freeman and Harold J. Chadwick, *Manners & Customs of the Bible* (North Brunswick, NJ: Bridge-Logos Publishers, 1998), 216.

15 "Prophet." *International Standard Bible Encyclopedia, revised edition*, Copyright © 1979 by Wm. B. Eerdmans Publishing Co. All rights reserved. *Easton's Bible Dictionary*, PC Study Bible formatted electronic database Copyright © 2003, 2006 Biblesoft, Inc. All rights reserved. *McClintock and Strong Encyclopedia*, Electronic Database. Copyright © 2000, 2003, 2005, 2006 by Biblesoft, Inc. All rights reserved. "Sons of the Prophets," from *Holman Bible Dictionary*. Copyright © 1991 by Holman Bible Publishers. All rights reserved [PC Study Bible © 2008, Biblesoft, Inc.].

16 Wikipedia contributors, "Harp and bowl," *Wikipedia, The Free Encyclopedia,* http://en.wikipedia.org/w/index.php?title=Harp_and_bowl&oldid=557424830 (accessed March 26, 2014).

17 There is a reason why Paul sought to regulate and limit the number of people prophesying during the course of worship gatherings at Corinth, and it wasn't because he was seeking to quench the Spirit (1 Cor. 14:23–30; 1 Thess. 5:19–22). This type of disorder does not originate with the Holy Spirit but is a manifestation of human carnality that violates biblical protocol and does not edify (1 Cor. 14:26, 33, 40).

18 An important principle to understand is that any prophet or gifted prophesier can prophesy seemingly at will, but an unction becomes even more evident during times of corporate worship, making it far easier and more compelling to want to prophesy. But having the ability or feeling the "anointing" to prophesy doesn't necessarily mean that you should, at least not at that particular

time or place. Therefore, no true (or mature) prophetic person will seek to monopolize or capitalize on every opportunity to stand before the people and say, "The Lord says…" Again, just because you can doesn't mean that you should. Get lost in worship, and allow others the opportunity to step forward and test their wings in prophecy as the Spirit will allow. By you seeking to monopolize every opportunity, you're not only quenching the Spirit, but you're preventing those who may be a bit more timid from coming forth.

19 It is important to note that true spiritual warfare is not self-focused or enemy-focused. One of the most common scriptural references to prophetic "warfare praise" is found in 2 Chronicles 20 in the battle of Jehoshaphat and Judah against a formidable league of foreign nations. After receiving clear prophetic affirmation and direction during a time of fasting, Jehoshaphat appointed singers *who should sing to the Lord, and who should praise the beauty of holiness*, and the song that they sang ahead of the army was "Praise the Lord, for His mercy endures forever" (2 Chron. 20:21). Notice that true spiritual warfare in this context was completely heaven focused. The unequivocal emphasis was upon praising the Lord, acknowledging His holiness, and magnifying His mercy. They weren't singing to the enemy; they were singing *to the Lord*! They weren't boldly declaring *their* promised victory; they were magnifying *the Lord's* mercy!

20 "Prophet," from *Fausset's Bible Dictionary*, Electronic Database Copyright © 1998, 2003, 2006 by Biblesoft, Inc. All rights reserved [PC Study Bible © 2008, Biblesoft, Inc.].

21 William Arndt, Frederick W. Danker, and Walter Bauer, *A Greek-English Lexicon of the New Testament and Other Early Christian Literature* (Chicago: University of Chicago Press, 2000), 8.

22 Wilhelm Gesenius and Samuel Prideaux Tregelles, Gesenius' Hebrew and Chaldee Lexicon to the Old Testament Scriptures (Bellingham, WA: Logos Bible Software, 2003), 475.

23 Spiros Zodhiates, Th.D., *The Hebrew-Greek Key Study Bible King James Version*, Copyright © 1991 by AMG Publishers, 4397.

24 Richard A. Taylor and E. Ray Clendenen, *Haggai, Malachi*, vol. 21A, The New American Commentary (Nashville: Broadman & Holman Publishers, 2004), 384.

25 David J. Clark and Howard A. Hatton, *A Handbook on Malachi*, UBS Handbook Series (New York: United Bible Societies, 2002), 433.

26 Mal. 3:2–5, *ESV Study Bible Online*, Copyright © 2001 by Crossway.

27 Ibid.

28 Wilhelm Gesenius and Samuel Prideaux Tregelles, *Gesenius' Hebrew and Chaldee Lexicon to the Old Testament Scriptures* (Bellingham, WA: Logos Bible Software, 2003), 679.

29 William Lee Holladay and Ludwig Köhler, *A Concise Hebrew and Aramaic Lexicon of the Old Testament* (Leiden: Brill, 2000), 383.

30 Kenneth S. Wuest, *The New Testament: An Expanded Translation*, Copyright © 1961 by Wm. B. Eerdmans Publishing Co. All rights reserved.

3

PRINCIPLES FROM THE LIFE OF JOHN

THE FACT THAT John the Baptist represents the third and final prophetic dimension recorded in Scripture—a dimension that finds its fullness of expression through the person of Jesus—means that a closer examination of John's life and ministry is absolutely necessary and essential to understanding the true character and architecture of the third prophetic dimension. It is stated that "Apart from Jesus Christ, John the Baptist is probably the most theologically significant figure in the Gospels."[1] Numerous parallels can be found in John's life when placed in juxtaposition with Jesus's, beginning with his supernatural birth and ending with his martyrdom. Of course, this should be expected since they both represent the same prophetic dimension. Just consider John as 3A and Jesus as 3B or John as version 3.1 and Jesus as version 3.2 (note that the number 3 is used to represent the third prophetic dimension). At times, what we find displayed in John's life in *practice* (practical demonstration) is displayed in Jesus's life in *principle* (spiritual application). Often, there is no difference whatsoever in practice or principle.

There are also a number of significant parallels that can be found in John's life and the previous prophetic dimension represented by Samuel, albeit with profound distinctions. For example, both Samuel and John were miraculously born out of barrenness, but

John's birth carried a greater (double) supernatural dimension reminiscent of Isaac's because not only was his mother barren, but both parents (father and mother) were also *well advanced* in age (Luke 1:7). Both were subjected to various aspects of *Nazirite* (meaning one separated or set apart unto God) separation (Num. 6:1–8). In Samuel's case, it was the outward and easily recognizable uncut hair, but for John, it was an internal matter of the consumption of wine or strong drink (1 Sam. 1:11; Luke 1:15). One (Samuel's) was given and driven by human compulsion; the other (John's) was given by divine command and motivated by the powerful divine influence of the Holy Spirit.

Samuel was very instrumental during his time in transitioning the people from theocratic nation to monarchic kingdom, even though begrudgingly so. John was instrumental in transitioning the people from earthly kingdom (Rome) to the spiritual or heavenly Kingdom of God. Samuel anointed the first two kings (Saul and David), but John baptized the King of kings (Jesus Christ). Also, both had strong ties to the Levitical priesthood, the exception being that John was a direct descendant of Aaron through both mother and father, while Samuel was a Levite grafted into the priesthood through adoption (1 Chron. 6:33–38, 24:1–10; Luke 1:5). In every respect of these parallels, John—including the prophetic dimension he represents—proves superior to Samuel.

The Fulfillment of Promise

One of the significant aspects of John's life and ministry is the fact that he represents prophetic fulfillment. Jesus confirmed that John was the fulfillment of the prophecy given hundreds of years earlier by the prophet Malachi regarding the apostolic-prophetic *messenger* who would *prepare the way* before the Messiah (Mal. 3:1; Matt: 11:10). After the promised Messiah and His Kingdom, the Jews most anxiously anticipated the coming of this great "Elijah" prophet. But Malachi's was not the only prophecy regarding this prophetic messenger and new prophetic dimension. There are various allusions to this messenger recorded elsewhere in Scripture, especially in the writings of Isaiah (Is. 40:3–4, 62:10). Even earlier than that, 1,500 years before the coming of John and Jesus, one of the most important references to this new prophetic dimension was given by the prophet Moses.

*The Lord your God will raise up for you a Prophet
like me from your midst, from your brethren. Him
you shall hear.* (Deut. 18:15)

Even though the word *Prophet* is grammatically singular in this text and has been specifically applied to a single individual—Jesus—in every New Testament reference (and rightly so), the full context of Moses's message is not, implying that the word can also be interpreted collectively, referring to a succession of prophets, just as the singular "king" in 17:14–20 refers to any and all kings (Acts 3:22; 7:37).[2] In other words, while the promised *Prophet* finds direct fulfillment in Jesus, it also carries a broader scope of application in reference to a new prophetic dimension manifested through a corporate company of prophets, John included. Expectation and anticipation grew with every passing generation regarding the fulfillment of this promise.

The fact that Moses identifies this *Prophet* as being on the same level ("like me") as himself is very significant. Although Moses was technically a prophet from the first dimension, he was, in reality, a prophet *par excellence.* Anyone who has studied the life and ministry of Moses will quickly realize that Moses was no "regular" prophet. No single individual or prophet of the old covenant was held in greater esteem by the Jews (Deut. 34:10). He was the lawgiver and the original mediatorial architect of the entire Judaic religious system and structure. He was not only the Old Testament type of an apostle, but his face-to-face communion with God, spiritual authority, and elevated dimension of sight placed him in a category above all others of his era. As such, Moses was a prophetic foreshadow of Jesus and the third prophetic dimension in fullness.

This prediction of a coming *Prophet* like unto Moses thoroughly confused the religious Jews in their eschatological expectations, as did the promise of both Elijah and the Messiah. They apparently weren't aware that the *Prophet* and the Messiah were the same. And they weren't sure what connection, if any, this *Prophet* had to the return of Elijah. Thus, the reason why the religious leaders questioned John regarding if he was the Christ (or Messiah), Elijah, or the Prophet (John. 1:19–21). What they failed to accurately discern or understand was that the presence of John in their midst signaled the threefold eschatological fulfillment of all three prophetic promises. John's presence meant Elijah had come and that the Prophet-Messiah was near.

The third prophetic dimension, therefore, is characterized by *fulfillment.* From the moment John and Jesus begin their ministries and are introduced upon our earthly stage, the process of prophetic fulfillment is exponentially accelerated. What was previously held back or delayed in the realm of promise quickly manifests itself in the realm of time. Over and over again in the New Testament—sixty-four times to be exact (compared to fifty-two times in the Old Testament, which is approximately three times the New Testament's size in volume and eighteen times the number of years in time span)—the word *fulfilled* or its related form is used. At no other time and in no other era had any other prophetic dimension brought this level of fulfillment in so short a span of time.

If you think this level of accelerated prophetic fulfillment was limited to Jesus and the first generation of believers, you're quite mistaken. God never intended for this momentum to be diminished for as long as this third prophetic dimension was in operation. But unfortunately, it did. The apostolic dimension of the early Kingdom Community deteriorated into apostasy. The prophetic became a deformed and dysfunctional display of something totally pathetic. The momentum of fulfillment John and Jesus ushered in eventually became stagnated and stifled by spiritual blindness and religious error. Without the *burning and shining lamp* of the third prophetic dimension continuing to function, God's corporate Community quickly plummeted into what has been historically described as the "dark ages," leaving them bereft of spiritual resource or any accurate understanding of God's Kingdom (John 5:35).

Lack of Fulfillment in the Current Movement

Prophetic fulfillment is sorely lacking even today in the current prophetic movement. The sad thing is, few seem to notice, and even fewer seem to care. Many lofty and flattering words are spoken, and at times, there are even warnings of coming disaster or judgment, but very few come to pass. Being satisfied with the few is like being satisfied with a broken clock that is right at least twice a day. What is worse, very seldom are these presumptuous prophets or prophesiers made to give an account for their false words. We have been taught, for the most part, to just quickly forgive or ignore the miss, so we just brush it off and move on to the next one. After all, prophets are only human. But when a "prophet" today says something vague that can eventually be applied to some major catastrophic or newsworthy future event by the stretch of one's imagination, he is quick to publicly demand credit for his "revelation." However, when he clearly misses it, he becomes deafeningly silent and pretends his error never took place.

About two or three years prior to the time of this writing, a "prophet" who trains students in the gifts and dream interpretation posted a video on his website clearly stating that the Denver Broncos would win the 2014 Super Bowl (XLVIII) against the Seattle Seahawks. He even went on to predict the final score. Of course, those of you who follow American football know that the Seahawks put quite a beating on the Broncos—the largest point differential in Super Bowl history—and won the championship. There are several things wrong with this prediction, the least of which is the fact that it didn't come to pass. However, what disturbed me the most was the prophet's response when everyone who saw his previous video realized he was wrong. Instead of humbly, contritely, and apologetically acknowledging his error, he quietly removed the video (which had already gone viral over the Internet) and proceeded to defend himself against his critics by making excuses and shifting blame away from himself, thus compounding his blatant error.

Facts versus Fulfillment

It is interesting that when Moses prophesied the coming of a *Prophet* like unto himself, he went on to describe fulfillment as a major indicator of an accurate prophetic dimension (Deut. 18:22). It is one thing to deliver a message with impressive facts (words of knowledge), but this alone does not necessarily imply an accurate prophetic dimension. I have seen many prophets impress in such a manner who turned out to be false. I can recall one prophet in particular who was very accurate in calling out names; however, many of the prophecies he gave were lacking in accuracy or fulfillment.[3] There are multiple avenues—both natural as well as supernatural—through which one can obtain valid facts. Even major corporations like Google, Facebook, and Amazon have developed technological algorithms through the mining of personal data in order to target their marketing specifically to your particular history, vocation, likes, or interests, but we all know that doesn't make them prophetic. There are also people well trained in the art of human analysis and behavioral science who are able to determine accurate facts about an individual with just a brief or simple encounter, but that doesn't make them prophetic either. Then there are the psychics and clairvoyants who tap into the lower and darker dimensions of the spirit realm. Many of them can give you very accurate information regarding your life, but like the other natural examples listed above, the creative power of fulfillment is beyond their reach. At times, they may be able to use these facts to make an accurate *guess* at the future, but they're often wrong (as guesses usually are). Even when they do manage to guess right, it is usually obscure or vague. This is why we can never judge a prophetic dimension by the accuracy of facts. The Scriptural requirement—though not the only requirement—is prophetic fulfillment.

When prophets like Agabus stood up and prophesied concerning an extensive famine, people took note because they knew his words carried weight. His words weren't obscure or vague but specific and precise. Therefore, Agabus's words could be recorded by the community of believers and people like Luke in order to properly validate its fulfillment. This type of response suggests that the prophetic dimension of that era carried weight and credibility. There was a healthy sense of fear and respect for the prophetic that is much different than the careless and irreverent response we see so much of today. This lack of godly fear or irreverence can be easily explained when we take into account Moses's message regarding the coming *Prophet*. When he identified fulfillment as a major characteristic of this prophetic dimension, he explicitly stated that we should not *be afraid* of the prophet who has spoken presumptuously (Deut. 18:22). The Hebrew verb translated as *be afraid* in that text means to *have a profound respect and reverence for another, with an implication of awe bordering on fear.*[4] In other words, implicit in Moses's statement is the principle that presumptuous prophecies and lack of prophetic fulfillment diminish healthy respect as well as holy and reverential fear for the prophetic in the hearts and minds of the people. This also means that prophets who are only accurate in giving detailed facts (names, phone numbers, addresses, etc.) without any true prophetic fulfillment are not worthy of our awe or respect.

The Rebirth of the Third Prophetic Dimension

The good news is that the third prophetic dimension is being birthed again to restore honor and integrity to the prophetic. Just as John was sent to prepare the way for Jesus's first coming and the inauguration of His eternal Kingdom, John—representing the third prophetic dimension embodied by a corporate company of prophets—is being sent again to prepare the way for Jesus's second coming and the consummation of His eternal Kingdom.

Every kingdom transition recorded in Scripture is precipitated by the birthing of a new prophetic dimension. When Israel first became a monarchic kingdom, it was precipitated by the birthing of a new prophetic dimension through Samuel. When the people of God were to be made ready for transition into a spiritual Kingdom, He sent a new prophetic dimension in the form of John and Jesus. Even Moses connected the promise of a future kingdom with the birthing of a new prophetic dimension (Deut. 17:14–20; 18:15–22). It is plain to see from these examples that the concepts of *kingdom* and the *prophetic* are parallel developments in Scripture. There is a dual dynamic in operation. One cannot emerge without the other. Therefore, if the Kingdom of God is to continue in its forceful advance toward eschatological fulfillment, it will require a new prophetic dimension at its vanguard once again. The progressive momentum of prophetic fulfillment that was lost just prior to the dark ages shall be restored in fullness once again. We are getting ready to step into a season of accelerated fulfillment. The fear of God and a reverential respect for the prophetic will once again be restored.

Fulfillment Despite Contradiction

It is worth noting that John's very birth was a sign of prophetic fulfillment in the midst of earthly contradiction (Luke 1:13–20).[5] Even the significant and high-ranking angel, Gabriel, had a difficult time convincing John's father of his impending birth due to the apparent earthly contradiction and militating natural evidence (Luke 1:18). Nothing in the natural seemed to line up with what was being divinely promised and declared. Expect the same contradiction today in the midst of the rebirthing of this third prophetic dimension. Not only will there be contradiction from a divergent prophetic order, but even natural conditions and occurrences will seem to defy the accelerated prophetic fulfillment of what has been promised. But we can take comfort in the fact that what God has promised, He will also perform.

As a matter of fact, *Zacharias*, the name of John's father, means *the Lord remembers*;[6] and *Elizabeth*, the name of John's mother, means *the oath of God*.[7] When there is an intimate marriage between divine *remembrance* and divine *promise* (oath), it produces the supernatural *fulfillment* of John (whose name means *Jehovah is gracious*).[8] In other words, the Lord will remember to perform the oath (or promise) He has spoken regarding (as well as through) John and the third prophetic dimension he represents, despite whatever seems to contradict it. And this fulfillment will be the result of God's immeasurable grace.

Departure from Established Religious Structures

The Gospel of Luke records of John that he *grew and became strong in spirit, and he was in the wilderness until the day of his public appearance to Israel* (Luke 1:80, ESV). This suggests that John basically grew up and lived in the wilderness from quite a young age. It also suggests that this "wilderness" was the sole or primary environment for nurturing and establishing John in spiritual maturity. As we study each of the various gospel records pertaining to John, including the prophecy given by the prophet Isaiah, we quickly discover that the *wilderness* concept is a very significant and important principle in the life of John and his ministry (Is. 40:3; Matt. 3:1–3; Mark 1:2–4; Luke 3:2–5; John 1:23). While there are numerous figurative shades of meaning for the concept of *wilderness* in Scripture, the primary principle being communicated by John is one of being isolated, separated, or apart from the established religious system. In short, it communicates the principle of divergence.

Let's put this in proper perspective. John is the son of Zacharias and Elizabeth—direct descendants of Aaron the priest—thus making John of pure priestly pedigree. Furthermore, John's father, Zacharias, had also been serving and functioning within the established priesthood. If anyone had reason or obligation to continue the family tradition and heritage of serving within the established religious priesthood, it would have been John. However, John chose to depart from and radically reject this religious system, opting instead for the obscurity of a wilderness ministry that was distinctly different, divergent, and disconnected from the traditionally established priesthood. Most people reading the account of John's wilderness ministry never pause long enough to consider what John was willing to give up. Being a functioning priest afforded one a certain degree of religious rank, recognition, and respect; while being in the wilderness meant reduced status and obscurity. Functioning priests were to be well supported and were allowed to partake of the offerings, but dwelling in the wilderness meant that John's diet consisted of *locusts and wild honey* (Ex. 29:26–34; Lev. 6:26, 29, 8:31–32; Num. 18:8–14; Matt. 3:4). Priests were clothed in easily recognizable religious attire made from a material (fine linen) usually worn by royalty and the upper class.[9] Their clothing communicated favor, honor, and respect. In comparison, John's clothing of "camel's hair" was very simple and coarse, used by lowly camel drivers and shepherds (Matt. 3:4).[10] Priests ministered within the comfort and "grandness" of the physical temple structures, but John chose to minister and operate within the harsh, uncomfortable conditions of the wilderness or desert.

As demonstrated by John, the third prophetic dimension cannot be effectively cultivated or matured within the context of traditionally established religious form or practice. The third prophetic dimension is not a product of the current religious system; it is a reformer of the system. It is distinct, divergent, and separate. Unlike Samuel and the second prophetic dimension that was birthed and assimilated into the current religious system, thus becoming similarly corrupted by reason of association and influence, the third prophetic dimension refuses to coexist with corruption. It is developed and established within the context of separation and obscurity. This is by God's design. If it appears deviant—as John most certainly did to the religious leaders of his day—it is because it most certainly is.[11] It is deviant to religious corruption! John, Jesus, and their disciples were, in reality, quite deviant to the corrupt religious practices of their day, and it will be no different in ours.

The wilderness separation of Moses

Before God could deliver Israel from the bondage and corrupt influence of Egypt, He first had to separate Moses and prepare him in the *wilderness* of obscurity for forty years. God could not nurture or develop the mature prophetic dimension that Moses walked in within the confines or context of a corrupt corporate community, which is what Israel was at the time. He had to be separated and set apart. There had to be a departure from the corrupt system he was being sent to reform. Even after Israel's exodus from Egypt, Moses continued to practice the principle of separation. Every major download Moses received from heaven was received outside or apart from the corporate community, on a mountain. Moses would never have been able to perform his ministry had he allowed himself to become assimilated into the congregation's corrupt religious culture inherited from Egypt. While Aaron was eventually influenced and seduced by this corruption due to his lack of separation from the community, Moses was able to maintain his integrity by virtue of this *wilderness* principle (Ex. 32).

The separation of Jesus and His disciples

Even though Jesus's separation was not as dramatic or overt as John's, this *wilderness* principle is, nevertheless, still demonstrated through His life and ministry. Jesus often frequented the temple and synagogues, even as a child, but He never ascribed to or validated the system (Matt. 21:12, 24:1; Luke 2:41–47, 4:16). On the contrary, He often criticized and condemned the false religious system represented by the scribes and Pharisees (Matt. 23). The chief priests, scribes, and elders didn't band together to plot Jesus's demise because He was closely associated with or friendly to the established religious system. They plotted His demise because He was antagonistic and appeared subversive and seditious to their religious practice (Matt. 26:3–4). Furthermore, none of Jesus's disciples (the original twelve apostles) were chosen from the priesthood or recognized religious community, thus demonstrating once again just how profoundly separate He and His followers were from the established religious order.

We need to stop viewing all aspects of separation or division as emanating from the flesh or devil. Separation and division can also be ordained of God, as proven by the examples above. One of the significant signs that give evidence of the approach of God's Kingdom is this principle of separation (Luke 17:34–37). Jesus Himself said that He came to bring separation and division (Matt. 10:34–36). For years, there has been a massive exodus of people away from traditionally established religious structures due to an overwhelming sense of discontent for the Church's lack of authenticity, yet many continue to view this as emanating from the devil or the Antichrist as a manifestation of the great "falling away" (2 Thess. 2:3). Yet prior to John's ministry, there was also a significant defection or separation by a community of Jews who also recognized the entrenched religious corruption within the system, known as the Qumran community.[12] It could be that God has been merely setting the stage for the birthing and development of this third and final prophetic dimension.

Kingdom Shift

With John's departure from empty religious form and practice came a significant shift from religious conformity to spiritual authenticity. A new spiritual order was being inaugurated and established, with a new line of demarcation emerging between religion and Kingdom. Though once hidden away in the wilderness of obscurity, multitudes were now flocking to John in the wilderness to be baptized (Matt. 3:1–5; Mark 1:1–5; Luke 3:7). They recognized that John possessed something that the priests, Pharisees, and religious leaders at the Temple in Jerusalem didn't have—spiritual authenticity and resource! Masses were willing to leave the comfort of the Temple in pursuit of an isolated man with no formal religious training, recognition, title, or degree. They were willing to brave the harsh conditions of the wilderness to receive ministry from a prophet without priestly privilege or prestige. This was a major shift considering the then current religious culture and context. John established a major movement away from the formal religious patterns and structures, with a massive number of followers. And so significant was this movement that John's disciples occupy a significant part of the Gospels, extending beyond his death and all the way into foreign lands as recorded in the book of Acts (Matt. 9:14; John 1:35–37, 4:1–2; Acts 18:24–25; 19:1–7).

The spiritual impact of this third prophetic dimension will be no less. The current emphasis on building and maintaining external religious structures, having "church," and conducting good Christian services without true spiritual authenticity or resource is being radically challenged by an emerging prophetic dimension, which is characterized by authentic Kingdom pursuit. Corporate gatherings are going to be radically redefined to operate within a Kingdom context. Our comfortable, entertaining, seeker-friendly services will only last so long before the people grow dissatisfied and weary, thus causing them to forsake the traditional religious structures in search of a prophetic dimension with true spiritual substance. This prophetic dimension will begin in obscurity, but it will not end in obscurity. If John's impact and influence was so extensive and great (as the former rain), you can expect the impact and influence of this latter-rain third prophetic dimension to be far greater. We are about to experience a massive movement away from dead religious patterns into powerful Kingdom experience.

Spiritual Rank and Authority

This divergent movement away from the traditionally accepted religious patterns and structures that was pioneered by John served to establish a "new" (in reality, it was the reestablishing of the old) principle and paradigm regarding spiritual government. In that particular time and culture (which was in many respects similar to our own), all spiritual rank or authority was perceived as being vested solely in those duly qualified and formally recognized by the established religious system—including the priests, elders, scribes, Pharisees and Sadducees—with the Sanhedrin representing the ultimate seat of power. Therefore, when John began preaching this new message on the *Kingdom*, while also practicing and promoting this novel spiritual principle of *baptism*, it alarmed the religious leaders. Even though masses were migrating toward John in order to submit themselves to this new spiritual teaching and principle, he was thoroughly rejected by the established religious system, including the chief priests and elders. Thus, they refused to publicly answer Jesus's question regarding John's baptism—whether it was divinely authorized and ordained by God [*from heaven*], or whether it was a self-appointed display of the flesh [*from men*] (Matt. 21:23–27). The people certainly recognized that John possessed spiritual rank and authority to pioneer and establish this "new" thing; however, the religious rulers refused to validate or endorse John's ministry because it was not rooted or grounded in their formal religious practice. In the end, what John establishes is a clear dichotomy between religious authority (based upon human [or religious] recognition, appointment, or position), and spiritual authority (based upon divine recognition, appointment, or anointing).

The Issues of Title and Office

Unlike the second prophetic dimension, the third prophetic dimension is not a group of formally recognized and accepted "professionals" who have been officially integrated into the established ecclesiastical religious system. They're not interested in titles, and they do not occupy any "office," as referring to any formal or official ecclesiastical position. This popular idea that the five-fold or ascension gift ministries are "offices" is an incorrect one that is based on error. While there is slightly greater opportunity to identify the prophet with such a position (untenable as it is) from Samuel's era in the old covenant, there is absolutely no ground in the new covenant for supporting any such idea. Just in case these statements are not plain enough, let me make it emphatically clear that there is no such thing as the "office of a prophet," as some claim to have. There is no such vocabulary or concept found in Scripture as pertaining to the prophet. This has been a major misconception among believers for as long as I can remember. Being a prophet is a matter of *function*, not position. Even when various Greek words are employed by Paul (and others) in reference to himself and members of the body, translated in some versions as "office," the sense and emphasis is clearly on function rather than position (Rom. 11:13, 12:4 KJV).[13]

This corrupt religious tendency of magnifying title and position over servanthood and function is characteristic of the current prophetic movement and religious Christianity as a whole. Many are seeking the latest and greatest titles or positions of prominence. When the current prophetic movement was first birthed in the late '80s, many went out and started printing business cards with the title "prophet" on them. It felt like almost every minister you met during that period was a "prophet" by title. Then the apostolic movement came around, and the majority of those who were once called "prophets" went out and "upgraded" their titles to "apostle." While it is not my intention here to debate the use of religious titles, I do wish to point out that Jesus addressed a similar principle with regard to the scribes and Pharisees.

> *But all their works they do to be seen by men. They make their phylacteries broad and enlarge the borders of their garments. They love the best places at feasts, the best seats in the synagogues, greetings in the marketplaces, and to be called by men, "Rabbi, Rabbi." But you, do not be called "Rabbi"; for One is your Teacher, the Christ, and you are all brethren. Do not call anyone on earth your father; for One is your Father, He who is in heaven. And do not be called teachers; for One is your Teacher, the Christ. But he who is greatest among you shall be your servant. And whoever exalts himself will be humbled, and he who humbles himself will be exalted.* (Matt. 23:5–12)

Beyond the very clear and explicit command given by Jesus in the text above—discouraging the seeking or use of religious titles of significance or honor, which inaccurately serve to elevate one member above another—is a much deeper spiritual principle. What is being primarily addressed here is the internal configuration of one's heart. The scribes and Pharisees were narcissistic and self-seeking. They took prideful delight in magnifying title and position because it brought them greater honor, afforded them greater prominence and privilege, and provided them with greater recognition and respect (vs. 6–7). Everything they did was toward this end (v. 5). In contrast, Jesus emphasizes the principles of humility and servanthood as the true Kingdom characteristics of greatness (Matt. 20:25–28). Even with all their religious recognition, lofty titles, and elevated ecclesiastical offices, the scribes and Pharisees were still invalidated and condemned by Jesus as being inaccurate and false. In other words, they had no real spiritual rank or authority. Therefore, spiritual rank and authority must never be defined by earthly or religious recognition, title, or position (office).

John rejected this corrupt spiritual principle of the scribes and Pharisees by forsaking the religious robes of recognition, the priestly positions of prominence and power, and the personal pleasures of priestly privilege. Even though John knew that as the son of a priest and an heir of Aaron he had a hereditary right to these things, he understood that true spiritual authorization comes from God alone, not from any religious office, title, or position. His ministry was characterized by humility and servanthood, and it will be the same in this third prophetic dimension.

There are many ministers today who will become angry or offended if someone chooses to address them without a title. If you are one of those, all I have to say to you is *get over it!* If you're angry or offended by that, it is a sure sign of religious pride. There is no indication that any of the apostles, prophets, or any of the other ministers of God in Scripture were ever addressed by a religious title. Agabus was called "Agabus," not "prophet Agabus" (Acts 11:28, 21:10). Peter was addressed as "Peter," not "Apostle Peter" (Matt. 17:24, 26). Paul was addressed as "Paul" or "Saul," not "Apostle Paul" or "Dr. Saul" (Acts 13:9, 13). Are you greater than them to require a title before your name?

Alexander Strauch, in his book *Biblical Eldership*, makes some interesting comments regarding this emphasis on titles in our current religious culture:

> The modern array of ecclesiastical titles accompanying the names of Christian leaders—reverend, archbishop, cardinal, pope, primate, metropolitan, canon, curate—is completely missing from the New Testament and would have appalled the apostles and early believers. Although both the Greeks and Jews employed a wealth of titles for their political and religious leaders in order to express their power and authority, the early Christians avoided such titles. The early

Christians used common and functional terms to describe themselves and their relationships. Some of these terms are "brother," "beloved," "fellow-worker," "laborer," "slave," "servant," "prisoner," "fellow-soldier," and "steward."

Of course there were prophets, teachers, apostles, evangelists, leaders, elders, and deacons within the first churches, but these terms were not used as formal titles for individuals. All Christians are saints, but there was no "Saint John." All are priests, but there was no "Priest Phillip." Some are elders, but there was no "Elder Paul." Some are overseers, but there was no "Overseer John." Some are pastors, but there was no "Pastor James." Some are deacons, but there was no "Deacon Peter." Some are apostles, but there was no "Apostle Andrew."

Rather than gaining honor through titles and position, New Testament believers received honor primarily for their service and work... The early Christians referred to each other by their personal names (Timothy, Paul, Titus).[14]

Debunking Ordination

It matters little that you were officially "ordained" to a religious office (with title) and you have a piece of paper hanging from your wall attesting to that fact. As a matter of fact, the solemn religious service we know and practice today as "ordination" finds very little precedence in Scripture and far less in the New Testament. Never mind the fact that the technical sense of the word *ordination* is found nowhere in the New Testament (where the term *appointment* is preferred), but more importantly, neither is the concept. To be "ordained" means that the person has met certain qualifications to be appointed a position in the church. Thus, ordination is the act of officially investing someone with religious authority. This act signifies selection and appointment to God's service.[15]

As we have already briefly discussed, ministry and leadership were concepts never viewed from a mentality of formal religious position or office among God's Covenant Kingdom Community in the New Testament. The emphasis was always upon *function* in the context of God-appointed service. There was no appointment to any formal position or office. Jesus chose and appointed His twelve apostles, but He never "ordained" them to any official position or office (John 15:16). When Matthias was chosen as Judas's replacement and Peter stood up and quoted from Psalm 109:8 regarding *another [to] take his office*, the intended sense was not an official position of authority but the *activity of witnessing* and the responsibility of caring oversight (Acts 1:20–26).[16]

> Though in some contexts *episcope* [office] has been regarded traditionally as a position of authority, in reality the focus is upon the responsibility for caring for others, and in the context of Acts 1:20 the reference is clearly to the responsibility for caring for the church.[17]

God is the One who ultimately chooses and appoints to ministries of service. All man can do is recognize and confirm His appointment. While man can confer *religious* authority through the formal act or rite of ordination, only God can confer *spiritual* authority through divine appointment. When the seven were chosen in Acts 6 and had hands laid on them with prayer, it did not bestow upon them greater grace, wisdom, or spiritual rank. They were already filled with the Holy Spirit and wisdom before they had hands laid upon them (Acts 6:3). What they received was a formal commissioning to a service they had already been divinely appointed and gifted for. The apostles simply acknowledged on earth what had already been established in heaven.

Similarly, Paul received his apostleship directly from God, not man (Gal. 1:1, 15). Paul was never "ordained" by any religious leader or ecclesiastical body to the "office" of an apostle. And contrary to popular religious opinion (many biblical commentators included), Acts 13:1–3 does not contradict this fact. Like with the seven in Acts 6, the leaders at Antioch simply acknowledged the grace that was already functioning in both Paul and Barnabas and corporately released (sent) them to fulfill their call.

If there is one ministry in the Bible that epitomizes this principle of divine authorization and appointment in contradistinction to the religious practice of "ordination," it is the prophet. There is no true prophet in Scripture who was ever chosen or "ordained" by man—including any leader or religious body. Therefore, to claim that you were religiously "ordained as a prophet" is an oxymoron of sorts. No man or religious body can "ordain" anyone a prophet, at least not a prophet of God. They can acknowledge or confirm, but they cannot ordain, for the simple fact that this is a spiritual ministry, not a religious position or office.

When the prophetic dimension is viewed or approached from a debased human mentality of religious professionalism—similar to the way that the prophetic companies or guilds first established by Samuel later degenerated into a group of formal religious professionals—error and corruption are the inevitable results. These formal or professional prophets later became a major snare and scourge to Israel, becoming the perpetuators of rampant and widespread apostasy and corruption. Thus, when the prophet Amos was rejected and rebuked by Amaziah the priest—representing the established religious authority in the region—on account of his ministry, he responded by saying, "*I was [am] no prophet, nor was [am] I a son of a prophet*" (Amos 7:14). By making this bold statement, Amos was clearly distancing and disassociating himself from the formally established prophetic order. He represented a divine divergence. In other words, Amos was saying, "I am not one of the professional and formally recognized prophets whose ministry is commonly viewed as an official vocation. I am not ordained or recognized by any formal religious institution, and I do not carry any card with the title 'prophet' or any other official credentials. I have no formal religious training or degree from the prophetic colleges as a *son of a prophet*, neither am I a member of any recognized prophetic network or guild like the one established at Bethel" (2 Kings 2:3). Amos understood that his authorization, anointing, and spiritual rank to minister as a prophet of God did not come from any human or religious agency. While the established religious order rejected his ministry and calling, heaven endorsed it. The irony is that while the religious order of that day rejected the ministry of Amos as being officially unqualified and false, while accepting the professional prophets as true, it was Amos who had heaven's genuine authorization while the other professional prophets did not.

The Melchizedek Dimension

Neither Jesus, John, nor any of the original twelve apostles had any formal religious recognition, training, or earthly ministerial credentials qualifying them in an official capacity for public ministry. They were patterned after the order of Melchizedek. In other words, the third prophetic dimension is a Melchizedek dimension.

> For this Melchizedek, king of Salem, priest of the Most High God, met Abraham returning from the slaughter of the kings and blessed him, and to him Abraham apportioned a tenth part of everything. He is first, by translation of his name, king of righteousness, and then he is also king of Salem, that is, king of peace. **He is without father or mother or genealogy, having neither beginning of days nor end of life**, but **resembling** the Son of God he continues a priest forever. (Heb. 7:1–3, ESV, emphasis mine)

Melchizedek was a king-priest with no earthly record of his pedigree or lineage and without any history of fatherly affirmation, identity, or inheritance. Contrary to various speculations from certain Bible commentators, he was not some angel or supernatural spiritual being like a pre-incarnate Christ, even though he clearly is a type of the latter by *resemblance*.[18] The clause *He is without father or mother or genealogy, having neither beginning of days nor end of life* does not mean he was an eternal being but refers to the fact that there was no historical record of his birth or of his death—very necessary and important factors in the ancient world for proving the legitimacy of one's priesthood.[19] It should be understood in the sense that his priesthood was isolated rather than a continuation of a priestly family line. Melchizedek had a priestly office [ministry] by special divine appointment and was thus a type of Jesus Christ in his priesthood.[20] In other words, his kingly authority and priestly ministry were not based upon earthly credentials or human validation, as is evidenced by Scripture and Abraham's significant response. By receiving Melchizedek's ministry and honoring him with a tithe of his booty or spoils, Abraham was acknowledging an authority and spiritual priestly rank that far superseded genealogical pedigree or earthly religious credentials.

It is for this very reason that Jesus is referred to in Scripture as *a priest forever, according to the order of Melchizedek* (Heb.5:6, 10). Jesus's high priestly ministry was never based upon earthly religious credentials because He was not a descendant of Aaron. By earthly religious standards, Jesus had no right at all to the priesthood. Even when He walked the earth as a man and worshipped at the Temple in Jerusalem, He was barred from entering into the inner sanctuary where the priests ministered because he was never acknowledged as a true priest (or minister) by the established religious systems of His day. In our current religious culture or terminology, we would say He was never officially "licensed" or "ordained." Thus, whenever He supernaturally healed a leper, He sent him back to the priest (who had credentials) so he could be officially certified as clean according to the law (Matt. 8:4, Luke 17:14 with Lev. 14). Even though Jesus had the spiritual authority to make the leper clean, He did not have the earthly or religious authority to certify the lepers' cleanness according to the requirements of the law. It would be the same as performing a marriage ceremony and signing the marriage certificate today. It does not matter how much spiritual authority you possess, you still have to have official credentials and satisfy the requirements of the law before it can be accepted by the State. Conversely, you may have all the credentials and religious authority on earth for legal or social acceptance yet still lack any true spiritual authority that is acknowledged as lawful in heaven. No level of priestly or religious certification would have been enough to make the leper clean had he not already been made clean by heaven's authority alone.

Like Melchizedek, Jesus's kingly authority and high priestly rank were not derived from earthly credentials or human validation but by divine appointment and authorization, which far exceeded Aaron's (Heb. 5:4–6). Jesus's priesthood, like Melchizedek's before Him, was far superior to anything in the Aaronic order (Heb. 7:1–28). Initially, He may have been withheld the honor and recognition He truly deserved. After all, He was "despised and rejected by men, a Man of sorrows and acquainted with grief" (Is. 53:3). The established religious priesthood despised and rejected Him. But just as Abraham was able to recognize the grace of God upon Melchizedek and give him due honor, even so shall the true sons and daughters of Abraham recognize the grace and anointing of God upon this despised but divinely appointed prophetic priesthood and give them true honor.

Recognition of Spiritual Rank

We find a remarkable example of such recognition demonstrated by a certain centurion—a commander of 100 men in the Roman army with extensive authority[21]—in Scripture.

> *"Now when He concluded all His sayings in the hearing of the people, He entered Capernaum. And a certain centurion's servant, who was dear to him, was sick and ready to die. So when he heard about Jesus, he sent elders of the Jews to Him, pleading with Him to come and heal his servant. And when they came to Jesus, they begged Him earnestly, saying that the one for whom He should do this was deserv-*

ing, "for he loves our nation, and has built us a synagogue." Then Jesus went with them. And when He was already not far from the house, the centurion sent friends to Him, saying to Him, "Lord, do not trouble Yourself, for I am not worthy that You should enter under my roof. Therefore I did not even think myself worthy to come to You. But say the word, and my servant will be healed. For I also am a man placed under authority, having soldiers under me. And I say to one, 'Go,' and he goes; and to another, 'Come,' and he comes; and to my servant, 'Do this,' and he does it." When Jesus heard these things, He marveled at him, and turned around and said to the crowd that followed Him, "I say to you, I have not found such great faith, not even in Israel!" And those who were sent, returning to the house, found the servant well who had been sick." (Luke 7:1–10)

Here is a military commander who, out of compassionate love and concern for his servant, is willing to do whatever is necessary for his servant to be healed. Up until this point, he had only heard about Jesus and His ministry, though He had never personally met Him. What makes this story even more interesting is the fact that this centurion is apparently, and at the least, familiar with the Jewish religion to have demonstrated such great love and support in building them a synagogue (v. 5). In all probability, he could have been a "proselyte of the gate, like Cornelius" (Acts 10).[22] Yet even though he understood the Jewish religious structure, he also understood its limitations. He knew that the official priests and elders had no spiritual authority to heal his servant. Therefore, instead of asking the Jewish officials (elders) to do what he knew they could not do, he sent them to ask Jesus on his behalf.

As Jesus follows these elders to the centurion's home, he sends a second contingent or delegation expressing his own sense of unworthiness in having a man of Jesus's authority and stature under his roof, requesting that He *say the word* only and his servant would be healed (vs. 6–7). Remember, this is a Roman military commander—an official representative of the Roman Empire and dominion—telling a militarily conquered Jew who is subject to Rome's power and dominion, and without any religious credentials, that he is unworthy to have Him in his house because He possesses far greater rank and authority than he does. No wonder he blew Jesus's mind (v. 9)! But pay close attention to what the centurion said, *I also am a man placed under authority* (v. 8). By using the word *also*, the centurion is clearly affirming a recognition that Jesus Himself is ministering and operating under authority. How was this centurion able to come to such a recognition when there was no earthly evidence of such in Jesus's life? By all appearances, Jesus was operating as a fringe religious rebel without any "spiritual covering" or accountability. He wasn't submitted to the Pharisees. He wasn't submitted to the Sadducees. He wasn't submitted to any religious leader, body, or organization. Yet this centurion was able to recognize and validate a principle of submission (being under authority) in Jesus's life and ministry even though it was not predicated upon earthly religious systems or principles. He was able to see beyond earthly titles, positions, and authority structures to accurately discern and recognize true spiritual rank and authority in Jesus through His submission to the ultimate authority—Father God. When such authority is recognized and honored, heaven responds, and the supernatural dimension is activated and released.

Had the *seven sons of Sceva*—a Jewish high priest—understood this spiritual principle, they could have saved themselves a lot of pain and embarrassment (Acts 19:13–16). Instead, these itinerant "deliverance ministers" (exorcists) presumed to possess a spiritual rank they did not have, probably on the basis of their priestly lineage and official religious credentials. While attempting to cast out demons "in the name of Jesus" *whom Paul preaches*, the evil spirit responded by acknowledging that it knew both Jesus and Paul—it recognized their spiritual authority despite their lack of earthly religious credentials—but it did not know these itinerant priests. This response is interesting considering the fact that the text seems to portray this group of itinerant exorcists as possibly having a considerable amount of fame and recognition in the city, thus causing their epic failure to go viral

(Acts 19:17). However, even though they may have been widely recognized by man, there was no recognition of them by either heaven or hell as possessing any spiritual rank or authority; thus, they were overpowered and assaulted by the demon. This means that hell also recognizes true spiritual authority. Neither heaven nor hell cares one iota what religious credentials you have, how popular or recognized you are, or what title(s) you carry. They only recognize and respond to true spiritual authority.

When Jesus submitted Himself to John's baptism, He demonstrated a recognition of spiritual rank and authority resident in John's person and ministry (Matt. 3:13). This required spiritual sight. Similarly, when John tried to prevent Jesus's baptism by acknowledging that Jesus possessed greater spiritual rank and authority than him, saying *"I need to be baptized by You, and are You coming to me?"* he was operating by prophetic insight (Matt. 3:14). There was nothing in the natural that made Jesus appear to be anything or anyone special. There was no visible halo around His head, and He had performed no miracle up until this point. Yet John was able to accurately discern deep spiritual resource in Jesus that elevated Him to a spiritual level far beyond John's present experience.

The Principle of Diminution

Perhaps the most remarkable aspect of John's accurate apostolic and prophetic witness is the principle of diminution it was both characterized by and built upon. It is a principle that is often rehearsed in the halls of Christendom. Numerous songs have been written and sung that include at least a portion of John's famous statement identifying and articulating this core spiritual value. Countless sermons have been delivered on this excellent spiritual virtue, yet few understand its true meaning. Even fewer have been able to progress beyond a mental or emotional religious petition to a meaningful internal posture, practically demonstrated and fleshed out in a selfless lifestyle.

When John first spoke these famous and often quoted words, *He must increase, but I must decrease,* he intended them to be understood within the particular context he spoke them in and not as an isolated statement detached from any practical reality. When examined within its particular context and then reconciled with what we know of John's ministry and lifestyle in Scripture, the depth and impact of these words become much more profound.

> *After these things Jesus and His disciples came into the land of Judea, and there He remained with them and baptized. Now John also was baptizing in Aenon near Salim, because there was much water there. And they came and were baptized. For John had not yet been thrown into prison. Then there arose a dispute between some of John's disciples and the Jews about purification. And they came to John and said to him, "Rabbi, He who was with you beyond the Jordan, to whom you have testified— behold, He is baptizing, and all are coming to Him!" John answered and said, "A man can receive nothing unless it has been given to him from heaven. You yourselves bear me witness, that I said, 'I am not the Christ,' but, 'I have been sent before Him.' He who has the bride is the bridegroom; but the friend of the bridegroom, who stands and hears him, rejoices greatly because of the bridegroom's voice. Therefore this joy of mine is fulfilled.* **He must increase, but I must decrease.**" (John 3:22–30)

Let's take a trip back in time for a moment in order to paint a vivid picture of what is happening here. We know from Matthew's account that John's ministry, at least up until this point, has been centered around Judea in a region close to the Jordan River. This is where he did most (or all) of his baptizing (Matt. 3:1–6). According to the text above, Jesus and His disciples shift their ministry focus from the Jerusalem capital to setting up a base of operations in the same general territory or vicinity where John's ministry was headquartered, basically in John's "backyard."[23] To make matters worse, they are shamelessly engaging in the very same ministry that was signature to John (thus the name "John the Baptist")—baptism!

Although the text itself does not make this clear connection, it would appear that John's relocation from the Jordan River—a place where he has historically experienced massive success in terms of numbers—to an alternate water source suitable for his ministry, was on account of Jesus and His disciples' recent occupation of that area around the Jordan where he once performed his baptisms. As one commentator describes it, "The importance of the note [v. 23] is to show that John moved from the south to the north, leaving Jesus to baptize in the area not distant from Jerusalem."[24]

John's ministry is no longer experiencing or enjoying the popularity it once had. It is now being eclipsed by a newer and greater ministry represented in Jesus. The masses that were once flocking to John by the Jordan are now flocking to Jesus, thus prompting the hyperbolic claim from John's disciples that *all are coming to Him* (v. 26). As a matter of fact, even some of John's loyal disciples had left him and were now following Jesus instead (John 1:35–40).

The remaining disciples of John no longer viewed Jesus and His disciples as ministerial colleagues or co-laborers but as disloyal competitors who once partook of the rich spiritual resource of John's ministry before turning around and starting their own. This apparently led to a jealous disputation (v. 25) originating with John's disciples regarding which baptism was greater (Jesus's or John's). As the original pioneers of the "water baptism movement" of that time, John's disciples obviously felt that their baptism was greater than any other, if for no other reason than the fact that they were the first to preach and practice it.[25] Of course, this type of carnal comparison is rooted in a competitive spirit and religious pride—the same kind that many of us are guilty of today.

The disciples of John finally bring their dispute directly to their leader (John), addressing him by the handle of *Rabbi*—the only place in the Gospel where the title [term] "Rabbi" refers to someone other than Jesus[26]—in a calculated attempt to reaffirm and reinforce the superiority of John's ministry (v. 26). Their argument and complaint would have been convincing in almost every religious context today:

(a) Jesus was once a member of John's ministry who submitted to John's leadership and baptism; (b) It could be argued that it was John's affirmation and testimony that brought Jesus such success; and (c) Jesus was now "stealing" John's ministry (baptism) and members (followers). Of course, we know that Jesus never stole anything or dishonored John in any way, but that doesn't change the way things appear from a purely—or rather, impurely—human perspective.

It is John's response, however, that will forever set him apart as the greatest born of a woman as he epitomizes a powerful spiritual principle that is at the heart of this prophetic divergence and third prophetic dimension. Instead of taking the bait and seeing himself either as a helpless victim or a deluded superior to Jesus (two opposite but similarly toxic extremes), he anchors himself in biblical faith by reaffirming the sovereignty of God (*A man can receive nothing unless it has been given to him from heaven* [v. 27]). He then poignantly reminds his disciples that he was "not the Christ" but one "sent before Him," indicating clear spiritual sight, perception, and recognition of Jesus being the Christ or promised Messiah who possessed a much higher spiritual rank and authority than he did (v. 28).

Friend of the Bridegroom

When John responded in such a noble manner, it was not an expression of false humility. His internal posture and outward perspective were correct because he was never intoxicated by his outward success (of literal masses once flocking to his ministry), deluded by an inflated ego or false sense of self-importance, or blinded by the lustful desire for power, position, popularity, or prestige. His concern was never on building an earthly empire or leaving a lasting legacy. He understood his clearly defined role as being a *friend of the bridegroom* (v. 29).

This ancient Hebrew concept of a *friend of the bridegroom* or *shoshben* (as referred by the Jews) that is employed by John as an analogy defining his prophetic role is quite profound. The challenge here is that there is nothing in our Western culture that is an accurate equivalent. The closest or nearest equivalent would be our traditional "best man" at weddings, but even this is a very meager and deficient representation that fails to capture even half of the Hebrew concept.

Here is one commentator's description of the *friend of the bridegroom*'s role in ancient Hebrew culture:

> According to the Hebrew custom, the Shoshben, a friend of the bridegroom, was a necessary mediator both in the formation and in the conclusion of the marriage. In behalf of his friend he made suit with the bride, and was the indispensable negotiator between the bride and bridegroom in relation to the wedding. At the wedding itself he was a chief manager of the feast, a necessary functionary at the inspection of the wedding-chamber, and even after the close of the marriage a mediator in misunderstandings and dissensions.[27]

It is clear that the *friend of the bridegroom* served and functioned in many diverse capacities (messenger, manager, mediator, etc.) "in behalf of his friend" throughout the length (not just the marriage ceremony) of his relationship with his bride. Despite these many functions, however, he occupied and fulfilled a single role—to seek after the will, interests, and pleasure of his close friend, the bridegroom. Regardless of his close involvement and very visible role in the formation, cultivation, and consummation of the relationship on behalf of his friend (the bridegroom), it was never to be about the friend of the bridegroom. The friend of the bridegroom was only there to elevate and magnify the bridegroom, not himself. If he performed his role selflessly and correctly, he would effectively fade into the background.

As a matter of fact, it was considered morally and culturally abhorrent in ancient times (more so than present) for the friend of the bridegroom (or best man) to betray the friendship of the bridegroom by pursuing the love or intimate pleasure of the bride for himself. Mesopotamian law forbade any marriage between the "friend" and the bride, even if the relationship or marriage had been aborted for whatever reason.[28] It was unlawful in any circumstance for the friend of the bridegroom to take the bride as his own. Therefore, when John boldly states that *I am not the Christ* (v. 28) and then closely follows it with the declaration that the bride belongs solely to the bridegroom (v. 29), he is reaffirming his covenant of honor with his friend by not seeking or desiring that which rightly belongs to the bridegroom—his bride! John's true joy and sense of fulfillment as the *friend of the bridegroom* comes from the satisfaction of the bridegroom. His pleasure comes from a posture of patiently positioning himself (standing) in close proximity to the bridegroom in order to accurately hear his voice (including commands), thereby determining his intent so he could effectively fulfill them. Then his ultimate pleasure came from the bridegroom's voice of satisfaction and delight when his desires were fulfilled.

The concept of being a *friend of the bridegroom* can be defined by one word—*selflessness*. It describes the ability to lay down one's own personal aspiration, ambition, or agenda for a higher, nobler purpose—the divine will and pleasure of the Bridegroom and the advancement of His Kingdom.

John the Baptist demonstrated this selflessness by never seeking to compete with Jesus, while at the same time doing everything within his power to ensure His success above his own. He surrendered his disciples, territory, and ministry for Jesus's benefit. He was never threatened by another's success because he understood his true role.

The warrior prince, Jonathan, demonstrated this selflessness when he willingly surrendered his right to the throne in preference of his close friend, David (1 Sam. 20). Jonathan recognized that the hand and calling of God was upon his friend, yet he never felt threatened by David's success or anointing like his father Saul. David's success and ascent to the throne meant the household of Saul's demise, yet even with this knowledge and understanding, Jonathan was willing to risk everything for David's safety and well-being. He too understood that *"A man can receive nothing unless it has been given to him from heaven."*

We see yet another example of this selflessness demonstrated by Philip after his successful outreach to Samaria (Acts 8:4–25). As powerful and effective as his ministry was to the Samaritans (with powerful and miraculous demonstrations of deliverance and healing), it was still limited. When the apostles at Jerusalem received word of Philip's ministry in Samaria, they sent an apostolic delegation to take the Samaritans to another level in their faith and experience (something Philip was otherwise unable to do as an evangelist because he apparently lacked the necessary grace). Instead of claiming ownership and resisting apostolic oversight and input, the people were given access to greater grace and a powerful apostolic dimension that they could not otherwise receive under Philip's leadership. Even though Philip's image and popularity could have waned after the apostles' visit (he was once the "man of power for the hour," but now there were greater "men of power for the hour"), this was never his concern. He never felt threatened by the apostles because his focus was on building the Kingdom, not building a following. Like John, he understood that *He who has the bride is the bridegroom*; therefore, despite the fact that the believing community in Samaria was founded by him, they were not his possession.

The entire principle of diminution is rooted and hinged upon the selfless internal posture of being a *friend of the bridegroom*. It is seeking His will, desire, and interests above our own. It means finding satisfaction solely in the Bridegroom's pleasure, even when that pleasure translates into our temporal pain and discomfort as we fade into the background. This cannot happen when ministry is still utilized or approached as a means of promoting ourselves and our interests, building an earthly legacy, immortalizing ourselves for our accomplishments and good works, attaining earthly significance and recognition, increasing followers and popularity, or exacting wealth.

This principle becomes especially challenging for those so blinded by earthly religion that they are incapable of recognizing Jesus in their brothers and sisters. John (the Baptist) recognized the grace and rank of Jesus and willingly submitted or subjected himself to a diminutive role. This, by the way, was done while Jesus walked the earth as *man* and not in His glorious state as God. In other words,

John was willing to decrease himself before another man's ministry while watching his brother's increase. How many of us are willing to do the same before our brothers and sisters? You cannot *decrease* before God until you're first ready and willing to *decrease* before men. The Bridegroom (and His Kingdom) cannot *increase* as in heaven unless we first learn to *decrease* (before men) on earth.

True Witnesses

There is, perhaps, no other ministry in Scripture that epitomizes this principle of diminution more than the prophetic. Prophets are the "friends of God (the Bridegroom)." John represents the third prophetic dimension. The sole purpose of an accurate prophetic dimension is to accurately represent, elevate, and magnify the Sender— never the messenger! Every human or earthly thing pertaining to the prophet or messenger in this context is insignificant and irrelevant. The minute a prophet of God deviates from this principle and begins to assert his own will, desire, interests, or ego above God's, both he and his ministry become false in direct proportion to the degree of the deviation. This means true prophets of God don't compete with each other; they submit to and complement each other. They are not concerned with building a personal following or promoting their ministries. Their meetings or ministry will not magnify the prophet; their meetings or ministry will seek to magnify God. This is the defining characteristic of the third prophetic dimension.

Earlier in this chapter, we mentioned about the prophet who made the incorrect Super Bowl prediction. Such a prediction, deliberately publicized and posted on the Internet, even if correct, would have served to magnify the prophet rather than God. Nothing in such a carnal prediction serves to magnify God or His Kingdom. This type of falseness, therefore, is indicative of human pride, ego, and self-centeredness resulting from the deviation we have just described.

Unfortunately, this type of deviation and self-promotion is rampant in the current movement. All too often, we encounter immature and/or inaccurate prophets who seek to bolster their public image by impressing their audiences with spectacular displays of supernatural knowledge or gifting. There is nothing wrong with revealing some-one's personal details like name, phone number, or address so long as that revelation serves to ultimately magnify the Father and advance His Kingdom on earth. Otherwise, the person who ultimately bene-fits when the ministry is over is the prophet.

When Jesus told the Samaritan woman at the well that she *had five husbands, and the one whom you [she] now have [had] is [was] not your [her] husband* (John 4:17–18), it was done privately and not before a crowd of people. He obviously wasn't trying to promote Himself or impress others with His gifting. This accurate word of knowledge was embedded in a much deeper and profound message that would serve to revolutionize, upgrade, and transform her wor-ship to the Father, thereby causing Him (not Jesus) to be magnified (John 4:20–24). A city was ultimately transformed and the Kingdom of God forcefully advanced in Samaria as a result of such an accurate prophetic witness (John 4:39–42).

John is identified in Scripture as a true prophetic *witness* because, as a *friend of the bridegroom*, he was never interested in pro-moting either himself or his ministry before men (John 1:6–8). John never sought to usurp the place of Christ by seeking the recognition or attention that belonged to Him alone. Rather, he was constantly diminishing himself before men, and so effective was he in this regard that *when the Jews sent priests and Levites*—the recognized and estab-lished religious leaders and ministers—*from Jerusalem* in an attempt to discover his true identity within their perceived eschatological framework, the only definitive information they were able to extract from him beyond who he was not (i.e. Christ, Elijah, or the Prophet) was that he was *the voice of one crying in the wilderness [of obscurity]* (John 1:23). It is important to note here that John never denied his role of being a prophetic forerunner in the spirit and power of Elijah. What he denied was being Elijah in the flesh. The principle here is that John rejected any title of significance or rank of importance. He wasn't passing out business cards with "Prophet John" posted in bold letters. He never responded by saying, "I am a prophet." He refused to ascribe any spiritual or religious significance or importance to himself before men.

While this type of behavior may appear foreign, or even ludicrous, in today's Western and narcissistic religious culture where earthly recognition and importance have become something to be grasped and where personal marketing and self-promotion have become the norm, it is totally in character with an accurate prophetic dimension. True prophets of God never seek recognition or notoriety. They do not promote themselves or their ministries in an effort to achieve greater popularity or exposure. As a matter of fact, there are several examples of anonymous prophets emerging in Scripture and performing their supernatural ministry while maintaining a diminished role so effectively that at the end of their ministry, people still had no detailed knowledge of their identity:

1. The author of Judges provides a detailed account of a prophetic message (rebuke) given by a *prophet* of God to the *children of Israel* during a time of apostasy, yet even though he is able to recount every word of the prophet's message and the fact that he was *sent* by God, he is apparently unable to identify the prophet by name (Judg. 6:7–10).

2. When a *man of God* (prophet) emerges during the early days of Samuel and issues a powerful and detailed prophetic rebuke to Eli—the senior member of the established religious priesthood of that day—and even confirms it with a prophetic sign, he quickly disappears (diminishes) into obscurity. While the adult Samuel is later able to fully recount this prophet's message, he is unable to identify this prophet by name (1 Sam. 2:27–36).

3. Our third example is a prophet or *man of God* whose ministry we have already briefly examined and discussed in the first chapter (1 Kings 13). He is credited with giving one of the most remarkable prophecies recorded in Scripture—identifying Josiah by name and describing his future actions in detail almost 300 years before he was even born. If that wasn't remarkable enough, he also demonstrated a powerful supernatural dimension of miraculous signs and wonders that would have made even the staunchest skep-

tic's jaws drop to the floor. He could have easily made a name for himself right then and there, but he didn't. He diminished himself and remained anonymous, even refusing the hospitality of the king when it could have easily elevated his wealth and reputation.

By today's carnal standards these prophets would be considered small and insignificant but not by heaven's reckoning. They never built themselves any earthly reputations or empires. They left no earthly legacies to be remembered or revered by. Like a *voice,* they came and then disappeared, leaving no earthly trace or record of their existence, not even a name. But we would be greatly mistaken if we assumed that their lives and ministries had little impact. Each of these prophets emerged during very key, pivotal, and critical times during the history of Israel. The record of their words and ministry lives on as a testament to the deeply profound impact they had on the nation of Israel for generations. By their *decrease,* God's Kingdom in the nation of Israel was able to *increase;* and by their examples, we are given greater insight into the architecture of the third prophetic dimension.

The Baptism of Repentance

It is impossible to have any intelligent discussion or examination of John's life and ministry, especially as it relates to and parallels the third prophetic dimension, without commenting on what is the most significant and notable aspect of his ministry—baptism! While it can be argued (among scholars) about who started the practice of water baptism first, there can be no argument regarding the uniqueness and significance of John's teaching and practice concerning it. John wasn't introducing some empty religious form or ritual, or else Jesus would never have subjected Himself to it. Have you ever wondered why God (The Father and Holy Spirit) waited until just that precise moment—when Jesus had entirely submitted Himself to the process of baptism under John's leadership—to open up the heavens and publicly affirm Him (Matt. 3:13–17)? Or why Jesus and His disciples continued the practice (John 3:22; 4:1–3).

John's baptism was prophetic in that it represented an access point to the Kingdom—i.e. righteousness—through the act of genuine repentance (Rom. 14:17). What Jesus submitted to and heaven endorsed in principle was the Kingdom prerequisite of righteousness that supersedes earthly religious pedigree, practice, or conformity (Matt. 3:15; 21:32). What was truly novel and revolutionary about John's message and ministry of baptism (repentance) was the fact that it viewed the very ones who considered themselves righteous—the Jews and especially the Jewish religious leaders—as the most corrupt and in need of repentance (Matt. 3:7–8). John emphatically challenged and discounted any misplaced confidence in Jewish religious heritage through Abraham, and this same misplaced confidence in our religious "Christian" heritage, doctrine, or denominations is going to be radically challenged by this new prophetic dimension emerging today also (Matt. 3:9–10).

The repentance that John demanded and the baptism he practiced was not something shallow or superficial like we often see in religious Christianity today. For example, water baptism today is practiced mostly as an empty religious ritual or ordinance publicly confirming one's decision to follow Christ, but the baptism John practiced was much more significant and profound. His concern was never about public (outward) confirmation but about deep internal transformation through genuine repentance. Genuine repentance, according to John's definition, would always be clearly demonstrated through a fruitful and accurate Kingdom lifestyle (Matt. 3:8, 10). In other words, the significance of being baptized in water was not necessarily in the act itself but in what the act was intended to represent. Divorced from its true substance—genuine repentance—the act of being dipped or submerged in water was inutile, insignificant, and irrelevant.

Furthermore, John's baptism was intended as a precursor to what Jesus (the promised Messiah and divine Prophet) would release in its fullness (Matt. 3:11; Acts 1:5, 19:4). It was a type and shadow of Jesus's supernatural baptism of the Spirit that would effect an internal purification and transformation of the heart and spirit of man. The emphasis, again, was always on the deep transforming power of the Holy Spirit and never on the external or outward "evidence." You will never find a single record of any apostle, leader, or early believer asking anyone whether or not they spoke in tongues; neither can anyone definitively prove it was ever implied. That was never the important issue. The question posed by Paul was, *"Did you receive the **Holy Spirit** [substance] when you believed?"* (Acts 19:2). Never once in that entire discussion or dialogue about the Spirit did Paul ever mention tongues, not even to prepare them in anticipation for an expected response. It was clearly never any priority or emphasis, regardless of how controversial this statement may sound to some segments of modern-day Christianity where the question is often asked, "Do you speak in tongues?" and the emphasis is on external "evidence" or manifestations—a sure formula for deception![29]

The principle here is that John's ministry was never focused or built upon externals, unlike his religious contemporaries (priests, scribes, Pharisees, Sadducees, and all the religious Jews) whose emphasis was always upon religious ritual and dead works. While John was very passionate about reforming the then current Jewish religious culture and society, he understood and practiced the principle that there can be no true reformation without internal transformation. Therefore, his emphasis was never simply upon behavioral modification or societal reform but upon heart transformation through genuine repentance.

John also understood that the greatest threat or impediment to true reformation and accurate Kingdom advance was organized and entrenched religion built upon a paradigm of what God had previously *said* instead of what He is currently *saying*. By calling the Pharisees and Sadducees—the established religious authority and government at the time—a *brood of vipers*, he was affirming the spiritual danger they posed and the fatally venomous poison such an inaccurate religious system possessed (Matt. 3:7).

Mainstream Christianity today has found itself in the same religious rut as the religious system represented by the Pharisees and Sadducees of old, producing with it a false and Pharisaic fatidic order, which focuses primarily on supernatural manifestation and self-gratification (2 Tim. 3:1–9). They love to be recognized and honored, and they love to be addressed with titles of significance (Matt. 23:1–12). They are foolish and blind prophets who are covetous and greedy, ministering out of their own self-interest and feigning piety while rejecting Kingdom principles of justice, mercy, and faith because they lack any genuine heart of compassion (Matt. 23:14–24). They outwardly appear righteous when internally, they are full of hypocrisy and lawlessness (Matt. 23:27–28). As such, they continue to reproduce themselves in others while perpetuating a false system of religion where the focus is on making the *outside* clean when the *inside* is still full of corruption (Matt. 23:25–26).

It is this very false religious system and fatidic order that the emerging third prophetic dimension is being called upon to boldly challenge and confront by laying the axe to the root and demanding deep, genuine repentance. And with this emergence will come a greater divergence—a greater division and separation initiated through judgment between that which is holy (accurate) and that which is defiled (corrupt)—thus signaling the "nearness" of the Father's Kingdom (Matt. 3:10, 12, 7:17–23, 10:34–36; Luke 17:34–36; 1 Pet. 4:17).

The Fruits of Genuine Repentance

When John demanded of those who came to be baptized of him *fruits worthy of repentance*—indicative of a genuine heart transformation—his expectations were much different from what was usually required from the established religious systems of his time, which required outward conformity to religious rules and ritual (Luke3:8).

> So the people asked him, saying, "What shall we do then?" He answered and said to them, "He who has two tunics, let him give to him who has none; and he who has food, let him do likewise." Then tax collectors also came to be baptized, and said to him, "Teacher, what shall we do?" And he said to them, "Collect no more than what is appointed for you." Likewise the soldiers asked him, saying, "And what

*shall we do?" So he said to them, "Do not intimi-
date anyone or accuse falsely, and be content with
your wages."* (Luke 3:10–14)

According to John, the true authenticity of repentance is revealed through the personal spheres of our diverse relationships and dealings within society as they are characterized by love, mercy, and compassion. These relationships also include our enemies (Matt. 5:43–48; Luke 6:35–36). There can be no greater evidence of repentance and Kingdom citizenship than to demonstrate the true nature and character of the Kingdom and its King—*love* (John 13:35; 1 John 4:8, 16).

As we examine each of the above requirements briefly, we will interpret these principles (fruits) in the context of being *imperatives for an accurate prophetic dimension.*

1. *The principle of shared resource* (v. 11). The willingness to part with food and personal items of clothing communicates a much higher principle than unselfish generosity, and it extends way beyond the boundaries of physical or earthly necessities.[30] This principle of shared resource (and the rejection of exclusivism in personal ownership) is noticeably demonstrated several times in the book of Acts, and it is indicative of a healthy and vibrant Kingdom community (Acts 2:42–47; 4:32–37). Only a mature and accurate prophetic dimension can promote or foster such an authentic Kingdom culture. It requires selfless love and compassion on the part of the prophet to offer his life and ministry in service to Christ's Bride without demanding remuneration or reward. The minute a prophet begins to deviate from this pattern and proceeds to minister out of his own self-interest or for financial gain, he becomes a false prophet and an agent of error. The prophetic anointing is a grace *freely* given by God. Contrary to popular belief, nobody has paid a price for anything they have received from God. If you paid for it, you earned it; and if

you earned it, it is no longer a grace from God. Therefore, *freely [as] you have received, freely give* (Matt. 10:8).[31]

2. *The principle of just stewardship* (vs. 12–13): Following closely upon the core values of the previous principle, the obvious emphasis here is on a prohibition against unjust exaction and greed. *Tax collectors* were those contracted to collect tolls and taxes on behalf of the Roman government.[32] These agents (or stewards) of the government were often dishonest and unjust in their practices, overtaxing others in order to pad their own pockets and increase personal profit. They represent a system of corruption and unjust exaction very similar to what we see practiced today among greedy prophets and ministers who employ manipulation, intimidation, and other forms of dishonest and questionable means in order to exact offerings for their own personal gain (disguised as legitimate "kingdom" business, of course). True prophets are faithful and just stewards, content with what God has allotted or appointed them. And an accurate prophetic dimension is one that challenges and confronts every form of corruption and injustice, especially when that corruption or injustice resides within the leadership of Christ's Community or within the structures of its worship.

3. *The principle of righteous authority*: Resident within the two prohibitions and one admonition given to the *soldiers* is a clear principle regarding the righteous exercise of delegated power and authority. These soldiers—regardless of whether or not they were actually Roman or Jewish—typified the exercise of delegated power and authority similar to how police officers and the military operate today. The authority they exercised and the power they wielded was not their own but was delegated to them by a higher (legislative or governmental) body to serve a purpose beyond themselves. This is called *righteous authority*. However, like today, some soldiers (or police officers) sought to abuse this "right" or privilege by misusing their authority for

their own self-interests, thus becoming *unrighteous author-ity*. The principle here is that righteous authority can only be exercised through selfless devotion in performing the will and intent of the One who delegated that authority—God! When the delegated authority we exercise becomes corrupted by our own self-interest or greed, it becomes unrighteous, and this unrighteousness is often mani-fested through *intimidation* (prohibition #1), *oppression* (prohibition #2)[33] and a covetousness or lust to acquire more—indicating a *lack of contentment* (admonition #1). An accurate prophetic dimension, therefore, is one that exercises righteous authority because it is completely devoted to pursuing the Father's will and intent above its own self-interests. It never employs acts (or prophecies) of manipulation, intimidation, or control in the dispense of its ministry, and the authority it exercises is never oppres-sive or overbearing but reflects the Father's heart of love and compassion.

There is much more that can be written concerning John and his ministry, including the "spirit of Elijah" dimension that he walked in, but we must now turn our attention to addressing commonly held misconceptions pertaining to prophets and personal prophecy.

Notes

1   William A. Simmons, "John the Baptist," in *Baker Theological Dictionary of the Bible*, ed. Walter A. Elwell (Grand Rapids, MI: Baker Books, 2000), 421.

2   Jeffrey H. Tigay, *Deuteronomy*, The JPS Torah Commentary (Philadelphia: Jewish Publication Society, 1996), 175.

3   Some of these prophecies were clearly identified as false for the simple reason that they never occurred within the specific time-frame given.

4   James Swanson, *Dictionary of Biblical Languages with Semantic Domains: Hebrew (Old Testament)* (Oak Harbor: Logos Research Systems, Inc., 1997).

5   Even John's death was on account of an oath made to Herodias's daughter, thus underscoring once again the principle that John represents the fulfillment of promise (Matt. 14:1–12).

6   Shuler, Philip L., and Mark Allan Powell. "Zechariah." Edited by Mark Allan Powell. *The HarperCollins Bible Dictionary (Revised and Updated)* (New York: HarperCollins, 2011).

7   "Elisabeth," from Smith's Bible Dictionary, PC Study Bible formatted electronic database Copyright © 2003, 2006 by Biblesoft, Inc. All rights reserved [PC Study Bible © 2008, Biblesoft, Inc.].

8   Spiros Zodhiates, Th.D., *The Hebrew-Greek Key Study Bible King James Version*, Copyright © 1991 by AMG Publishers.

9   Youngblood, Ronald F., F. F. Bruce, and R. K. Harrison, Thomas Nelson Publishers, eds. *Nelson's New Illustrated Bible Dictionary* (Nashville, TN: Thomas Nelson, Inc., 1995).

10 Ibid.

11 William A. Simmons, "John the Baptist," in *Baker Theological Dictionary of the Bible*, ed. Walter A. Elwell (Grand Rapids, MI: Baker Books, 2000), 423.

12 Alexander, T. Desmond, and Brian S. Rosner, eds. *New Dictionary of Biblical Theology* (Downers Grove, IL: InterVarsity Press, 2000).

13 See also Acts 1:15–22 where both the context as well as the Greek definition of the word *office* relate very clearly to function rather than title or position.

[14] Alexander Strauch, *Biblical Eldership: An Urgent Call to Restore Biblical Church Leadership* (Littleton, CO: Lewis and Roth Publishers, 1995), 302.

[15] Eugene E. Carpenter and Philip W. Comfort, *Holman Treasury of Key Bible Words: 200 Greek and 200 Hebrew Words Defined and Explained* (Nashville, TN: Broadman & Holman Publishers, 2000), 352.

[16] Arndt, William, Frederick W. Danker, and Walter Bauer. *A Greek-English Lexicon of the New Testament and Other Early Christian Literature* (Chicago: University of Chicago Press, 2000).

[17] Greek-English Lexicon Based on Semantic Domain. Copyright © 1988 United Bible Societies, New York. Used by permission [PC Study Bible © 2008, Biblesoft, Inc.].

[18] Alexander, T. Desmond, and Brian S. Rosner, eds. *New Dictionary of Biblical Theology* (Downers Grove, IL: InterVarsity Press, 2000).

[19] Ibid.

[20] Walter A. Elwell and Barry J. Beitzel, *Baker Encyclopedia of the Bible* (Grand Rapids, MI: Baker Book House, 1988), 1434.

[21] Ibid., 421.

[22] Lange, John Peter, and J. J. van Oosterzee. *A Commentary on the Holy Scriptures: Luke.* Translated by Philip Schaff and Charles C. Starbuck (Bellingham, WA: Logos Bible Software, 2008).

[23] Note that the word *remained* (v. 22) and the imperfect tenses used to describe this event are indicative of prolonged activity or continued action.

[24] George R. Beasley-Murray, *John*, vol. 36, Word Biblical Commentary (Dallas: Word, Incorporated, 2002), 52.

[25] Note that while it is arguable among scholars whether or not Jewish proselyte baptism predates John's, there is no argument regarding the fact that the baptism that John taught and practiced was distinct, separate, novel, and unique in almost every regard to the ritualistic practices of the Essenes (Qumran community) and others before or during that time. For one thing, "Until John's appearance, neither in Judaism nor in the world around had anyone baptized other persons" (Stegemann, 218).

26 Gerald L. Borchert, *John 1–11*, vol. 25A, The New American Commentary (Nashville: Broadman & Holman Publishers, 1996), 190.

27 John Peter Lange and Philip Schaff, *A Commentary on the Holy Scriptures: John* (Bellingham, WA: Logos Bible Software, 2008), 143.

28 A. Van Selms, "Friend of the Bridegroom," ed. D. R. W. Wood et al., *New Bible Dictionary* (Leicester, England; Downers Grove, IL: InterVarsity Press, 1996), 386.

29 It is beyond the scope of this current writing to fully address this issue of speaking in tongues. Sufficed to say, while speaking in other tongues is a valid, biblically based, Holy Spirit manifestation, it is incorrect to assume that such "evidence" always equates to a genuine Holy Spirit baptism or transformation in the life of an individual. Just as someone can prophesy without the Spirit (or by a human or evil spirit), someone can speak in tongues in the same manner. Outward evidence was meant to *confirm* inner substance, not substitute it. You can manufacture evidence without substance, but you can never possess substance without manifesting some kind of evidence. Therefore, evidence (tongues or prophecy) without internal substance (The Holy Spirit and His deep internal transformation) translates to *having a form of godliness but denying its power* (2 Tim. 3:5). Unfortunately, there are millions of tongue-talkers today who believe they are Spirit baptized yet have never experienced any genuine encounter with the Holy Spirit and are, therefore, void of any true substance. They may flaunt tongues like a wedding band (evidence), but in reality, they are separated or divorced (lack of true spiritual substance) from the One whom the "band" was meant to express covenant with.

30 The Greek verb, **metadidōmi**, translated *to give* (NKJV) or *to share* (ESV) is used in the New Testament to refer both to material possessions as well as divine resource (Rom. 1:11, 12:8; Eph. 4:28; 1 Thess. 2:8).

31 The scriptural command for prophets and ministers sent by God to give *freely* is a two-way street. Often when this scripture is

quoted, it is isolated from the larger unit of thought it is contained within. The very next two verses are explicitly clear that a minister should not have to provide for himself because *the workman deserves his support [his living, his food]* (Matt. 10:10, AMP). In other words, the ethical imperative given to ministers to share their spiritual resource freely is balanced by an equally ethical responsibility upon those receiving this resource to reciprocate honor and blessing by ministering to their natural and physical needs. This principle will be expounded upon much more fully in an upcoming volume.

[32] Jeffrey E. Miller, "Tax Collector," ed. John D. Barry et al., *The Lexham Bible Dictionary* (Bellingham, WA: Lexham Press, 2012, 2013, 2014).

[33] Gerhard Kittel, Geoffrey W. Bromiley, and Gerhard Friedrich, eds., *Theological Dictionary of the New Testament* (Grand Rapids, MI: Eerdmans, 1964–), 759.

4

PUTTING PROPHETS AND PROPHECY
IN PROPER PERSPECTIVE

A NEW— *THIRD*—PROPHETIC DIMENSION is emerging in the earth, and with this new emergence comes a fresh, updated, and, in many ways, divergent understanding of many core concepts and principles pertaining to its operation. We have discussed several of these concepts and principles in the previous three chapters. We have also identified a key Kingdom principle that whenever God seeks to reemphasize, redevelop, or reform a key spiritual ministry in the earth, it is always accompanied by a redefinition of principles, patterns, and paradigms pertaining to that ministry's operation.

One such area of redefinition in the prophetic pertains to our understanding of prophets and prophecy. Despite the numerous number of seminars, conferences, and published material on the subjects, a large degree of confusion, misunderstanding, and misconception abounds—due in large part to the incorrect teaching and misinformation involved. In the first chapter, we took a broad-brush approach to addressing these prophetic concepts, but from here on, we will be applying much finer and detailed strokes as we attempt to recalibrate and readjust our perspectives into more informed and biblically accurate ones.

The Elementary Principle of Prophecy

For many believers today, there is an apparent sense of wonderment and awe when they see prophecy being discharged, or when the personal details of one's heart and life are made known through words of knowledge by certain individuals usually recognized as "prophets." Not that there is anything necessarily wrong with being in awe of God's power and goodness, but when we begin to develop a "hero worship" mentality or form incorrect and unhealthy assumptions regarding the men (or women) giving these prophecies—viewing them as some type of special or super saint because of their ability to prophesy—something has gone awry.

The assumption that accuracy in detail (prophesied) equates to accuracy in ministry, character, or prophetic dimension is a very subtle and dangerous lie. It reflects an unbiblical, undeveloped, and juvenile understanding of the prophetic that is inconsistent with reality. The reality, as we explained very early in the first chapter, is that the gifted ability to prophesy accurate details or foretell future events is only the "tip of the iceberg" (less than one-tenth of the hidden mass) regarding what it means to be truly prophetic.

Furthermore, the ability to prophesy, and to do so accurately, is not some mystic art that is relegated only to a select few. The Scriptures are very clear that we *may all prophesy* (1 Cor. 14:31). In fact, far from being an indication of one's level of spirituality, maturity, or doctrinal accuracy, prophesying is an elementary principle or activity in the Kingdom of God.

The Ephesian Believers

When Paul encountered a group of John's disciples in Ephesus who had not yet been upgraded into the present truth of Christ Jesus, the very one who John the Baptist was sent to prepare the way for, his efforts to remedy this situation marked the beginning and birthing of a new Kingdom community in this region.

> *And it happened, while Apollos was at Corinth,*
> *that Paul, having passed through the upper regions,*
> *came to Ephesus. And finding some disciples he said*
> *to them, "Did you receive the Holy Spirit when*
> *you believed?" So they said to him, "We have not*
> *so much as heard whether there is a Holy Spirit."*
> *And he said to them, "Into what then were you bap-*
> *tized?" So they said, "Into John's baptism." Then*
> *Paul said, "John indeed baptized with a baptism*
> *of repentance, saying to the people that they should*
> *believe on Him who would come after him, that*
> *is, on Christ Jesus." When they heard this, they*
> *were baptized in the name of the Lord Jesus. And*
> *when Paul had laid hands on them, the Holy Spirit*
> *came upon them, and they spoke with tongues **and***
> ***prophesied.*** (Acts 19:1–6, emphasis mine)

Not only had this group of *disciples* not been introduced to the gospel of Jesus, but also, they had never even *heard whether there is [was] a Holy Spirit.* They had repented of sin according to the teachings (baptism) of John and were devotedly positioned at the door of the Kingdom, but they had never fully entered in because they were still ignorant of the finished work of Jesus Christ. This deficiency necessitated a spiritual upgrade from Paul, who proceeded to lead them into present truth before rebaptizing them in the name of Jesus—a unique occurrence that is never repeated anywhere else in the New Testament—thus ushering them through the Door (Jesus) and into the Kingdom of God. These new converts then had hands laid upon them by Paul for the baptism of the Holy Spirit when something interesting happens—not only did they speak in other tongues, which is an activity believed by many to be the initial evidence of the Holy Spirit's baptism, but they prophesied also!

These newly born-again believers were able to speak in tongues **and prophesy** upon their initial entry into the Kingdom of God. They did not have to enroll in a series of "new believer" classes, complete any form of Bible school/college curriculum, or obtain any predetermined level of religious maturity or experience in order to participate in this spiritual activity. As a matter of fact, up until minutes ago, they were not even aware of the Holy Spirit's present existence, yet the scriptures tell us that they were still able to prophesy. Based upon this principle, it is clear that prophesying is not as complicated or advanced as many of us have been led to believe it is, but is in fact, an elementary spiritual principle that can be activated and practiced by even the newest convert, regardless of age, gender, or any other social factor or status.

Most Pentecostal or Charismatic believers today would never dream of placing a person on some type of pedestal simply because of their ability to speak in other tongues. It is understood that this type of activity should be commonplace and expected in every believer. It should be no different with prophecy because it is the same Holy Spirit who empowers both. In the same way that there is no elevated or inflated opinion of others when they speak in tongues, there should be no elevated or inflated opinion of others when they prophesy. Both manifestations function according to the same spiritual principle and should be just as frequent.

Issues of Maturity and Character

In our example above regarding the Ephesian disciples (Acts 19:1–6), we provided scriptural evidence supporting the truth that prophecy is an elementary principle able to be activated and practiced by any believer regardless of their spiritual maturity. We will continue to elaborate upon this principle, but what part does character play in all of this? Can such a Holy Spirit–inspired gift be discharged through an unclean or unholy vessel also? I'm glad you asked, and the answer is yes! Even though it was never God's intention for us to operate this way, a lack of holiness or Christlike character does not impede or restrict your ability to prophesy any more than it does your ability to speak in other tongues.

When King Saul was in a demonized and murderous state, rejected by God and consumed with a jealousy so deep and evil that he was intent on hunting and killing innocent blood, he was still able to prophesy (1 Sam. 19). From a holiness and character standpoint, it doesn't get much worse than Saul. How could such a demonized man intent on committing murder and thoroughly rejected by God still be able to prophesy? Because prophecy is an elementary principle that does not require godly character or holiness by which to operate on a base level.[1] None of the gifts of the Spirit do.

If you read the text regarding Saul's prophesying in this particular instance, similar to the time when he prophesied just after being anointed king by Samuel (1 Sam. 10:1–11), no mention is made of him prophesying inaccurately. We have to assume, then, that Saul's prophesying was spot-on even in his demonized and murderous state. Of course, this raises the question as to how the Spirit of God could still come upon and flow through an individual in such a depraved condition, but it is beyond the scope of this writing to address that question.

We encounter a similar occurrence of this principle in operation in the Corinthian community of believers. The Corinthian community (church) was a very spiritually gifted company (1 Cor. 1:7, 12–14). Not only did they speak in unknown tongues quite frequently, especially during public gatherings, but it is quite apparent from Paul's letters that they were quite familiar in the exercise of prophecy also (1 Cor. 14). Because of their many excesses and the fact that seemingly every member of the community was capable and willing to participate, Paul had to outline clear instructions and guidelines for the exercise of their vocal gifts—tongues and prophecy—during public worship gatherings in order to prevent any further disorder (1 Cor. 14:26–33). Undoubtedly, this was a community of believers where almost every member could speak in tongues or prophesy (1 Cor. 14:5, 23–24, 26, 31).

There are many people today who would describe such an assembly as being a "prophetic church" due to the frequency and totality of their gifted manifestations in prophecy. There would have been resident and/or itinerant "prophets" in their midst. Perhaps they even hosted prophetic training seminars or conferences like many similar-type churches do today. Whatever may be the case, there is no denying the fact that they did prophesy and that the exercise of prophecy within their corporate gatherings was commonplace. But does this truly make them prophetic? Note that Scripture uses no such adjective in its description or depiction of this Covenant community.

Far from being an iconic, prophetic, or prototypical Kingdom community, however, the Corinthian believers had many spiritual, moral, and doctrinal issues. These included sectarianism and division (1 Cor. 1–4); sexual immorality—including such despicable and perverse forms as incest (1 Cor. 5); irreconcilable personal disputes, which escalated into lawsuits due to selfishness, unforgiveness, and greed (1 Cor. 6:1–11); marital issues and divorce (1 Cor. 7); prideful abuse of one's personal liberties and willful offense (1 Cor. 8); false accusation (1 Cor. 9); idolatry (1 Cor. 10); violation of God's divine order and creation pattern (1 Cor. 11:1–22); desecration of the Lord's Supper (1 Cor. 11:23–34); misunderstanding and misuse of spiritual gifts (1 Cor. 12–14); lack of true love (1 Cor. 13); and doctrinal heresies regarding the resurrection of the dead—one of the six foundational or *elementary* principles of the faith (1 Cor. 15:1–19; Heb. 6:1).

Most would agree that these are some very serious issues mentioned above and the sins or spiritual shortcomings are numerous. Not only were these Corinthian believers deficient in biblical holiness and moral character, but they had major doctrinal and internal issues as well. Yet in spite of the aforementioned, they were still able to prophesy just as easily, just as frequently, and just as accurately. Neither spiritual immaturity, doctrinal deficiency, nor immoral character were able to hinder or impede these believers' ability to continually exercise spiritual gifts, including prophecy. Rather than being a prophetic community, this was mostly a *pathetic* one. But the point is crystal clear—prophecy can be manifested or exercised by any believer regardless of their level of immaturity or sinful character. It is an elementary spiritual principle.

Let me interject that the principle remains the same with regard to physical maturity. There is no physical age requirement for prophesying. I have seen children as young as three or four years old prophesy corporately and effectively. They may not have been as articulate as an older, more mature individual, but they were able to effectively communicate the basic truth that the Holy Spirit was seeking to convey.

The Threefold Purpose of Prophecy

One of the more common misconceptions regarding prophecy relates to its primary purpose and function. Many believers today ascribe to the incorrect theological position that prophecy was intended by God to be *blessing* oriented. As such, prophecy is expected to be soft, flattering, and full of "encouraging" words describing all the goodness and blessing God wants to pour upon the recipient's life. Areas of sin and disobedience are, therefore, either ignored or completely disregarded altogether as the primary emphasis remains fixated after this model.

I remember reading the work of one particular author who was attempting to teach on the "prophetic" while promoting a message of blessing, goodness, and peace. This author ascribed to the above position and proceeded to misinterpret or misapply the text, which states that *the goodness of God leads you [men] to repentance* (Rom. 2:4). The hypothesis was that it is the goodness and blessing of God—as opposed to His correction or judgment—that causes a person to recognize their error and repent. When viewed in its proper context, however, this particular scripture says nothing of the sort. What the author (i.e. God, through the apostle Paul) was really saying is that *it is the mercy of God that allows men time and space to repent.* In other words, He delays His judgment and withholds his wrath for a season to allow us time to repent—not so that we can presume upon His mercy and goodness to continue in sin but to allow us time to see the error of our ways. God's patience should never be misconstrued as a lack of intent to judge, and neither should prophecy.

As a matter of fact, the preponderance of Scriptural evidence supports and favors prophecies that include rather than exclude words of correction or judgment. The rebellious inhabitants of Nineveh, for example, would never have repented had Jonah prophesied words of only blessing and favor (Jon. 3). As it turns out, it was a prophecy of correction and impending judgment that became the vehicle or catalyst through which the Ninevites could appropriate God's grace and mercy. When there is an incorrect understanding or overemphasis on these divine virtues (grace and mercy), it often results in lawlessness (Rom. 6:1).[2]

Prophecy, ever since its inception, was always intended to serve a single threefold purpose which will be detailed below. There is nothing in Scripture that indicates otherwise. However, proponents of the blessing-oriented view of prophecy would have us believe that this purpose was somehow altered or changed with the ratification of the new covenant. Prophecy under the old covenant, they claim, served a purpose of mostly correction and judgment under a dispensation of law; but under the new covenant, prophecy is supposed to be encouraging as well as spiritually and emotionally uplifting because it operates under a dispensation of grace. This misunderstanding or divergence of opinion can be easily rectified by reexamining Paul's original teaching on the purpose of prophecy.

> *But he who prophesies speaks edification and exhortation and comfort to men.* (1 Cor. 14:3)

According to the apostle Paul, the purpose of *all* prophecy—irrespective of dispensation or covenant—is threefold:

1. Edification
2. Exhortation
3. Comfort

At first glance, Paul's definition of prophecy's purpose appears to be very clear and concise, which it is, but it also appears to contradict, or at very least diminish, what we know of how prophecy was exercised and employed under the old covenant. This apparent "tension" or "contradiction" has led many sincere Bible teachers to postulate what I refer to as the "covenant dichotomy of prophecy" theory.[3] However, an appearance to the contrary, there really is no contradiction. The main source of the confusion is our English translation. As you know, Paul didn't speak or write these words in English; he communicated his message in Greek. This is one of those cases where the true meaning got lost in translation. Each of the three words Paul used to communicate the purpose of prophecy (like many other words in ancient Greek or Hebrew) carries with it an idea or thought that cannot be fully or accurately expressed by a single English word. Therefore, in order to understand what Paul was seeking to communicate, it is imperative that we perform a word study on each of these three words.

Edification

The word *edification* is translated from the Greek word, **oikodomē**, and literally conveys the idea of *architecture*[4] and the process of *building* or *construction*.[5] In the Greek, the word is often used to communicate not only the process of building but also *the finished building which is the result of [the] building [process]*.[6] In other words, the building activity being represented here is purposeful, strategic, and long-term; it has sight of the finish! This means that temporal satisfaction or fulfillment is never the objective but a complete and finished (perfect) building. While these temporal aspects may often occur, they represent a small part of a much bigger and eternal picture.

Furthermore, the building in contextual view here relates to the corporate whole rather than the individual member. When contrasting prophecy against the personal or individual aspect of tongues in the next verse, the author (Paul) is very explicit in stating that *he who prophesies edifies* [the verb form of oikodomē, meaning "build"] *the church* [corporate Kingdom Community] (1 Cor. 14:4). This does not mean that individual members are excluded from the building process (each individual part must be built up to create a finished and complete corporate whole), but it does suggest that the activity of building transcends the limited scope of personal or individual reception—even involvement—to address a much bigger corporate picture. In other words, while prophecy may often be "personal" or directly address a specific group or individual, it is ultimately always corporate in its architectural intent and design. The objective is a completely finished house (corporate community) and not just a perfectly aligned panel or post (individual member).

The purpose of prophecy, therefore, is not to provide some fleeting emotional high or produce some "feel-good" soulish state defined by some as encouragement or upliftment. It is not even for the purpose of boosting or affirming one's personal self-esteem. It doesn't take a spiritual dynamic such as prophecy to produce any of the above. These things can easily be accomplished through carnal knowledge alone, which has the ability to inflate personal egos and self-esteem—*puff up* (1 Cor. 8:1). The overarching purpose or concern of prophecy, however, is to reproduce the elevated spiritual architecture of heaven in God's Covenant Kingdom Community here on earth. This is accomplished through purposeful, intelligent, and strategic building activity that is motivated and fueled by a prophetic sight of the finish. Prophecy has one single end-goal in mind, and that is the perfection or completion of God's spiritual House. Simply put, prophecy was intended to *build up*, not *puff up*!

Every God-breathed prophecy given or recorded in Scripture—whether under the old covenant or the new—served to accomplish this goal. The presence of correction or judgment—aspects of prophecy that are generally considered to be negative—in no way altered or hindered this divine purpose. On the contrary, these negatively perceived elements, as was the case in Nineveh, often served to accelerate and effectively accomplish this objective. Even under the new covenant, when Peter rebuked Ananias and his wife, Sapphira, for their unrighteous deeds through words of knowledge and prophecy, the effect was a reproduction of Kingdom architecture (the fear of God), powerful supernatural manifestations and accelerated numerical growth (Acts 5:1–16). The entire Kingdom community (church) in Jerusalem was built up as a result of prophecy that included words of correction and judgment.

As we saw in chapter 1 while discussing the Jeremiah principle (Jer. 1:10), any successful building or construction initiative must first be preceded by the negative aspects of destruction. Land has to be cleared, existing and rotting foundations removed, etc. They all have a part to play in the building process, and ultimately, they will all be viewed as positive in light of the finished product—a complete and perfectly built house.

For example, here in the Walton County of Florida where I currently reside, they are constructing a new bridge to help ease the traffic congestion and aid in faster evacuation routes. One of the results of the current construction process is long traffic delays on the existing bridge due to one of the two lanes being closed. Even though the *purpose* of the construction is to help ease the flow of traffic, the *process* of the construction has inevitably (though temporarily) restricted its flow; thus, apparently making things worse. County residents are willing to patiently submit to the negative process, however, because we understand that the end product will be significantly positive.

Another example comes from a television program I recently saw my wife viewing. It was about a struggling businessman who sought the help of a professional "shark" to help finance and grow his family business. The shark offered him the capital to pay off his debts and finance his business for a percentage of the company. However, he required full control of the business operations to make the business successful, which he eventually did. But the process and pathway to success was a very negative and bitter one (especially for the business owner), involving redefining the vision and completely tearing down the existing structures so that they could rebuild from the ground up. This is the principle of the prophetic.

Building involves both positive and negative aspects that are mutually dependent upon each other. Therefore, it is both unbiblical, as well as foolish, to view prophecy as merely a "feel good" or "bless me" ministry that focuses solely upon positive affirmations while disregarding or excluding what we generally consider to be negative—words of rebuke, correction, or judgment. This doesn't mean that prophecy has to be harsh, critical, or offensive (which it generally shouldn't). Neither does it mean that prophecy was intended to expose others' sins, faults, shortcomings, or weaknesses (which is both folly and error); but it does mean that the underlying ethic behind all true prophetic activity should be to build according to God's design without excluding any aspect of prophecy that we find unfavorable.

There is a reason why *oikodomē* (edification, or rather, *building*) was listed first among the other two, and it is because it represents the primary or principal aspect of prophecy's purpose. It can be viewed as the governing principle. When this fundamental prophetic principle is ignored and the building ethic that both defines as well as underscores prophecy's true purpose is absent, lawlessness expressed through self-centeredness is the result. Jesus Himself warned of this lawless dimension being present and active among able or gifted prophesiers ministering in His name.

> *"Many will say to Me in that day, 'Lord, Lord, have we not **prophesied** in Your name, cast out demons in Your name, and done many wonders in Your name?' And then I will declare to them, 'I never knew you; depart from Me, you who practice [work or labor to perform]*[7] *lawlessness [iniquity, wickedness or transgression]*[8]*!'"* (Matt. 7:22–23, emphasis and parentheses mine)

You will notice in this passage that the ability to have *prophesied* is mentioned first. This would seem to indicate that this was the primary gift or ministry of the group in question. Coupled with the fact that this warning follows directly on the heels of a previous warning concerning false prophets (Luke 7:15–20), it is safe to conclude that Jesus is addressing (or describing) a false or lawless prophetic dimension. This doesn't necessarily mean that their prophecies were false, inaccurate in content, or didn't come to pass. On the contrary, we have to assume the opposite since the text clearly implies that they were able to successfully perform other supernatural activity in Jesus's name such as casting out devils and the working of miracles. The issue is not in their gifting but in the lawlessness they were promoting and building (working or laboring to perform). Their prophecies may have been specific and accurate in content, but they were deficient in reproducing or constructing the architecture of heaven within the lives of their hearers or within the corporate community as a whole. While this principle of building may not be overtly apparent here, it is definitely being alluded to by Jesus considering the Greek word translated as *practice* in the text carries the idea of *work* or *labor*, as in the process of building.[9] Then in the verses immediately following this pericope, Jesus elaborates further upon this issue of building as He differentiates between the wise and the foolish (Matt. 7:24–27).

Jesus's entire teaching here is reminiscent of Ezekiel's earlier prophetic rebuke and condemnation of Israel's false or corrupt prophetic order (Ezek. 13). Once again, the relationship between building and the prophetic comes into view. The prophets here are described as *jackals among ruins* (Ezek. 13:4, ESV), indicating not only a lack of desire or capacity to build (v. 5) but also a nature and predisposition toward exploiting such ruinous conditions.[10] Ezekiel then goes on to explain more plainly that even when these prophets appear to be building, what they are building is futile and superficial. They simply cover up or hide the holes, deficiencies, and shoddy workmanship (poor construction) with *untempered mortar* (v. 10). However, like the wise and foolish in Jesus's teaching who built their houses and then later had the integrity and foundation of them tested by violent storms (Matt. 7:24–28), even so shall the superficial and poorly constructed walls of this false prophetic order be tested and judged by violent storms sent by God in order to expose its true foundation (vs. 11–14).

All prophecy is actively building something—whether good or bad, holy or profane, righteous or unrighteous, the Kingdom of God or the kingdom of man. Both groups of lawless prophesiers described above were building in others (as well as the corporate whole) what had already been built in themselves—an iniquitous disconnect from accurate Kingdom values, culture, and architecture. However, on the *surface*, they *appeared* to be building accurately, producing activity that appeared righteous and kingdom-like but was internally deficient, corrupt, and wicked. What we have here is the perfect description of the old "prophetic" order, where overemphasis is placed on prophesying and other supernatural manifestations while disregarding or ignoring the true purpose of prophecy and the divine requirements of God. They are spiritually impotent due to a relational disconnection from the Head. The words *I never knew you* issued by

Jesus imply the absence or true intimacy or deposit of spiritual seed that produces (as well as reproduces) Christlikeness. The words of God must be able to penetrate and transform our hearts first before they can be effective in building or transforming others. Otherwise, our hypocrisy is magnified and reproduced through prophecy, and we end up building iniquitous structures or patterns in the earth.

Does God want accurate (as in content or detail) prophecies? Of course, He does! Is it God's will that we manifest supernatural ministry? Without a doubt, it is! But our ability to produce that which only *looks* like God, or outwardly appears to be what God requires, is of no eternal value if what we are building is inaccurate, and there is no relational intimacy with the Head that gives life to all our activity and truly validates all of our efforts.

In other words, one of the most defining characteristics for determining or identifying a true and accurate prophetic dimension (or prophecy) is underscored by the question, "How accurate is your building?" rather than "How accurate is your prophesying?" We seem to forget that psychics and clairvoyants have the ability to convey accurate personal or factual details through their readings as well, yet what they are building remains perverse because of a relational disconnect from the true God. If the true purpose of prophecy isn't being fulfilled, then it isn't true prophecy.

I know (or have heard) of some "prophets" and ministers with very accurate and mind-blowing factual detail in their personal prophecies, prophesying full names, addresses, phone numbers, birth dates, etc. Perhaps you have even seen some of them on YouTube or Christian television. Let me reemphasize again that there is generally nothing wrong with such personal detail. Personal details can often serve to open up the recipient's heart to receive the word of the Lord and confirm that God is truly speaking. However, we are mistaken if we believe that accurate detail is the sole defining characteristic of true prophecy. Prophecy is defined by its purpose, and there is nothing in Scripture that states that prophecy was given for the purpose of divulging or confirming what we already know. Heaven's concern is on what is being built, and what I have often found in these specific yet spiritually shallow prophecies is that when all is said and done, there is no genuine or profound spiritual deposit from heaven and nothing constructive (from a Kingdom viewpoint) being built in earth. Rather, they often served to magnify and elevate the "prophet's" own image through sensational and spectacular displays of knowledge. Something was being built, but it wasn't God's Kingdom. When an overemphasis is placed on factual detail, we become prime candidates for deception (Deut. 13:1–3).

Exhortation

The word translated as *exhortation* in our English Bibles is a somewhat familiar one in the Greek. It is the word ***paraklēsis***, and its nuances are so varied and broad that it often poses a challenge for translators who are left with no English equivalent. This word can refer to the *act of emboldening another in belief or course of action, encouragement, exhortation; a strong request or appeal*; or even *the lifting of another's spirits, comfort or consolation.*[11] Considering the context and the fact that *paraklēsis* (exhortation) is used in distinction from another Greek word translated as *comfort*, it would seem that the primary sense of the word in 1 Corinthians 14:3 is the act of exhorting, encouraging, or effecting a particular response or action. Or as one commentator puts it, *the sense of urging people forward in a positive and helpful way for their good.*[12] Based upon this definition and what we have already discovered about prophecy's overarching purpose of building, we understand from this word one of the most important aspects of how this purpose is fulfilled. Prophecy was intended to procure a correct and accurate response of obedience—in both belief as well as behavior—as it pertains to the divine requirements of God and the reproduction of the elevated spiritual architecture of heaven in the lives of the individual members as well as the corporate whole.

In other words, if the principal and fundamental purpose of prophecy is to build, secondary to that purpose—or the primary means through which the principal and fundamental aspect of building is fulfilled—is the reinforcement and/or adjustment of belief and behavior until there is perfect alignment with heaven's decree. Just as building requires a blueprint of architecture (heavenly insight) by which to measure accuracy and completion, *exhortation* requires a corresponding response (of obedience) by which to measure its effectiveness. Whenever someone attempts to embolden, exhort, or encourage another person, or even put forward a strong request or appeal, they do so with the hope and expectation of producing a desired response. It is not an audience they are after; it is the response. A correct response entails receiving the word (belief) and then acting on it (behavior). That is what true prophecy is after—not to enter-tain an audience but to effect accuracy in response!

Again, what is being described here is not some "feel good" blessing activity often ascribed to prophetic ministry. The emphasis is clearly on engaging and affecting belief and behavioral patterns in man so that an internal reformation and transformation process occurs. God doesn't speak because He likes to be heard; God speaks because He expects—or rather, demands—an obedient response. And even though His will is paramount in every declaration, it is always ultimately for our own benefit and good. With this emphasis in mind, it would be incorrect to assume that *paraklēsis* (exhortation) excludes any sense of correction or judgment. On the contrary, since belief and behavior are the principal targets of biblical *exhortation*, adjustment—including correction or judgment—is implied.

Those who would feel inclined to reject this important principle due to a theological "blind spot" or ungodly mentality of equating correction and rebuke with a lack of love would do well to remem-ber that *the opposite of love is not correction but indifference.*[13] From a biblical and heavenly perspective, love—especially God's love—is profoundly expressed through chastening or correction.

> *And you have forgotten the exhortation which speaks to you as to sons: "My son, do not despise the chas-tening of the Lord, Nor be discouraged when you are rebuked by Him; For whom the Lord loves He chas-tens, And scourges every son whom He receives." If you endure chastening, God deals with you as with sons; for what son is there whom a father does not chasten? But if you are without chastening, of which*

all have become partakers, then you are illegitimate and not sons. Furthermore, we have had human fathers who corrected us, and we paid them respect. Shall we not much more readily be in subjection to the Father of spirits and live? For they indeed for a few days chastened us as seemed best to them, but He for our profit, that we may be partakers of His holiness. Now no chastening seems to be joyful for the present, but painful; nevertheless, afterward it yields the peaceable fruit of righteousness to those who have been trained by it. (Heb. 12:5–11)

As a matter of fact, when the writer of Hebrews gives this message and quotes from the original text in Proverbs (Prov. 3:11–12), he identifies this text as *exhortation—paraklēsis* (v. 5)! In other words, he associates a biblical text or message regarding rebuke and correction as a valid expression of *exhortation*. Furthermore, all of Scripture is actually a *paraklēsis*, an exhortation, admonition, or encouragement for the purpose of strengthening and establishing the believer in the faith (Rom. 15:4; 1 Thess. 2:3; 1 Tim. 4:13; Heb. 12:5, 13:22).[14] Who among us would limit Scripture to simply an encouragement or "feel good" text for claiming the promises of God? That would be ludicrous at best, as well as totally contradictory to the text that states: *All Scripture is given by inspiration of God and is profitable for doctrine, for* **reproof***, for* **correction***, for instruction in righteousness...* (2 Tim. 3:16; emphasis mine). Thus, prophecy operates and functions according to the same spiritual principle as Scripture.

If we were to delve even deeper, we would discover that the official designation for the Holy Spirit as *Helper* or *Comforter— paráklē-tos*—that was given by Jesus is derived from the same root word for *exhortation* (*parakaléō*) and conveys a similar meaning. Thus, when Jesus identifies the work and ministry of this coming *Helper* or Paraclete, the very first thing He outlines is *convict[ion] of sin [correction]*, followed by *righteousness* and *judgment* (John 16:8, parentheses mine). Based upon the context, *paráklētos* (comforter, helper) implies much more than what the English words convey. In my opinion, these English words can be somewhat misleading regarding the Holy Spirit's true function and purpose. Even if they're not, it should be understood that *helping* often requires honest exposure, challenge, or bracing exhortation "to help" in long-term rather than short-term ways.[15] Whatever the case may be, it is clear that prophecy also operates according to the same spiritual principle as the Holy Spirit, and this implies that correction and judgment are valid spiritual aspects of *exhortation.*

If the idea of prophecy being inclusive of correction or judgment makes you fearful or uncomfortable, it really shouldn't. As we have already discovered from Scripture, prophecy was never intended for the ignoble purpose of tickling our ears. It serves a much higher and elevated purpose of bringing necessary alignment or adjustment to our lives in accordance with God's divine intent, purpose, and design. We can trust in God's love that He has only the best of intentions for us, regardless of the vessel He uses. I mention "vessel" here because it is commonly taught in some circles that God only trusts correction to the mature, especially in spirit and character. But if that was the case, prophecy would be limited to only the mature. We already explained very early in this chapter that prophecy is an *elementary* principle that can—as well as should—be practiced by any believer regardless of age or spiritual maturity. Paul's teaching on prophecy in 1 Corinthians 14 was intended for the benefit of every born-again believer or member of that community. Never once did Paul place any restriction on prophecy for the younger, immature believers in their midst. This means he expected *edification, exhortation, and comfort* (according to the original Greek meaning and definition) from their prophecies also.

Furthermore, the idea that the ability to identify or confront error is a sign (mark) of maturity is a very erroneous one. While wisdom and maturity can often play a part in identifying (as well as addressing) the more ambiguous or subtle errors that others often miss, all that is really required is sight. And proximity often affords us a better vantage point to *see*. Therefore, those closest to us—even our kids or subordinates if we are parents or leaders—are much more aware of our faults and shortcomings than the rest of the world with which we interact. As a matter of fact, the boy Samuel's first revelation (prophecy) from God was received while in a state of great immaturity. Samuel couldn't even tell God's voice apart from rejected Eli, yet despite his immaturity, the first revelation he received and prophecy he delivered was a word of judgment against Eli and his entire household for sins that could never be atoned for (1 Sam. 3:1–18). To Eli's credit, he never rejected the word of the Lord from Samuel based upon the severity of the message, the immaturity of the messenger, or the misunderstanding of his motives (as a true son motivated by love for God and his leadership rather than an ungrateful son seeking to only criticize and judge the current leadership so as to promote his own ministry).

The point here is that while the mature may be the best qualified to give correction, there is no age (or spiritual maturity) limitation or restriction imposed upon others giving correction in Scripture. God will choose whatever vessel is available, even if that vessel happens to be a *dumb ass* like in the case of Balaam (2 Pet. 2:16, KJV, with Num. 22:22–33). If God can use a dumb ass to bring correction to a blind prophet, God can use anyone to bring correction to you. Don't let your spiritual pride or arrogance cause you to reject the true word of the Lord. And don't be deceived into believing that prophetic correction will only come from a mature, recognized prophet or from those above or on par with you. The Holy Spirit is no respecter of person, position, or title and will speak through whomever He deems fit at the time, even if the vessel is considered lesser in our eyes or has been placed in a subordinate position under our charge.

For those giving words of correction or judgment through prophecy, let your words be seasoned with grace. Speak as the Holy Spirit would, with gentleness and love. Learn from the pattern recorded in John's revelation to the seven churches. Every message begins with a recognition of something they were doing well [pat on the back], followed by a criticism or rebuke (when applicable) for something they were not doing well [kick on the butt], and then ended on a positive note again for something they were doing well or with a promise [pat on the back] (Rev. 2–3). Someone once referred to this as the "correction sandwich" and it is very effective. Minister to others in the way you would like to be ministered to yourself.

Comfort

The word *comfort* is translated from a Greek noun, **paramythia**, that occurs only once in the entire New Testament. Even though the word is often translated as *comfort* or *consolation* in various Bibles and lexicons, the actual meaning of the word more closely relates to the previous word we examined in the Greek for *exhortation* (*paraklēsis*), referring to *any address*, whether made *for the purpose of persuading*, or *of arousing and stimulating*, or *of calming and consoling*.[16] *The Theological Lexicon of the New Testament* (TLNT) provides some interesting insight into the true meaning of the word:

> In these words (*paramythion, paramythia, paramytheisthai*), there is more than comfort or encouragement, but a real stimulation, [or] strength for overcoming difficulties. The word is used not only for reassurance, and for encouraging and prodding to action; but for supplying a lack, [or] bringing help...The meaning "sustenance, support" is attested especially for *paramythia*. In the Byzantine period, *paramythia* referred to the compensation or surety on a mortgage (*P.Flor.* 382, 65), the security, which was an application of the classical notion of *paramythia;* and the word came to mean "salary, compensation," especially in the bookkeeping formula *hyper paramythias.*[17]

As you can see, there is much more to the Greek meaning of *paramythia* (*comfort*) here than the English translation would lead us to assume, at least according to our modern English usage. In the older, Middle English (1175–1225) that reflected more of the original Latin meaning, "comfort" was a compound word (prefix *com* [completely] + *fort* [strong]) meaning "to strengthen."[18] This is more in line with the Greek meaning where the six New Testament uses of the cognate forms (of *paramythia*) suggest the bracing, strengthening, and supportive activity of the older English.[19] However, beyond this strengthening and supportive aspect of *paramythia* is the activity of persuasion, admonition, and exhortation that often accompanies or precedes it (1 Thess. 2:11, 5:14). What this means is that biblical *comfort* is a fortifying process that has only the end in view, not our immediate satisfaction. Surety on a mortgage debt (see Byzantine usage of *paramythia* outlined in the TLNT definition above) is necessary for providing a security or assurance in the event of one's inability to repay his/her debt in the *future*. Likewise, salary or compensation speaks of a reward or remuneration for services rendered and usually due upon completion (in the future). In other words, comfort and consolation are the end results of a process started with persuasion, admonition, and exhortation. In New Testament reality, admonition becomes genuine comfort so that it is hard to separate or distinguish between the two.[20]

In the context of prophecy, this means that *comfort* relates to the end product or result of its threefold purpose—producing a spiritual building that is not only accurate in heavenly architecture as well as perfectly aligned in belief and behavior but which is also thoroughly fortified and spiritually impregnable against the enemy. Biblical, prophetic comfort was never about our personal or emotional feelings as if our immediate emotional or psychological state was heaven's primary concern. It is not some type of spiritual "Prozac" intended to temporarily medicate us so that we feel better about ourselves or perceived future. The emphasis and objective of prophetic comfort is to strengthen us at our core—spiritual inner man—and the process of doing so may not be at all emotionally "comforting." But the ability to strengthen us at the core is what separates biblical or prophetic comfort from every other human or medicated kind with a very shallow (and temporary) reach of targeting only the mind or emotions. When the core is truly strengthened, every other part of our being follows, including our mind and emotions.

The best human analogy I can think of that somewhat captures this prophetic principle pertains to a person with a dislocated shoulder. A dislocated shoulder can cause intense physical pain and emotional distress for the afflicted person. Such a person would be in desperate need of "comfort" and would face two options: either treat (medicate) the pain with painkillers, thus providing only temporary relief while never fixing or curing the problem; or go to a doctor or chiropractor who would immediately pop the shoulder back into its correct position—a very painful experience—thus correcting the underlying problem and providing permanent future relief (provided the shoulder is never dislocated again). What is believed, taught, and practiced in large part among believers today as it pertains to prophecy as comfort relates to the first option described above. We have opted for the immediate and temporary. We have focused on prophecy making people feel better without adequately addressing the core issues that have brought them out of divine alignment (including their emotional or mental state). Scripture describes this shallow and ungodly approach as *vain comfort* with *false* revelation, and it has been practiced by false prophets and the religious minded for ages (Zech. 10:2; Jer. 6:13–15, 8:11–12; Ezek 13:8–16).

True prophetic comfort has the end in view and cares very little about one's immediate emotional disposition. It can be likened to the second option described above regarding the person with the dislocated shoulder. Its focus is on strengthening your inner core and correcting any issues that have weakened you or brought you out of perfect structural alignment. This corrective process might be very uncomfortable and painful, with an apparent lack of regard for your current suffering or struggles, but it is actively working for your good to provide a more permanent and lasting future comfort. It is not concerned with providing temporary relief or superficial comfort like the first option. So rather than just "cheer you up," prophetic comfort was meant to *fix you up*! Thus, when the prophet Isaiah prophesies of *the voice of one crying in the wilderness*—the third prophetic dimension—and prefaces his prophetic proclamation with the word *comfort* (as a command from God), he is not contradicting himself (and neither is God) by including words of correction and judgment as part of the message (Is. 40:1–5). And when the psalmist David pens his most famous psalm regarding the Great Shepherd (Ps. 23), expressing faith and confidence in His divine *comfort* when walking through *the valley of the shadow of death*, he employs the key symbolism of **rod** *and staff*—an instrument(s) that represented not only protection but also correction and discipline (Ps. 23:4; 2 Sam. 7:14; Job 9:34; Prov. 10:13, 13:24; Is. 11:4; Ezek. 20:37; 1 Cor. 4:21).

Thus, the movement's current emphasis of delivering flattering and "feel good" prophecies with empty promises of blessing and breakthrough, while disregarding the core (and often corrupt) internal and/or behavioral conditions that are antagonistic to the same, is a violation of the principle of prophecy and, therefore, false. According to Scripture, the true purpose of prophecy is threefold:

1. To build correct internal architecture according to heaven's design (edification)
2. To procure an accurate response of obedience while bringing adjustment to belief and behavior (exhortation)
3. To fortify and strengthen the inner man until it is impregnable against the enemy (comfort)

It is interesting to note that there is nothing in prophecy's declared purpose or definition that insists on prophecy being predictive. While prophecy can often foretell, it is by no means limited to this function. Whether prophecy is predictive or not, its purpose doesn't change. Therefore, it is incorrect to judge prophecy solely on whether or not it comes to pass. There are false prophets, psychics, clairvoyants, and other occult practitioners who can foretell quite accurately, but the real test of prophecy is how well it conforms to the threefold prophetic principles of purpose described above. Jonah's prophecy to Nineveh of impending judgment never came to pass (for the current generation), yet the purpose of prophecy was powerfully fulfilled. Conversely, Moses warned of prophets who were accurate in prediction or powerful manifestations but were deviant regarding God's prophetic purposes by leading people into apostasy and corruption (Deut. 13:1–3).

The Requisite of Judgment

One of the most glaringly obvious weaknesses or shortcomings of the current prophetic movement has been its inability to adequately prepare and equip believers to exercise judgment in prophecy. Of those who have been "taught" or "trained" in this regard, many are misinformed. For the vast majority of believers I have encountered—even those from established "prophetic" circles—the emphasis has been on the *spectacular* (specific or accurate details), the *sensational* (the type of emotion or excitement it immediately produces), or the *supernatural* (miraculous demonstrations and/or accurate fulfillment). As a matter of fact, many believers today erroneously substitute the *sensational* for the *spiritual* (inner witness or leading of the Holy Spirit). Thus, when a genuine word of prophecy fails to generate the type of (fleshly) emotional response expected due to the accurate prophetic frequency of the word in shifting the emphasis from what we want (or hope for) to what God wants (or expects), therein challenging us or making us uncomfortable, it is usually rejected on the false premise that "it didn't bear witness with my spirit." It is similar to how many preachers can immediately get an affirmative answer from God when invited to minister at a popular event or dream location like Hawaii but require significantly more time to "pray about it" when there is nothing appealing or the location is dangerous or not as enticing.

True prophecy can generate negative emotions

This may come as a surprise to you, but a true word from God can generate many negative emotions in the same way that the converse is also true. Pharaoh was *troubled* (disturbed) or *agitated* on account of a dream (revelation) received from God (Gen. 41:8). Daniel was so spiritually and emotionally distraught after the divine revelation he received from God through a vision that he was physically sick for several days following (Dan. 8). There are many today who would have wrongly attributed such revelation to witchcraft due to the great distress and resulting sickness, but this revelation was divine in origin. Often when the prophets prophesied in Scripture, their words generated an emotional response from the hearers of anger, hatred, or cynicism. Even the apostle Peter experienced the negative emotions of offense, sadness, and anger when Jesus began to prophesy His impending suffering and death. Peter was so distraught that he took Jesus aside and began rebuking Him (Matt. 16:21–23). On another (later) occasion when Jesus prophesied (foretold) that **all** of His disciples would *be offended and stumble and fall away* on account of Him that very night, even using the prophetic scriptures as confirmation (Zech. 13:7), Peter—as did the other disciples—adamantly rejected and disputed the word because he could not "witness" or identify with the negative aspect of the prophecy (Matt. 26:31–35). Jesus's prophecies clearly evoked a series of negative emotions among His disciples, but that never disqualified His prophecies as false. Also, the witness of the Holy Spirit is much more than an emotional response.[21] If, as a believer, you are still unable to differentiate between the two, it is a clear indication that you are still spiritually immature (Heb. 5:12–14).

The need for spiritual maturity

Admittedly, one's ability to effectively judge is usually commensurate with one's level of spiritual maturity. Those most qualified in this regard are usually *those who by reason of use have their senses exercised to discern both good and evil.* The mistake we often make, however, is to assume that *all* spiritual leaders (pastors, elders, etc.) are spiritually mature and then defer all judgment to them. We teach those receiving prophecy to submit them to their spiritual oversight (assuming they're mature) for wisdom and counsel. But what happens when these leaders are too (spiritually) immature to offer sound wisdom or judgment? Or worse, what if they are cessationists—those who believe that spiritual gifts such as tongues or prophecy have ceased with the original twelve apostles—who dismiss the prophecies altogether as false? What do we do then?

Biblical principles and precedents

The first thing we need to settle within our hearts and minds is that ALL prophecy must be judged, without exception! It doesn't matter if the prophecy originated from the most recognized or accurate prophet in the world or from a new beginner or believer just uttering their first word of prophecy; the principle remains the same. The biblical precedent of Scripture is that prophecy requires judgment.

> *Do not quench the Spirit. Do not despise prophecies. Test all things; hold fast what is good. Abstain from every form of evil.* (1 Thess. 5:19–22)

> *Let two or three prophets speak, and let the others judge.* (1 Cor. 14:29)

> *Beloved, do not believe every spirit, but test the spirits, whether they are of God; because many false prophets have gone out into the world.* (1 John 4:1)

In each of the scriptural references listed above, there is a clear and very explicit apostolic admonition to *test* or *judge* all prophecy.[22] Taking the Thessalonian pericope as our primary reference or example, it is clear that the apostle intended ALL prophecy to be judged, without exception.

> The apostle did not even exempt himself or the other apostles from such scrutiny by the congregation. He also did not limit scrutiny to visiting teachers and prophets. Those in the congregation, its members, and its leaders as well were apparently included in the apostle's command to examine "everything."[23]

I have known many spiritual leaders, pastors and prophets who have encouraged judgment for everyone else's ministry but their own. Paul, however, teaches that there should be no discrimination, nepotism, or favoritism in the exercise of prophetic judgment. Any deviation from this pattern, under the guise of false loyalty or submission, is a violation of prophetic protocol and clear Scriptural command.

The second thing that needs to be firmly established within our hearts is exactly who the responsibility of judgment falls upon. There is nothing in Scripture to support the notion that it is the leadership's sole responsibility to judge prophecy. On the contrary, and as supported by the scriptural references listed above, the responsibility for judging prophecy falls upon the entire spiritual community or congregation of believers, including every individual member. Therefore, we have a responsibility as prophets and leaders to teach, train, and equip those within our sphere of influence not only how to prophesy but, more importantly, how to identify and participate in an accurate prophetic dimension. With that will come the understanding of how to exercise apostolic and prophetic judgment in prophecy.

Fortunately for us, Paul shares some insight regarding this in his apostolic letter to the Thessalonian covenant community. His command to not *quench the Spirit*—a very clear, unambiguous allusion to the Holy Spirit's ministry or activity of fire and often rendered as "Do not put out the Spirit's fire"—or *despise* [reject or treat with contempt] *prophecies* carries profound implications for what Scripture defines as Holy Spirit inspired prophecy.

Contrary to popular belief, even among many respected Bible scholars and commentators, Paul is not addressing the issue of allowing charismatic manifestations during corporate gatherings. As a matter of fact, the entire context of Paul's writing has to do with the purification and sanctification of the covenant community rather than the liberal exercise of spiritual gifts (1 Thess. 3:13, 4:3, 5:5–10, 14–15, 23–24). In general, whenever the Holy Spirit (or God) is identified with fire in Scripture, it is in the context of the purification and sanctification of His people or judgment (Deut. 4:23–24, 5, 9:3–4; Is. 4:4, 29:6, 30:30, 33:14–16; Matt. 3:11–12; Luke 3:16–17, 12:49; 2 Thess. 1:3–8; Heb. 12:25–29). When this biblical motif and understanding is coupled with what we have already identified as the primary objective regarding the ministry and activity of the Elijah-John (the Baptist) third prophetic dimension (Mal. 3:1–5; Matt. 11:8–11)—to purify and refine *the sons of Levi*—it is clear that Paul was seeking to validate a prophetic dimension that was otherwise being invalidated and despised by the Thessalonian community. He was alluding to the fact that Holy Spirit–inspired prophecy is like a refiner's fire intended to purify God's covenant people of everything that defiled. This conforms to what we have recently discovered regarding the threefold purpose of prophecy as defined by Paul.

Instead of rejecting, resisting, or restricting *all* prophecy like many have assumed, it is possible that the Thessalonian believers discriminated against prophecy based on the appeal factor of the word, thus rejecting any prophecy that either overtly or covertly carried the "negative" aspect of a purifying or cleansing fire in seeking to bring any form of correction or judgment. Paul, therefore, admonishes the community of believers to stop extinguishing or putting out the Spirit's fire through their contemptuous disposition to an accurate prophetic dimension.

Like the children of Israel before them and many churches in operation today—including many who identify themselves as being "prophetic" or are otherwise participants under that banner—the desire to protect and preserve their mortal existence (experience) created a natural fear and resistance to the holy fire of God (Deut. 5:23–25). In other words, even though we may claim to want or desire God's presence or glory in our midst, we are secretly fearful and resistant to God's fire due to the death (to self), destruction (to selfish ambition and the works of the flesh), and discomfort (of suffering) it brings. This fear causes us to instantly reject or resist Spirit-inspired prophecies infused with God's holy fire, opting instead for the poor fleshly substitute of carnal prophecies intent on doing the opposite (of true prophecy) by telling us what we want to hear.

Paul's solution to this issue was not to simply object to the quenching of the Holy Spirit's fire and rejection of an accurate prophetic dimension but to encourage sound judgment by the entire community of believers. Instead of advocating a blanket, gullible acceptance of every prophecy claiming divine authority or the indiscriminate rejection of all prophecy as false, Paul's command is to *test all things*. The Greek verb translated as *test* here is **dokimazō**, meaning to make a critical examination of something in order to determine its genuineness.[24] It is used, for example, in speaking of a moneychanger testing the genuineness of a coin.[25] Money changers had to always be on guard against false or counterfeit coins (money), thus requiring an expert ability on their part to distinguish the real coin from the counterfeit. The more knowledgeable and familiar they were with the real, the easier it became to identify the counterfeit, even when it appeared almost identical to the real. This type of testing required the money changer to look past the outer appearances of the coin (or who it came from) through critical scrutiny in order to determine (discern) its authenticity (true nature or source). This is the same type of critical scrutiny that Paul is espousing regarding prophecy in this context, and it is a Kingdom characteristic that is noticeably absent from the Thessalonian community, as scripture itself testifies (Acts 17:10–11). Readiness to *receive* the word must be equally balanced with a readiness to *judge* [test] the word. Unfortunately, the Thessalonians appear to have been deficient in both.

Implicit in Paul's command to *test* is the criteria necessary for the testing. All true prophecy will have the Holy Spirit as its source (v. 19). Since the true nature and purpose of Holy Spirit–inspired prophecy is likened to fire, it is safe to conclude that such prophecy's major emphasis and concern will be on our purification, sanctification, maturation, and/or judgment. When the Holy Spirit is not at the source and center, the opposite will occur, masquerading itself as godly, spiritual, and even "kingdom" when its true nature is one of rebellion against God through self-indulgence (personal blessing), selfish ambition (personal breakthrough), and pride (personal recognition).[26] Even though these characteristics may not necessarily appear evil—after all, God is not necessarily opposed to personal blessing or breakthrough—at their core is often a principle that is antithetical to true prophecy and Kingdom architecture, thus the need for sound judgment (intense scrutiny) and discernment. Any spirit or prophecy that emphasizes our personal comfort or well-being over Christ's lordship is not from God (1 Cor. 12:3; 1 John 4:2–3).[27]

Note again that this *testing* is all-inclusive and is to be applied indiscriminately to *all things* (prophecy), regardless of the speaker or apparent accuracy in detail (whether through prediction or words of knowledge). Judging prophecy solely by the accuracy of detail is juvenile at best, which is why Paul never espoused such superficial judgment. The devil isn't stupid enough to try to deceive you with blatant error. Some of the most destructive prophecies I have seen (or heard) were wrapped or encased in very accurate personal details, thus allowing the spirit of error to slip through unnoticed. Why should the enemy try to convince you to drink the contents of a bottle that is clearly marked poison when he can easily mix a tiny portion into a food or drink that you find "good" and "tasty?" We must be able "money changers" who are capable of seeing past the external appearances in order to identify the prophecy's true nature and source. Does the prophecy serve to being purification, sanctification, maturation, or (godly) judgment? Or does it serve to sensationalize, impress, flatter, or magnify the "prophet" and the needs of man? Does it fulfill the threefold purpose of prophecy as taught by Paul? Or does it simply tickle our ears? Is the prophecy redemptive in nature? Or does it promote self-righteousness or condemnation? These are the types of piercing questions that should be asked in critical analysis every time we hear a prophecy spoken. Only then will we be truly able to determine what is *good*—morally excellent and beneficial to both the individual and corporate community—for acceptance, as opposed to what is inherently *evil*—despite the fact that it often appears "good"—and from which we are commanded to abstain (1 Thess. 5:21–22).

Prophesiers Versus Prophets

If you have been reading from the start, it should already be veridically established within your heart and mind that it requires significantly more (remember the iceberg principle) than an ability to prophesy accurate details to make one truly prophetic. At the very beginning of this chapter, it was proven that prophecy is an elementary spiritual principle that can, and should, be practiced by any (every) believer regardless of age, moral character, or spiritual maturity. Unfortunately, there is a general tendency among both believers as well as unbelievers alike to confuse gifted prophesiers—even genuinely prophetic ones—with ascension gift (normally referred to as five-fold) prophets. This happens when we make the lowest common denominator—prophecy—the major deciding or validating factor. But just as one's ability to prophesy does not necessarily make one prophetic (in the complete sense of the word), it would be ludicrous to believe that it would make them a prophet. Every prophet will be a gifted prophesier, but not every gifted prophesier will be a prophet.

This confusion is further exacerbated from the misinformation that is often spewed from pulpits and text books in portraying the Holy Spirit gift of prophecy as something lower or lesser in grace (power) or efficacy than Jesus's ascension gift of prophet. Based upon this principle or logic, prophecies emanating from the Holy Spirit gift of prophecy have an inferior anointing to bring change or "breakthrough" than those from Jesus's ascension gift. They are also more limited in scope. This means that we can determine whether or not someone is a prophet by the quality and scope of their prophecies. Hogwash! Not only is this totally unbiblical, it is also totally unethical. Since when is the Godhead in competition with itself? Since when is the Holy Spirit inferior to Jesus? Since when is the Holy Spirit lacking in power or efficacy? Members of the Godhead may not be equal in rank, but they are all equal in Person and Power. No Member is superior or has greater ability than the other.

As a matter of fact, there is no "gift" of prophet (or apostle, evangelist, teacher, or pastor) as far as it being something to be desired or possessed like the other charismatic gifts. The prophet becomes the *gift* and ministers with the same charismatic graces (gifts) given by the Holy Spirit to other believers (Eph. 4:8–11). In other words, a person doesn't possess the gift or grace of a prophet; he is the prophet, and his ability to prophesy comes from the Holy Spirit's gift of prophecy (or combination of gifts like word of knowledge, word of wisdom, etc.) and not from some other source (1 Cor. 12:7–10).

The Godhead complements each other; they (the members) don't compete with each other like carnal man. So the dichotomy some have tried to create pertaining to prophecies originating from the Holy Spirit gift of prophecy being distinct from the ascension gift of prophet is a false one. As far as prophecy is concerned, no such distinction exists since the Holy Spirit is the source of *all* true prophecy. This is why prophetic gifting or ability should never be used as a litmus test for identifying whether or not someone is a prophet. Prophets don't have to prophesy better than everyone else because that is not what defines them as a prophet. Their ministry transcends mere gifting to become an embodiment of Jesus's ministry.

The biblical account of the disciple Ananias provides us with an excellent example:

> *Now there was a certain disciple at Damascus named Ananias; and to him the Lord said in a vision, "Ananias." And he said, "Here I am, Lord." So the Lord said to him, "Arise and go to the street called Straight, and inquire at the house of Judas for one called Saul of Tarsus, for behold, he is praying. And in a vision he has seen a man named Ananias coming in and putting his hand on him, so that he might receive his sight." Then Ananias answered, "Lord, I have heard from many about this man, how much harm he has done to Your saints in Jerusalem. And here he has authority from the chief priests to bind all who call on Your name." But the Lord said to him, "Go, for he is a chosen vessel of Mine to bear My name before Gentiles, kings, and the children of Israel. For I will show him how many things he must suffer for My name's sake." And Ananias went his way and entered the house; and laying his hands on him he said, "Brother Saul, the Lord Jesus, who appeared to you on the road as you came, has sent me that you may receive your sight and be filled with the Holy Spirit." Immediately there fell from*

his eyes something like scales, and he received his
sight at once; and he arose and was baptized. (Acts
9:10–18)

You will notice that Ananias received very detailed revelation from God by means of a vision. Not only did God supernaturally provide him with Saul's name and physical address of his present location, but God also revealed to Ananias exactly what Saul was doing at the time—praying! Ananias's natural knowledge of who Saul was caused him to be apprehensive at first, but when he finally obeys God and finds Saul exactly where God told him that he would, he receives even more revelation (words of knowledge) regarding Saul's experience on the Damascus road—information that was not previously contained in the original vision. Ananias then proceeds to lay hands on Saul and supernaturally heals him of his blindness by imparting sight. I don't know about you, but I know very few prophets who can operate in such detail. This guy received names (both Saul's as well as the name of the person with whom he was staying), address, and everything but Saul's blood type and birth date. He knew what Saul was doing, what Saul had recently experienced, Saul's true spiritual condition, and what was afflicting Saul's body. Yet despite the broad scope and impressive quality of his revelation, Ananias is described by Scripture as nothing more than a *disciple*. He was not a prophet! If he was, Scripture would have informed us so, like it did with Agabus (Acts 11:27–28, 21:10), especially considering the significance of Ananias's character in the text.

Think about that for a moment. Think about the level of accuracy and supernatural power Ananias displayed in his ministry to Saul. The blind was healed and the believer filled (baptized) with the Holy Spirit. His prophecy was more detailed and powerful than anything John the Baptist demonstrated, and he (John) was described by God as being the greatest prophet born of a woman (Luke 7:28). How could this guy prophesy or minister in such an impressive way and not be a prophet? Because prophecy (revelation) is a *manifestation* of the Holy Spirit's grace, not an *attestation* to the ascension gift of prophet. It is the same Holy Spirit who is prophesying through them as is prophesying through the prophet. Therefore, being more detailed or accurate in one's prophesying is a matter of grace through faith (Rom. 12:6), not rank, authority, or maturity.

It is interesting to note that Ananias was not the only one to receive detailed revelation in the pericope above. Saul, who was just a three-day-old new convert at that time and not even water or Spirit baptized yet, had also received a vision from God. In his vision, Saul received supernatural information regarding Ananias, his name, and the method by which he would impart sight unto him (v. 12). Neither Saul's spiritual immaturity nor his lack of Pentecostal experience (Holy Spirit baptism or speaking in tongues) were enough to disqualify him from receiving detailed revelation from God. Most people who prophesy never receive anything as detailed as a name, yet Saul was able to receive such revelation in a state of blindness. Since Saul's physical blindness was indicative of a much deeper spiritual condition (spiritual blindness), it is safe to conclude that even the spiritually blind can receive specific and detailed revelation from God regarding people, occurrences, or situations. We obviously need to develop a more biblical view of revelation—including prophecy, words of knowledge, words of wisdom, etc.

Let us examine this principle from a different angle, focusing our attention primarily upon the prophet. Agabus is one of the few individuals mentioned by name who is identified in the New Testament as being a prophet, and he is probably the most recognized as such in the entire book. Scripture records him prophesying to Paul and warning him of the impending persecution that awaited him when he returned to Jerusalem.

> *And as we stayed many days, a certain prophet named Agabus came down from Judea. When he had come to us, he took Paul's belt, bound his own hands and feet, and said, "Thus says the Holy Spirit, 'So shall the Jews at Jerusalem bind the man who owns this belt, and deliver him into the hands of the Gentiles.'"* (Acts 21:10–11)

The interesting thing about this story is that there was nothing distinctly unique about the prophetic message given by Agabus to Paul with regard to detail or content. Paul had already received this exact warning several times and in multiple different cities before by what would appear to be regular saints prophesying by the Holy Spirit—the same Holy Spirit through whom the prophet Agabus prophesied (Acts 20:22–23). The point is that even though Agabus was clearly an ascension gift prophet, his ability and anointing to prophesy was no different than any regular saint (believer), as evidenced by the similarity of detail and content in their prophecies. The same Holy Spirit who empowers one also empowers the other, thus causing similar results. Thus, the saints in the various cities through which Paul journeyed were able to prophesy the same as Agabus even though they were not necessarily prophets.

The Prophet's Ministry and Function

A lot more is required of a prophet than just an ability or anointing to prophesy (in the traditional sense of giving a personal prophecy) because if such was the case, we would all be prophets. The fact that personal prophecy is one of the lowest forms of prophetic ministry can no longer be argued in light of the biblical evidence provided throughout the pages of this book. While personal prophecy may be the most commonly recognized aspect of prophetic ministry today, it is still an elementary spiritual principle that can be practiced by any and all believers. When it comes to the prophet's ministry, however, the bar is raised much higher, and personal gifting becomes less of a factor in light of his overall mission. This is because the ministry of the prophet, from a full biblical perspective, involved far more than just giving personal prophecies to individuals or corporate communities. Even when such personal prophecies were employed, it was in the context of a much grander scheme. The focus and emphasis of the prophet's ministry were usually directed toward correcting the error, complacency, injustice, and spiritual backsliding of God's people. Words given to leaders, kings, and other individuals were given with a corporate view in mind and often in the context of the nation as a whole. In this sense, prophets really acted as heavenly ambassadors, charged with accurately representing as well as communicating the interests and desires (or rather, demands) of the King of Heaven to all mankind.

In order to accomplish this grand task of being an ambassador of heaven, the ministry of the prophet, unlike mere prophetic gifting, requires maturity and accuracy that transcends mere words. They needed to be an accurate reflection as well as an intelligent representation of the very nature, culture, and values of the King (God) and country (Heaven) they were called to represent. This, of course, required maturity of character and total submission to Christ's lordship in their lives. They couldn't be unstable or flaky. Their lifestyles had to match their words. They had to first know and then be able to teach the laws and requirements of God to the people. In other words, they couldn't be biblically ignorant (Deut. 4:5; 31:19–22). They had to be able to interpret the law (2 Chron. 34:20–28). They had to be impartial (unbiased) and have wisdom in judgment as they judged both people and nations (Ex. 2:13–14, 18:13; Num. 11:16–17, 25–30; Judg. 4:4; 1 Sam. 7:15–17; 1 Cor. 14:29). This meant that they were far more than just able prophesiers; they were godly leaders and spiritual fathers (e.g. Moses, Samuel, Elijah, Elisha, etc.), in addition to being worshippers and watchmen (Ex. 15:1, 20–21; Ezek. 3:16–21), or even musicians and psalmists (Duet. 31:22, 30, 32:44; 1 Sam. 10:5; 1 Chron. 25:1–5; Psalms).

This level of maturity that is expected as well as demanded of the prophet is alluded to by Paul in his letter to the Ephesian community of believers:

> *And he gave the apostles, the prophets, the evangelists, the shepherds and teachers, to equip the saints for the work of ministry, for building up the body of Christ, until we all attain to the unity of the faith and of the knowledge of the Son of God, to mature manhood, to the measure of the stature of the fullness of Christ.* (Eph. 4:11–13, ESV)

According to the text, prophets—in concert and collaboration with the other four ministries—are tasked with the primary responsibility of equipping or perfecting the body of Christ until it ultimately arrives at a place (or rather, state) scripture defines as *mature manhood*. And lest we be confused or unclear on exactly how both the author and the Holy Spirit intend for us to define "mature manhood," added detail is provided articulating a maturity and completeness that is equivalent to Christ's own—*the measure of the stature of the fullness of Christ*. In essence, Jesus gave (or divided Himself into) the five ministries—each representing and manifesting that particularly unique dimension of Christ's ministry—in order to reproduce Himself through His body, as depicted in the chart below.

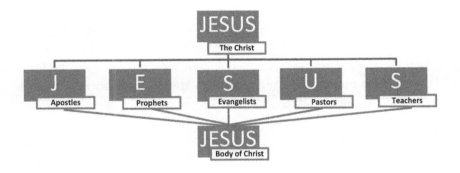

It stands to reason that if a minister or leader is called to bring a people into what the scriptures define as *mature manhood*, that minister or leader must first be mature himself. You can minister, teach, preach, or prophesy what you know (or have), but in the final analysis, you will only be able to reproduce who (or what) you are. It is impossible for any immature prophet to bring any person into maturity. Therefore, spiritual maturity is an unequivocal requirement of every New Testament prophet or ascension gift ministry. Of course, this does not necessarily mean that any of us this side of eternity will ever be able to claim ultimate "arrival" or "attainment," but it does imply a certain degree of maturity coupled with a relentless and progressive spirit of migration and pursuit toward Christ (Phil. 3:7–16). In any event, according to God's prophetic purpose for His

Bride, there is a measurable and clearly defined point of maturity—a final place or destination, as it were—that is expected *first* of Christ's ascension gift ministers before it can be reproduced in His Body, and this maturity is so effulgent with heavenly substance that it is equivalent to Christ's own.

You will notice also from the pericope above that the prophet's clearly defined ministry and assignment is not to simply prophesy (in the traditional sense of delivering personal or corporate prophecies) but to build accurate Kingdom architecture into the lives of God's people until they are a mature and accurate representation or, if you may, reproduction, of Jesus Christ in the earth.[28] Of course, every aspect of the prophetic dimension—including personal prophecy—may be employed and should serve in this regard; however, there is nothing in this text or even Scripture as a whole that even remotely suggests that a prophet's primary mission is to run around giving people personal prophecies. The failure to properly understand this principle has led to many errantly labeling every good prophesier a "prophet" or making personal prophecy the chief defining factor for prophetic ministry today.

Gift Versus Office

It is interesting to note, referring back to the Ephesians 4:11 text, an important point that was briefly discussed in the preceding chapter. Since this principle is directly related to a correct understanding of the prophet's ministry and function, I would be remiss to not mention or reiterate it here. When Paul identifies the five ascension gift ministries, including the prophet, in this text, his emphasis is clearly on describing and portraying these ministers as gifts of the exalted Christ, as opposed to ecclesiastical officers created or appointed by some religious (church) body, denomination, or network.[29] Even the Greek verb translated as *gave* retains its general sense of "to give" rather than "to appoint" in the immediate context.[30] Some Bible scholars and commentators, however, continue to argue in defense of the "office" position, even though at least one of them concedes that Paul's emphasis in Ephesians 4:11 is on these ministries functioning as gifts rather than as officers.[31] Unsurprisingly, most of these same Bible scholars and commentators also argue that there are no longer any apostles or prophets today. As a result of this misunderstanding, many believers today view these five ministries as offices or positions they can be appointed (ordained) to by a governing religious body.

It requires much more than head knowledge or seminary training to accurately interpret Scripture, which is where the apostolic and prophetic dimensions come into play with their elevated sight and revelation. Let's take a brief look at the biblical evidence without venturing too far into the area of church polity in our assertion of gifted function over office:

1. First and foremost, if apostles, prophets, or any of the other five ministries are to be thought of as offices, "one has to first demonstrate that there were 'offices' in the New Testament church. There is no Greek word in the New Testament corresponding to 'office'. The term did occur in the King James Version, but without warrant in the Greek text."[32]

2. The concept of ecclesiastical office or position is inextricably linked to institutionalized religion, which is **not** something Jesus came to build or establish. Jesus didn't come to earth to establish a new form of Judaism. The Kingdom Community (Ekklesia) Jesus came to build is spiritual yet organic, reflecting the very architecture (nature, values, culture) of heaven itself (Matt. 16:17–19, 23:1–12; Luke 22:24–27).

3. Even if one ascribes to the position that there are legitimate church offices (e.g. elders [also called bishops] and deacons), one still has to acknowledge the fact that occupation of these "offices" came by appointment (Acts 14:23; Titus 1:5) or election (Acts 1:26; 6:3; 1 Tim 3:1–13), whereas gifts are bestowed by God (Rom 12:6; 1 Cor 12:11, 18, 28).[33] This is why Paul could boldly declare regarding his apostleship: *"Paul, an apostle (not from men nor through man, but through Jesus Christ and God the Father who raised*

Him from the dead)...For I neither received it from man, nor was I taught it, but it came through the revelation of Jesus Christ" (Gal. 1:1, 12).[34]

4. Following on the previous point, there is no Scriptural record of any person being ordained or appointed to any of the five ministries so as to legitimize the concept of office.[35] For example, Philip was elected to serve in the capacity of what some would describe as "deacon;" however, his functional ministry as evangelist came directly from God without any need for the approval of man (Acts 6:1–5; 8:5–13, 26–40, 21:8). Furthermore, if the deliberate rejection of the use of titles in the New Testament is any indicator, as is clearly evidenced, then it was the wrong concept of offices as well as the institutionalizing tendency they represent that they were seeking to avoid.[36]

5. Perhaps the greatest argument in support of gifted function over office is Jesus's own personal experience and example. Jesus functioned effectively in the earth as Apostle, Prophet, Evangelist, Pastor, and Teacher; however, as we discussed before, He occupied no officially recognized religious position or office. As far as the established religious leaders were concerned, Jesus was just a regular layperson leading multitudes into error. If Jesus's fivefold ministry depended on human or religious appointment or approval, Jesus would have had no ministry. Even Jesus's priesthood was a matter of spiritual function rather than earthly position (office), as evidenced by the fact that He had no priestly authority (credentials) in the religious sense or any access into the inner sanctums of the Temple in Jerusalem where the priesthood ministered after the order of Aaron.

As we come to the close of this chapter, I would like to reiterate the fact that while the ability to prophesy and being a prophet may appear to be synonymous in Scripture, a careful examination, such as we have done in this chapter, proves that they are not. If we are to put prophets and personal prophecy in proper perspective, we must understand this core concept. Only then will we be able to interpret scripture correctly. For example, when scripture identifies Philip the evangelist as having *four virgin daughters who prophesied*, it was careful not to identify any of them as being prophets (Acts 21:8–9). It would be incorrect to assume that an ability to prophesy equates to ascension gift prophet in this (or any) context. However, there are many—including well-meaning Christian egalitarians—who would lead us to believe that these were four female ascension gift prophets. But to equate the act of prophesying with that of being a prophet in this instance would make every prophesier a prophet, and this is simply not so.

As a new prophetic company emerges in this third prophetic dimension, the need for greater or more elevated sight and understanding has never been greater. As a matter of fact, it is this elevated dimension of sight that truly distinguishes and separates the third prophetic dimension from those of the old prophetic order.

Notes

1   While neither holiness nor godliness are prerequisites to the ministry of prophecy at its lowest level, it is impossible to be truly prophetic without submitting to every aspect of the Holy Spirit's work, including holiness of character and lifestyle. The same Holy Spirit who empowers us to *do* also empowers us to *be*.

2   Any truth that is overemphasized or taken to an extreme leads to error.

3   This simply means that the purpose of prophecy (and how it was exercised) changed with the covenants.

4   James Strong, *A Concise Dictionary of the Words in the Greek Testament and The Hebrew Bible* (Bellingham, WA: Logos Bible Software, 2009), 51.

5   William Arndt, Frederick W. Danker, and Walter Bauer, *A Greek-English Lexicon of the New Testament and Other Early Christian Literature* (Chicago: University of Chicago Press, 2000), 696

6   Gerhard Kittel, Geoffrey W. Bromiley, and Gerhard Friedrich, eds., *Theological Dictionary of the New Testament* (Grand Rapids, MI: Eerdmans, 1964–), 145.

7   Spiros Zodhiates, *The Complete Word Study Dictionary: New Testament* (Chattanooga, TN: AMG Publishers, 2000).

8   James Strong, *A Concise Dictionary of the Words in the Greek Testament and The Hebrew Bible* (Bellingham, WA: Logos Bible Software, 2009), 12.

9   H.G. Liddell, *A Lexicon: Abridged from Liddell and Scott's Greek-English Lexicon* (Oak Harbor, WA: Logos Research Systems, Inc., 1996), 311.

10   Jackals are creatures known for scavenging and making dens among ruins. They represent a false prophetic company preying on the people for their own greed and self-interest.

11   William Arndt, Frederick W. Danker, and Walter Bauer, *A Greek-English Lexicon of the New Testament and Other Early Christian Literature* (Chicago: University of Chicago Press, 2000), 766.

12   Derek Prime, *Opening up 1 Corinthians*, Opening Up Commentary (Leominster: Day One Publications, 2005), 125.

13 Anthony C. Thiselton, *The First Epistle to the Corinthians: A Commentary on the Greek Text*, New International Greek Testament Commentary (Grand Rapids, MI: W.B. Eerdmans, 2000), 1089.

14 Spiros Zodhiates, *The Complete Word Study Dictionary: New Testament* (Chattanooga, TN: AMG Publishers, 2000).

15 Anthony C. Thiselton, *The First Epistle to the Corinthians: A Commentary on the Greek Text*, New International Greek Testament Commentary (Grand Rapids, MI: W.B. Eerdmans, 2000), 1089.

16 Joseph Henry Thayer, *A Greek-English Lexicon of the New Testament: Being Grimm's Wilke's Clavis Novi Testamenti* (New York: Harper & Brothers., 1889), 485.

17 Ceslas Spicq and James D. Ernest, *Theological Lexicon of the New Testament* (Peabody, MA: Hendrickson Publishers, 1994), 34–35.

18 Comfort. Dictionary.com. *Dictionary.com Unabridged.* Random House, Inc. http://dictionary.reference.com/browse/comfort (accessed: June 07, 2015).

19 Anthony C. Thiselton, *The First Epistle to the Corinthians: A Commentary on the Greek Text*, New International Greek Testament Commentary (Grand Rapids, MI: W.B. Eerdmans, 2000), 1089.

20 Gerhard Kittel, Geoffrey W. Bromiley, and Gerhard Friedrich, eds., *Theological Dictionary of the New Testament* (Grand Rapids, MI: Eerdmans, 1964–), 821.

21 The Holy Spirit active within us will often trigger an emotional response; however, not every emotional response is rooted in the Holy Spirit.

22 The two Greek words translated as *test* and *judge* are synonymous in nature and carry the same connotation of scrutiny and judgment.

23 D. Michael Martin, *1, 2 Thessalonians*, vol. 33, The New American Commentary (Nashville: Broadman & Holman Publishers, 1995), 185.

24 William Arndt, Frederick W. Danker, and Walter Bauer, *A Greek-English Lexicon of the New Testament and Other Early Christian Literature* (Chicago: University of Chicago Press, 2000), 255.

25 Paul Ellingworth and Eugene Albert Nida, *A Handbook on Paul's Letters to the Thessalonians*, UBS Handbook Series (New York: United Bible Societies, 1976), 124.

26 See Jeremiah 28:1–16.

27 Note that the principle of "saying" or "confessing" in these scripture references extends far beyond the vocalization of mere words to the architecture of character and lifestyle in willing submission to Christ's lordship (ownership) over our lives. When Christ is truly *Lord,* the emphasis becomes Him instead of ourselves (including our needs, wants, and desires).

28 Note that the Greek word translated as *building—oikodomē*—is architectural terminology that conveys a process of skillful building or construction. It is the same word translated as *edification* in 1 Corinthians 14:3 that we examined earlier in this chapter.

29 Andrew T. Lincoln, *Ephesians*, vol. 42, Word Biblical Commentary (Dallas: Word, Incorporated, 1990), 248–249.

30 Ibid.

31 William Hendriksen and Simon J. Kistemaker, *Exposition of Ephesians*, vol. 7, New Testament Commentary (Grand Rapids: Baker Book House, 1953–2001), 195.

32 Walter L. Liefeld, *Ephesians*, vol. 10, The IVP New Testament Commentary Series (Downers Grove, IL: InterVarsity Press, 1997), Eph 4:11.

33 Charles H. Talbert, *Ephesians and Colossians*, Paideia Commentaries on the New Testament (Grand Rapids, MI: Baker Academic, 2007), 112.

34 J. Vernon McGee, *Thru the Bible Commentary: The Epistles (Ephesians)*, electronic ed., vol. 47 (Nashville: Thomas Nelson, 1991), 120.

35 The only possible exception would be Judas's replacement, Matthias, but this was clearly a unique situation pertaining to the original twelve and what they represented (Acts 1:15–26).

36 John Muddiman, *The Epistle to the Ephesians*, Black's New Testament Commentary (London: Continuum, 2001), 199.

5

DIMENSIONS OF SPIRITUAL SIGHT

LONG BEFORE THERE was ever a need for prophets or prophetic ministry, man lived and functioned in a realm of unbroken and unhindered fellowship with God. The first man—Adam—was afforded the privilege of having direct face-to-face communication with God, far removed from the fleshly encumbrances that afflict us today. Adam, being a resident of both heaven and earth in the garden of Eden (the portal to heaven), was able to seamlessly interface between both realms naturally and effortlessly.[1] Every dimension of man's being, including his brain and physical senses, were tuned to the frequency of heaven without static or distortion. Adam could commune with God and hear His voice just as easily as he could commune with his wife, Eve. There was never any need for a mediator or a go-between like a priest or prophet because Adam had direct access to God at the highest possible level—face-to-face communication. As such, what we now describe and Scripture also defines as prophetic was a natural and normal experience for Adam that was essentially effortless.

For example, Adam's ability to accurately and effectively name *every beast of the field and every bird of the air* didn't just come from his human intellectual or scientific capacity to observe or analyze the outward characteristics of each species. The insight that Adam demonstrated when he named these creatures was prophetic in nature, indicative of an elevated dimension of spiritual sight. The names that he chose (or rather, used) were neither fanciful nor frivolous but reflected the true nature and character of each species. Adam simply spoke what he had heard and seen in heaven (where these creatures already existed). Thus, it was by heavenly insight that Adam was able to call every living creature by its true name (Gen 2:19–20).[2]

The more apparent prophetic display comes directly after Adam has named all of the various creatures. Scripture records that *the Lord God caused a deep sleep to fall upon Adam, and he slept*, meaning that from a purely physical or human standpoint, Adam was unconscious or anaesthetized while God performed the surgery to remove one of his ribs in order to make the woman (Gen. 2:21). In other words, each of the five human senses by which mankind interacts with the physical world were neutralized during this point in time that Adam slept. However, when Adam awakes from his sleep and is presented with his new companion, the woman, he responds (prophesies) insightfully regarding the woman's name (*Woman*), her origins (*bone of my bones and flesh of my flesh*), and also her future destiny as both a mother and wife in the newly established institution of family (Gen. 2:23–24). There was no natural means by which Adam could have received this insight, so it clearly came from heaven and his face-to-face communication with God.

Unfortunately, man was not able to maintain this high spiritual dimension of intimate communion and proximity with God. When Adam sinned, he was expelled from the garden and barred from accessing the elevated spiritual dimension of heaven or having face-to-face communion with God like he did before (Gen. 3:22–24). From this point on, man became more earthly or carnal in his existence as the veil of flesh and sin further separated us from God and the high spiritual dimension where He resides. Man's spiritual senses and ability to seamlessly interact with the heavenly realm became dulled and continued to gradually deteriorate or decline as he became more reliant on his five physical senses and capacity for human reasoning to live and interact with God's creation on earth. In effect, sin brought spiritual death in not only separating us from God but also impeding or completely neutralizing man's ability to see, understand, respond, or otherwise interact with the spiritual realm.

Of course, this degradation of spiritual sight and inability to interact with the heavenly realm was not immediate but a gradual process. Adam didn't wake up the next day unable to hear God or otherwise communicate with Him. As a matter of fact, Adam's first sons (Cain and Abel), as well as generations after them, were able to effectively communicate with God and hear His voice while interacting with the heavenly realm, albeit at a lower or inferior dimension to Adam before the fall (Gen. 4:1–16). Thus, when Cain kills his brother Abel and is judged by God, his sentence is described as being *hidden from Your [God's] face* (Gen. 4:14) and removed *from the presence of the Lord* (Gen. 4:16). Since Adam had already been expelled from Eden and barred access to the portal of face-to-face communication with God, the implication is that Cain was being driven even further from the divine presence symbolized by the garden than his parents were.[3] The spiritual separation and degradation were accelerated for Cain because of his sin, causing him to be further removed—decreased spiritual proximity—from God and His elevated spiritual dimension than Adam.

Exactly how Adam and his earlier descendants were able to communicate with God (i.e. hear His voice) and interact with heaven's elevated spiritual dimension without the close (face to face) proximity represented by the garden of Eden is not expressly stated. Scripture merely asserts that they did with no explanation as to how. Statements like, *"So the Lord said to Cain"* (Gen. 4:6), *"Enoch walked with God"* (Gen.5:24), and *"God said to Noah"* (Gen. 6:13) affirm this reality but provide no clue as to the actual process. It is not until Abram (Abraham) and after a prolonged period of spiritual degradation that necessitated the ministries of priest and prophet that scripture finally identifies man's new process of hearing. According to scripture, *the word of the Lord came to Abram in a vision* (Gen. 15:1).

While our father of faith—Abraham—was still able to interface with the elevated spiritual dimension of heaven through what scripture defines as *visions*, he was still far removed from Eden and

Adam's face-to-face proximity to God. This spiritual separation and degradation was expectedly worse for mankind in general and the heathen nations in particular where the first mention of God speaking directly to anyone after Abraham is a heathen king by means of a *dream by night* (Gen. 20:3). Are you noticing the downward spiral? Man starts off with the most intimate relationship with God possible, face-to-face communication with God in Genesis chapter 2. By Genesis chapter 15, God is now communicating with man through visions. By the time we get to Genesis chapter 20, dreams are now introduced as a vehicle for divine communication. And if you read the Old Testament all the way through until the end of the book of Malachi, most reference works attest to a long period of silence lasting approximately 400 years following this writing.[4] In other words, by this time, God was apparently not speaking at all.

The principle here is that there are measurable degrees of intimacy with, and proximity to, God, that directly determine the overall context or parameters for how we communicate with God and spiritually interface with the elevated dimension of heaven. This principle is explicitly yet poetically articulated by God Himself in his rebuke of Miriam and Aaron for their unrighteous opposition of Moses.

> *Then He said, "Hear now My words: If there is a prophet among you, I, the Lord, make Myself known to him in a vision; I speak to him in a dream. Not so with My servant Moses; He is faithful in all My house. I speak with him face to face, Even plainly, and not in dark sayings; And he sees the form of the Lord. Why then were you not afraid To speak against My servant Moses?"* (Num. 12:6–8)

Notice how each of these three methods of divine communication (dreams, visions, and face to face) are juxtaposed in the text in such a way that there is a distinct difference expressed in the degree of intimacy, revelation, clarity, rank, and authority represented by each dimension. For example, while God is said to merely *speak* to someone (in this context, a prophet) by a dream, the language is more forceful regarding visions where God is said to *make Myself [Himself] known*—*yāḍa* (Heb). This Hebrew word, *yāḍa*, communicates a much deeper sense of knowledge, understanding and revelation than the dark speech usually associated with dreams. When God proceeds to define Moses's relationship as being very personal and intimate, however, his degree of proximity and corresponding method of communication with God is described as *face to face*, thus entitling him to not only a greater level of rank and authority but also greater clarity of revelation and a much higher dimension of sight.

Think about it, having someone speak to you does not necessarily imply that you have any personal knowledge, history, or relationship with them. I have heard numerous voices speak through various forms of media (Internet, television, radio) without ever actually meeting or personally knowing the vast majority of speakers. It is the same principle with dreams; it requires very little—if any—intimacy, proximity, or relationship with God to function. Also it is the lowest spiritual frequency by which to interface with heaven, having the most amount of earthly static and often requiring a descrambling (interpretation).

Visions are more personal and assume a much higher degree of knowledge—like Adam *knew* [*yāḍa*] Eve his wife—intimacy and understanding (Gen. 4:1). Personal relationship is not only implied; it is positively required. The revelation received through this medium is clearer and more refined, with less static and distortion than dreams. The higher the dimension, the less human or earthly static there is to contend with that serves to distort, scramble, or muddy the spiritual frequency. It is no accident that the dimension of sight God associates first with the prophets is visions considering that there is an overwhelming amount of evidence in Scripture proving that visions are the primary method by which prophets receive divine revelation.

Then, of course, we have "face to face," which is unequivocally the highest and most intimate dimension of communication there is. It is one thing to have God speak *to* you but another thing to have God speak *with* you like is described with Moses. This type of speaking implies not only proximity but mutual understanding and dialogue. It describes the ultimate dimension and design for man from which Adam fell. At this level, communication is crystal clear with absolutely no room for distortion of any kind.

Now that we have established the principle of varying degrees or dimensions of sight (divine communication), let us proceed to examine these various dimensions in greater detail while continuing to identify key areas of divergence with regard to the third prophetic dimension. We will begin with the lowest and then end with the highest.

Dreams

A dream can be defined as "a state of mind in which images, thoughts, and impressions pass through the mind of a person who is sleeping."[5] From a purely human or natural point of view, dreams are common to all men and can be triggered by almost anything—including various stimuli upon the physical senses (e.g. touch, odor, sound) and one's physical or emotional condition during sleep.[6] In the words of the author of Ecclesiastes, *"For a dream comes through much activity [burden, cares]."* In other words, dreams are often the product of whatever our hearts and minds are fixed or focused upon, thus causing them to be extremely deceptive.

Spiritually speaking, dreams can also be a valid medium or vehicle for receiving divine revelation from God, as we alluded to before while tracking the deterioration of man's ability to communicate with God and interface with the elevated spiritual dimension of heaven after the fall. By the time of Moses, it is clearly identified by God as one of the ways that He speaks, specifically to prophets (Num. 12:6). Then as we progress to the period around Samuel and Saul, we notice a commonly held belief or expectation in Israel that the Lord would speak through dreams as another established method of communication besides the Urim and prophets (1 Sa. 28:6).[7]

The significance of dreams in the biblical cannon is attested to by the fact that there are approximately 116 references to the word in Scripture (according to *Young's Concordance*), almost half of which occur in Genesis alone.[8] The majority of the remaining occurrences appear later, in the book of Daniel, and number 29 references.[9]

To the casual observer (reader), it may appear as if both God and Scripture ascribe great value to the dream phenomenon as a spiritual resource, but you would be greatly mistaken. This misconception is rampant in Christianity today, particularly in the current (old order) prophetic movement where great emphasis is placed on dreams and dream interpretation. The large number of seminars being taught and books written on this subject—especially from so-called "prophetic" camps—is quite alarming, and is indicative of the subtle syncretism that has crept into the movement with regard to pagan beliefs and practices.

Pagan origins and connections

The fact that dreams are mentioned over a hundred times in Scripture in no way amplifies its value. While the Bible clearly ascribes a certain measure of significance to the topic based upon its frequent mention, it is incorrect to assume that this significance, to whatever degree, translates into the phenomenon being a Kingdom principle worthy of pursuit or practice. Money is mentioned hundreds of times in Scripture, yet few would argue that its biblical significance does not lie in it being something to be cherished, valued (from a Kingdom perspective) or pursued but in the fact that it represents a concept that is common and easily recognizable to all men. It is the same with dreams. The Bible, contrary to commonly held opinion, "attaches relatively little religious [spiritual] significance to dreams."[10]

As a matter of fact, the weight of Scriptural and historical evidence identifies dreams and dream interpretation more closely to pagan religion and practice. From the very first time that dreams are introduced in Scripture as a medium for divine communication, it is identified with a heathen (pagan) king named Abimelech (Gen. 20:3). Based on the "law of first mention," this is very significant. Then when we take into consideration the fact that of the approximately 116 references to the word *dream* in Scripture, which we mentioned above, that more than two thirds (2/3) of the time these references occurred within a pagan and foreign context (i.e. Egypt and Babylon), we begin to see a pattern unfold. It is interesting that "during the approximately 1,000 years between Joseph [in Egypt] and Daniel [in Babylon], only two dreams are recorded."[11] The first reference takes place within a pagan or foreign context again, this time from the Midianite/Amalekite military camp Israel was commanded to destroy (Judg. 7:12–14). The next occurrence pertains to Solomon during a period of his life where, despite his love for God, he was still influenced by pagan religion and had clearly adopted some of their customs (1 Kings 3:3–5).

Since divination was very much a part of pagan religion and culture in the ancient world, it comes as no surprise that dreams—including the interpretation thereof—became closely associated with the dark arts and continued in that vein even "within [the] Graeco-Roman society."[12] Here is how one Bible scholar describes this connection between divination and dreams/dream-interpretation, as well as Israel's apparent ambivalence regarding them:

> In the ancient Near East generally, dreams and the interpretation of dreams must be considered in the wider category of omens and omen interpretation (including reading liver deformities, the shapes and patterns of smoke, oil in water, flights of birds). However, dreams were considered among the least trustworthy forms of divining.
>
> Although there are occasions where dreams (Heb. *hălôm*) are important communications from God to Hebrews (Jacob's famous dream in Gen. 28:12), this form of communication is contrasted with the directness with which God spoke to Moses (Num. 12:6–8), and dreams are certainly condemned as less than trustworthy by Jeremiah (Jer. 23:27, 32; 29:8) and of little value to the Psalmist (Ps. 73:20; 90:5). From the suspicions of prophecy by omen and dream in Deut. 13:1–5 to the late opinion of Sir. 34:7 ("For dreams have deceived many, and those who put their hope in them have perished"), one can trace

this early Hebraic ambivalence with regard to dreams as trustworthy sources of information.[13]

Joseph and Daniel

One of the reasons why both Joseph and Daniel were able to quickly (and easily) climb the ladder of success in these foreign (pagan) nations and be appointed to high political positions in government was because of their (God-given) ability to effectively and accurately "divine" (interpret) dreams. "According to biblical testimony, the royal courts of both Mesopotamia and Egypt had among their wise men and prognosticators [political court officials] those who professionally interpreted [divined] dreams."[14] These dream diviners or interpreters were to "be consulted at the highest level of government for important decisions," which explains why these pagan rulers wanted Joseph and Daniel in their political courts or at their right hand.[15] The Hebrews—by the Spirit of God—proved to be far more accurate and effective than the "wise men" (occult practitioners), sorcerers, magicians, and astrologers who usually occupied this position (Gen. 41:8, 24; Ex. 7:11; Dan. 2:2, 27, 4:7). However, had either Joseph or Daniel been back in their own home kingdom where a theocratic philosophy of government existed both in the patriarchal as well as monarchic periods respectively, they would have been unemployed in such a context. In the kingdom of Israel, the kings and leaders surrounded themselves or consulted with priests, prophets, and elders, not dream interpreters (2 Sam. 8:15–18, 19:11; 1 Kings 1:23, 32, 2:26; 12:6; 2 Chron. 29:25). There was never any need for such a ministry in Israel because the revelation they received from God—even when such revelation came through the medium of dreams, as seldom as that was—usually required no interpretation or outside interpreter. The messages they received from God were a lot less scrambled or obscure. There is not a single record of any Hebrew in Scripture ever requiring an interpretation for a dream they or someone else received. On the contrary, when Joseph received his two dreams about the *sheaves* bowing down to his, followed by *the sun, the moon, and the eleven stars* doing likewise, his father and brothers immediately understood what the dreams meant without requiring someone to interpret them (Gen. 37:5–10).

In contrast, whenever a foreigner or non-Israelite received a dream in Scripture, it usually required an interpretation from an outside source (interpreter). Thus, the baker, the butler, and even Pharaoh himself in Egypt required the interpretive insight of Joseph (Gen. 40–41); Nebuchadnezzar required assistance from Daniel (Dan. 2); and the Midianite soldier needed the help of his companion (Judg. 7:13–14). Also, unlike the Hebrews, pagan cultures employed the use of "divinatory dream interpretation" manuals ("dream books") they developed, thus, bolstering their understanding of dream symbols to interpret dreams, as evidenced by the numerous documents of such kinds discovered by archaeologists in the Near East.[16] Their approach to interpreting dreams was remarkably similar to what is commonly taught and practiced today in the current prophetic movement as well as some other Christian circles. However, when you examine the Hebrew approach, you discover a marked difference and divergence. In the case of the two foremost dream interpreters in all of Scripture—Joseph and Daniel—their interpretations are explicitly attributed to God rather than human wisdom or their understanding of the science of symbolism (Gen. 41:16, 38–39; Dan. 2:27–28, 47).[17] Joseph and Daniel never escaped into their personal studies and began leafing through dream books or dictionaries of symbolism in order to ascertain the meaning or interpretation for the dreams of the two pagan monarchs. And there is nothing in the biblical narratives to lead us to believe that these men somehow acquired this knowledge or understanding during their time of captivity in these foreign kingdoms. It is clear from both historical records and Scripture that the Hebrews thoroughly rejected this "secular approach" to dream interpretation, and so should we. Joseph and Daniel were able to accurately interpret dreams by the Spirit of God, "not by research in dream books or by natural human ability."[18]

In case this hasn't fully sunk in or registered yet, let me state categorically and emphatically that any attempt to interpret dreams through research in dream books (this relates to any form of material addressing the subject of dreams or dream interpretation) or the study of dream symbols—including those resources which originate from within the "Christian" community—is an exercise in divination and an expression of pagan religion. It really doesn't matter just how you try to spiritualize this evil practice by adding prayer or meditation to the mix. At its core is a principle that is antithetical to both Kingdom and Hebraic culture. Dreams are to be interpreted by the Spirit of God or not interpreted at all. The fact that Scripture is heavily interwoven with symbolism or symbolic language expressed through numerous examples of literary types, shadows, and symbols in no way negates this principle. While the understanding of biblical symbolism is not only tolerated but encouraged due to its ability to greatly enhance our understanding of Scripture, it is not the basis upon which we interpret Scripture. Neither is biblical symbolism, for that matter, the same as dream symbolism. They both operate according to different principles. Whereas biblical symbolism is generally consistent in its application and interpretation depending on the usage and context, dream symbols tend to be unique to the individual dreamer.[19] The failure to understand this particular dream dynamic has led to many false interpretations. Only the Spirit can interpret the Spirit. You cannot interpret the Spirit (or spiritual communication) by the flesh; therefore, it is ludicrous to believe that a dream from God—spiritual communication—can be accurately interpreted through human understanding or fleshly research.

Dreams in the New Testament

"The NT [New Testament] gives still less place and importance to dreams than the OT [Old Testament]," with the only "six references" on the subject occurring in the Gospel of Matthew alone.[20] It is interesting that of the six references, not a single one pertains to Jesus or any of His followers. With the exception of Joseph, pagans are once again the candidates of choice (Matt. 1:20, 2:12, 13, 19, 22, 27:19). This is not surprising considering it is clearly the only way that God is able to communicate with an unregenerate sinner or someone who is outside the household of faith. Every single time that God communicates directly with such a person in Scripture, it is through this means. For example, Abimelech (Gen. 20:3–7), Laban (Gen. 31:24), the chief butler and baker (Gen. 40:5), Pharaoh (Gen. 41:1–8), the Midianite/Amalekite (Judg. 7:13), Nebuchadnezzar (Dan.2:1), the magicians/astrologers/sorcerers/wise men (Matt. 2:12), and Pilate's wife (Matt. 27:19).[21] This is the primary reason it is considered the lowest dimension of divine communication. In addition, it is also impersonal and one dimensional in nature, occurring in the unconscious and impressionable state of sleep rather than in a state of mental awareness or understanding. Based upon the principle enunciated by Paul in 1 Corinthians 14 regarding the significance of our understanding being engaged in spiritual activity, this diminishes or lessens the value of dreams.

Not only are dreams noticeably absent as a method of divine communication for Jesus, but even more significant is the fact that "Jesus nowhere refers to dreams, evidently attaching little if any importance to them."[22] After the resurrection of Jesus and the birth of His Covenant Kingdom Community, dreams are never again mentioned or referred to as a vehicle for divine communication in Scripture, the only exception being the single citation occurring in Acts 2:17. Some scholars interpret this silence as a reflection of "a certain early Christian hesitancy to be associated with pagan practices."[23] Whatever the case may be, trances and visions are mentioned within God's Kingdom Community but never dreams.

In light of this discovery regarding dreams and how they are negatively portrayed or devalued under both Covenants (Old Testament and New Testament), one of the obvious questions that arises is how then do we reconcile this to the citation of Joel 2:28 in Acts 2:17 where dreams are identified with the outpouring of the Holy Spirit? In order to answer this question, we need to take another (brief) look at the two texts. There's a key word employed in both instances intended to convey a truth or principle that is often missed.

*And it shall come to pass afterward That I will pour out My Spirit on all flesh; Your sons and your daughters shall prophesy, Your **old** men shall dream* *dreams, Your young men shall see visions.* (Joel 2:28, emphasis mine)

*And it shall come to pass in the last days, says God, That I will pour out of My Spirit on all flesh; Your sons and your daughters shall prophesy, Your young men shall see visions, Your **old** men shall dream dreams.* (Acts 2:17, emphasis mine)

Firstly, you will notice that Peter's quotation of Joel's prophecy contains very minor but, nevertheless, still significant alterations. Whereas Joel places dreams before visions in his original prophecy, Peter reverses the order. Coincidence? Hardly likely considering what we have already discovered regarding dreams in the New Testament. It is not unreasonable to surmise that Peter intentionally placed dreams last as a mode of revelation since it was clearly ascribed lesser value in Hebraic culture and even lesser still in the New Covenant Kingdom Community of believers. Peter's order is not only consistent with the New Testament position but with the Bible as a whole. Whereas Joel's original audience—the children of Judah—would have immediately understood this principle regardless of where dreams were placed within the order of the prophecy, Peter's audience consisted of both local and international Jews and proselytes from many different (pagan) nations of the world (Acts 2:5–11). They would have needed this interpretive clarity from Peter in order to accurately understand the message he was trying to convey.

Secondly, you will notice that I emphasized the word *old* in both passages. This word is significant to the interpretation of the texts. In Scripture, the word *old* is often employed idiomatically to convey impotence (Gen. 18:11; 2 Kings 4:14; Luke 1:18, 36), weakness (Ps. 71:9), and diminished sight or blindness (Gen. 27:1; 1 Sam. 4:15).[24] Like Jesus's use of the term in *old garment* and *old wineskins*, there is a not-so-subtle requirement for the rejection of the old due to its inherent weakness and inferiority in comparison to the new (Matt. 9:16–17).[25] Of course, the term *young* in the texts above is used in a similar way to *old* but with the opposite connotation of vigor and strength in being representative of the new (Prov. 20:29). These terms (young and old) have very little to do with physical age or maturity and almost everything to do with one's spiritual mentality and internal architecture, heart condition, or posture.[26] In other words, even though the outpouring of God's Spirit was initiated by God and intended to make everyone participators, we are the ones who ultimately determine the extent, dimension, or level of our participation based on our internal posture and mentality. God will initiate, but we must appropriate! We will elaborate a bit more upon this human component of responsibility later in this chapter; however, the point of emphasis here is that the prophetic citation in Acts 2 should not be interpreted as a final endorsement or encouragement for dreams as a valid method of receiving divine revelation, which we already know it is, but as a confirmation of its inferiority and inherent weakness as a vehicle for divine interface.

This brings us to another equally obvious question that I am almost certain constitutes one of the major points of contention for those arguing in support of dreams as a major emphasis or practice in the current prophetic movement: If dreams are as weak and inferior as stated, why then are they so closely identified with the prophetic dimension by God Himself in Numbers 12:6? Since we have already discussed the principle of varying degrees or dimensions of spiritual sight (divine communication) in our brief examination of this text at an earlier point in this chapter, I will not attempt to rehash it here. Sufficed to say that it was never God's intention to ascribe undue significance to dreams in the context of the prophetic or in any context for that matter. The assumption that dreams played an important or significant part in the prophetic dimension of Scripture is an incorrect one. "The prophets generally do not speak of dreams as the source of their inspiration [revelation]" in Scripture, and when dreams are mentioned in such a context, it is usually in the negative sense of false prophets and/or prophecies (Deut. 13:2–6).[27] Thus when the prophets Jeremiah and Zechariah denounce the false prophets for their reliance upon dreams—which, as we already mentioned, are extremely deceptive by nature—they (the false prophets) are lumped together and identified with soothsayers, sorcerers, and diviners (Jer. 23:25–28, 32, 27:9–10, 29:8–9; Zech. 10:2).[28]

Again, this does not necessarily mean that dreams are all bad or that a true prophet of God will never receive genuine divine revelation from heaven through this means. It does, however, imply that the significance of dreams in the prophetic dimension has been grossly exaggerated and that the dream form of revelation was highly minimized or rejected—even forbidden as a trusted source[29]—within Israel's prophetic history, as it should also be in ours.

Visions

Visions are, by far, the most common and established medium for divine interface between God and His covenant people—especially his holy prophets—in all of Scripture. While the word itself is used a little over a hundred times in the New King James Version (NKJV) of the Bible, the principle or concept is far more prevalent, as we will soon discover.

In some theological circles, it has been a commonly held belief for many years that dreams and visions are fundamentally the same, the only difference being that one (dreams) occurs during sleep and the other (visions) while awake. While it is certainly true from a biblical standpoint that *night* visions are often equated with dreams due to the fact that the experiences were so similar that they were virtually indistinguishable by the participants, dreams and visions are far from synonymous (Job 4:13, 7:14, 20:8, 33:15; Is. 29:7; Dan. 7:1–2).

Most of the misunderstanding regarding visions today has to do with the very narrow, limited, and restricted sense in which we have come to define the term. This misunderstanding is strikingly similar, and closely related, to the "prophets versus seers" fallacy we addressed in the second chapter. If you remember (if not, please mark this page and go back and read it again), one of the root causes for that error was an incomplete and, therefore, incorrect definition of the Hebrew words related to *sight* or *seer*. These Hebrew words conveyed a much broader and expansive definition than the limited English translations, thus the misunderstanding. Truth be told, even without the

Hebrew definitions, the scriptural usage and contexts surrounding these words should have been sufficient for debunking the error. Nevertheless, it is not surprising that the word *vision* has been subject to similar error of interpretation considering it is also rooted in, as well as translated from, the same Hebrew words (along with a few others, including Greek).

Divine revelation

Based on the biblical evidence, including the wide variety of usage and contexts in which the word *vision* has been employed in Scripture, it can be defined simply—though quite accurately—as divine revelation. You will notice that this definition is very broad and leaves open the assumption that there can be more than just a visual experience involved. This is because the word *vision*, while clearly referring to sight in the literal (or spiritual) sense of the word in certain contexts (Ezek. 1:1; 43:3), is often used simply as a technical term for any verbal communication from God.[30] Thus, the young Samuel's divine encounter where he first *heard* the *audible* voice of the Lord is described in scripture as a *vision* even though there was absolutely nothing visual about the experience (1 Sam. 3:15). We see this principle again with Nathan where *words* are identified or described as *vision* (2 Sam. 7:17). Even some prophetic books— written revelation—are labeled or described as *visions* even though the majority of the revelation contained therein did not come by any visual experience (Isa. 1:1; Obad. 1; Nah. 1:1). The point here is that visions are not necessarily visual but can describe revelation given by heaven through any context. As a matter of fact, even when the vision consisted of a distinct visual element, there was usually a degree of hearing involved as a verbal message or audible discourse was communicated (1 Kings 22:19–22; Isa. 6).

When the biblical vocabulary of *visions* is understood and interpreted outside of its usually narrow confinement of visual activity to encompass what is clearly a very broad spectrum of prophetic revelation and supernatural insight, it dispels the error and confusion propagated by an old prophetic order seeking to create a false dichotomy between prophets and seers. Furthermore, a biblically correct understanding of visions being representative of divine revelation serves to eliminate the false perception that any visual experience—supernatural or otherwise—constitutes a heavenly vision. In order for one's experience to be accurately classified as a true vision, it must first meet the biblical prerequisite of conveying divine revelation. Experiences may differ from person to person in the way a vision from God is communicated (seeing, hearing, feeling, sensing, etc.), but the one singular, non-negotiable constant of a vision from God is that it constitutes divine (or prophetic) revelation. Without this divine element, the presumed vision is false. Thus, when we approach scriptures like the often quoted—or rather, misquoted— proverb rendered "Where there is no *vision*, the people perish," (Prov. 29:18) we understand that the term "vision" cannot refer to the literal sense of perception through the physical organs of sight or to the human aspect of imagination or future planning. To remain consistent with its biblical usage and definition, the word *vision* can only be accurately interpreted as referring to divine, prophetic revelation received from God.[31]

This begs the question: What is divine revelation and how can it be distinguished from those that are merely false claims? There are numerous occasions in Scripture where the visions propagated and proclaimed as "divine revelation" by the established prophetic order were identified as false because they did not, in fact, emanate from God (Jer. 14:14; 23:16; Lam. 2:14; Ezek. 13:7; 22:28; Zech. 13:4).

A vision can come from one of three sources:

1. Divine influence (Acts 18:9)
2. Human imagination or self-delusion (Lam. 2:14)
3. Demonic influence and spiritual deception (Jer. 14:14)

Everything that originates from God carries His nature and heaven's divine architecture (Jam. 3:17). This means that all divine revelation will manifest the character of Christ (*good fruits*) and seek to reproduce it in others. It is not empty, shallow, frivolous, or self-serving. Rather, it is full of spiritual density, weight and divine purpose as it brings guidance (Gen. 46:2–5), direction (Acts 16:9–10), encouragement (Acts 18:9–10), warning (Is. 21:2–4), judgment (1 Sam. 3:1–15), and apostolic fervor (Acts 26:19–20). It is given "to develop the Kingdom of God by revealing the moral and spiritual deficiencies of the people of God in light of God's requirements for maintaining a proper relationship with Him."[32] As such, not only will it conform to Scripture, but it will also be non-hypocritical and impartial, as opposed to being characterized by narcissism, favoritism, cronyism, nepotism, nationalism or chauvinism—issues of spiritual blindness and internal corruption.

Conversely, whatever is not from God is carnal and reflects human (earthly) or satanic architecture that is antithetical to everything the Kingdom of God represents. It is not only empty and shallow but ultimately self-serving and self-seeking (Jam. 3:14–16). It may be able to "see" or describe in detail earthly facts (like a PO Box or telephone number), but it is incapable of manifesting or reproducing Christ's character and Kingdom here on earth. Its purpose is to impress man and honor or elevate self, regardless of the religious rhetoric employed. Its emphasis is usually on personal or corporate blessing and breakthrough, ignoring the sin, rebellion, and iniquity running rampant beneath the surface (Lam. 2:14). And it is often characterized by partiality and human bias as it is blinded by its own carnal preferences and self-interests. These types of "visions" have become all too common in an age and prophetic movement today where success is defined by popularity, acceptance, and social network followers rather than by internal correctness, accurate building, and complete obedience.

Variations in visionary process

The word *vision* in Scripture can also refer to the process "through which supernatural insight or awareness is given by revelation."[33] This process can range anywhere between two extremes. At one extreme, the visionary process is so vivid, overpowering, heightened, and intense that the participant is unable to distinguish it from a literal experience (Luke 24:1–8, 23; Acts 12:9). Thus, the apostle

Paul describes his Damascus road experience as a *vision* (Acts 9:1–9, 26:12–19) and also expresses difficulty in determining whether or not his *third heaven* visionary experience was a literal *out of the body* one or a divine download received while *in the body* (2 Cor. 12:1–4). As a matter of fact, as far as Scripture is concerned (primarily the New Testament), there is hardly any distinction between this type of vision from God—especially when multiple participants are involved who may have seen or experienced the same thing—and an actual angelic visitation or heavenly encounter like what happened with Jesus at the transfiguration (Matt. 17:1–9; Luke 1:11–22; 24:1–8, 23; Acts 10:3–8).

Slightly less extreme, but extreme nevertheless, is what scripture describes as a *trance*. The word *trance* is translated from the Greek word **ekstasis**, from which we get our English word *ecstatic*. It literally means "standing outside" or "being put outside" of one's normal state of mind.[34] It describes "a state of being in which [human] consciousness is wholly or partially suspended,"[35] or "the state of being removed from the awareness of the mundane perceptions of the sensory world and awakening to the perception of the extrasensory world."[36] This is what happened to Peter on the housetop as a result of divine action (Acts 10:9–16). Peter's human or earthly consciousness was temporarily suspended or overridden by a divine awareness, enabling him to "step outside" of his earthly dimension of existence to a higher spiritual dimension of divine interface with God. The experience can be so powerful and sudden that it can feel as if someone flipped a switch that immediately transported us to another place or realm.

The ecstatic visionary experiences of prophets like Ezekiel and Daniel, which seemed to involve translation to other places, also fall within this category (Ezek. 8:3; 40:2; Dan. 8).[37] It is not surprising, therefore, that one particular theological lexicon provides a literal translation of the Greek word *ekstasis* as "change of place."[38]

Based on the narrative of Acts, powerful visions like the kinds mentioned above were quite commonplace among the early Covenant Kingdom Community of believers. As a matter of fact, it was expressly this type of revelation from the Spirit of God that acted as a catalyst for initiating key new developments in God's Kingdom Community after it was birthed.[39] This includes Philip's evangelistic initiatives (Acts 8:26–40), Paul's conversion and reception into the Kingdom Community (Acts 9:3–17), Paul's apostolic mission to the Gentiles (Acts 22:17–21), Peter's ministry to Cornelius, thereby breaking down long-standing ethnic boundaries and establishing new precedent that God's Spirit and Kingdom were available to the Gentiles also (Acts 10:3–6, 9–16), and Paul's apostolic witness in Rome (Acts 23:11; 27:23–24).[40]

You will notice that these visionary or ecstatic experiences were in no way limited or exclusive to the prophets. Not a single prophet is mentioned in any of the New Testament references above. Anyone could participate! Visions had now become the new normal for God's Kingdom people, far removed from the previous 400 years of spiritual silence that had ended only decades earlier. These experiences served to reinforce and confirm their convictions in the invisible, eternal dimension of God, allowing them to withstand the criticism and hostility of their spiritually blind antagonists as well as legitimize their break with the established religious order.[41] Peter's ecstatic vision, in particular, is explicitly mentioned as "an essential part of his defense before the 'circumcision party,' clarifying for them and the reader that he was acting not on his own initiative but rather following the legitimate and unimpeachable authority of the Spirit" (Acts 11: 2–18).[42] With the confirming and validating evidence of the Spirit's outpouring, his testimony was received. As it was then, so shall it be today in this new reformation and prophetic divergence. Expect these kinds of visions to increase for essentially the same purpose in the days ahead. These types of visions will once again become the new normal in God's Kingdom Community.

At the other extreme—the opposite end of the spectrum—are visions that are characteristically much more subtle, intuitive, and benign. These visions have been classified by some scholars as "symbolical perception."[43] They usually operate in such a way that "a prophet sees an ordinary object which is part of the natural world, but sees it with a heightened significance beyond the normal."[44] In other words, even though the prophet or visionary recipient is still fully conscious, engaged or aware (of his natural world and surroundings), his spiritual senses and intuitive perception are elevated to a new heavenly dimension. He receives a "distinctive worldview or perception of reality" that is prophetic in nature.[45] This is how Jeremiah could view seemingly common earthly objects or processes like the *branch of an almond tree, a boiling pot*, or even a *potter* working on his clay and receive divine revelation and insight that would have otherwise been impossible to access by human observation alone (Jer. 1:11–16; 18:3–11). The same with Amos when he viewed *a basket of summer fruit* (Amos 8:1–3).

This elevated dimension of spiritual sight where there is an afflated confluence between physical awareness and amplified spiritual sensitivity is probably the greatest distinguishing characteristic separating visions from dreams. In the dream state, there is no physical awareness or human consciousness as all five physical senses are dormant or inactive during sleep. This not only makes dreams fundamentally one-dimensional as opposed to visions, which are often two-dimensional, but it also informs us as to why God is only able to communicate with an unregenerate or unbeliever through this medium. Since unbelievers are "dead in sin" (Eph. 2:1) and thus incapable of seeing, hearing, or otherwise interfacing with God or His heavenly dimension in any physically conscious state, the only way for God to get a message through to them is to completely bypass their consciousness or physical awareness during sleep by means of a dream. This essentially places dreams on a lower level than visions since dreams are common to all men and visions are exclusive to God's covenant people, His holy prophets in particular. There is not a single record in Scripture of God ever communicating with an unregenerate sinner or unbeliever by means of a vision, and understandably so, since visions require closer proximity (to God) and spiritual sensitivity in order to operate.[46]

As a matter of fact, it is this closer proximity and spiritual sensitivity that makes visions a lot less ambiguous or obscure than dreams. Because there is less human static or distortion, visions from God never require any outside interpretation since the wisdom, understanding, and insight necessary for accurate interpretation always accompany the vision. In other words, when it comes to visions, the interpretation usually comes directly from God Himself. Again, Scripture establishes unequivocal precedent by the very fact that there is not a single account of any visionary recipient ever needing or requesting an interpretation (from any human individual) for a vision received from God.

These key points not only reinforce the principle that visions are superior to dreams on every level—as *wheat* [divine revelation] is to *chaff* [dreams] (Jer. 23:28)—but it also establishes the existence of a clear biblical paradigm where visions are the recognized and accepted standard for divine interface with God in the New Testament. Even so, there is still more. There is a higher dimension of divine communication with God than both visions and dreams, and few are they who find it.

Face-to-Face

For many today, the idea of being able to communicate with God face-to-face resides somewhere in the realm between impossibility and naiveté—humanly unattainable and beyond natural reach, at least in this life, or else a fanatically hyperbolic embellishment concocted by the super/spooky-spiritual. We have become so far removed from Adam's original Eden experience and so misinformed on account of Scripture's apparent contradiction on the subject—the foremost being, "*You cannot see My [God's] face; for no man shall see Me [God] and live*" (Exod. 33:20)—that we have resigned ourselves to lower or inferior dimensions of communication with God. These apparent scriptural contradictions, by the way, can easily be resolved when we understand how the ancient Hebrew idiom *face-to-face* is employed in Scripture.

Adam, as we all know, enjoyed unbroken and unmitigated fellowship with God prior to the fall. But after Adam and Eve disobeyed God by eating of the forbidden fruit, they both *hid* or withdrew themselves *from the presence of the Lord* (Gen. 3:8). The word for *presence* here can literally be translated *face*, and it is often used in this symbolic and "theological sense with regard to the person or presence of God" in Scripture (Gen. 4:16; Exod. 33:14).[47] As a matter of fact, even "in the tabernacle, the 'shewbread' (KJV) or 'Bread of the Presence' (RSV), was a local manifestation of the presence of God. The literal Hebrew reads 'bread of the faces.'"[48] Thus, the *face* of God is symbolically representative of God's personal presence or proximity, with "face-to-face" signifying "the most direct and personal encounter" one is able to have with the Father.[49] It is an expression not only of the deepest intimacy with regard to relationship but also the greatest insight (understanding) with regard to revelation, as everything is made perfectly clear in such a context (Num. 12:8; 1 Cor. 13:9–12).

When Scripture asserts, quite emphatically, that *no man shall* (Exod. 33:20) and *no one has* (John 1:18; 1 John 4:12) *see(n) God* and be(en) able to live through that experience to tell about it, it is obviously not referring to the sight of God or face-to-face experiences of Adam and others (Gen. 32:30; Exod. 24:9–11, 33:11; Isa. 6:1). If it were, Scripture would be directly contradicting itself. Most Bible scholars are in agreement that the sight of God being prohibited or denied access to mankind in these verses pertains to the unveiled or unbridled "essence of deity."[50] Not even Moses was permitted to look upon God in His fullness, or it would have killed him instantly (Exod. 33:20). Scripture seems to imply that even Adam, prior to the fall and in his sinless state, was not permitted to gaze upon God in this fashion either or his flesh—sinless as it may have been at the time—would have been consumed also.[51] It is not that God does not desire to provide full disclosure of Himself to His Bride; it is that we have no capacity as finite beings to either process, handle, or endure such an infinite disclosure. But thanks to Jesus and the redemption purchased by His sinless blood, our fragile earthly bodies shall one day be transformed into new, infinitely better and glorious ones, thus enabling us to gaze upon God in His fullness and abide in His presence forever (2 Cor. 5:1–8; Rev. 21:1–3; 22:3–4).

This means that while we are not permitted, in our present earthly bodies, to gaze upon God in His fullness, we have, however, been granted access to a personal and intimate face-to-face encounter with God similar to what Adam experienced in the garden. If this concept is still difficult to grasp and seems beyond reach in your present reality due to the fact that Adam was in a perfect and sinless environment without the added weight of sinful flesh (at the time), consider the fact that there are at least two other examples—both living under an old and inferior covenant—who were able to transcend their earthly limitations and encounter God in such a way. They are Jacob and Moses.

Jacob's face-to-face encounter with God

> *And he arose that night and took his two wives, his two female servants, and his eleven sons, and crossed over the ford of Jabbok. He took them, sent them over the brook, and sent over what he had. Then Jacob was left alone; and a Man wrestled with him until the breaking of day. Now when He saw that He did not prevail against him, He touched the socket of his hip; and the socket of Jacob's hip was out of joint as He wrestled with him. And He said, "Let Me go, for the day breaks." But he said, "I will not let You go unless You bless me!" So He said to him, "What is your name?" He said, "Jacob." And He said, "Your name shall no longer be called Jacob, but Israel; for you have struggled with God and with men, and have prevailed." Then Jacob asked, saying, "Tell me Your name, I pray." And He said, "Why is it that you ask about My name?" And He blessed him there. So Jacob called the name of the place Peniel: "For I have seen God face to face, and my life is preserved." Just as he crossed over Penuel the sun rose on him, and he limped on his hip. Therefore to this day the children of Israel do not eat the muscle that shrank, which is on the hip socket, because He touched the socket of Jacob's hip in the muscle that shrank.* (Gen. 32:22–32)

In the case of Jacob, the account of his face-to-face encounter with God is so mysterious and ambiguous that the reader is left with more questions than answers. For example, Jacob is described as wrestling with a mysterious *Man*, but this *Man* is also described as both an *Angel* and as *God* Himself (Gen. 32:28, 30; Hos. 12:2–4). How is a mortal man able to go toe-to-toe with an immortal being, much less when that immortal being is God in the flesh? Furthermore, the text gives us no information on how this *wrestling* match started or what precipitated it. It is just stated matter-of-factly. How long did this wrestling match last (we know when it ended, but we have no information about what time of the night it started)? The questions go on and on. Nevertheless, there is sufficient information in the text for us to extract some very key principles relative to divine face-to-face encounters.

1. *The Principle of Emptiness.* According to the narrative, the vicinity of the *Jabbok* River is identified as the scene or location for Jacob's face-to-face encounter with God. While some commentators debate exactly which side of the river he was on, that is irrelevant to the story. What is important is what the Jabbok represents (Hint: It's more than a Hebrew pun on Jacob's name). The name *Jabbok* means "pouring out or emptying."[52] It represents an internal place of being broken, empty, and "poured out" before God. Jacob had come to the end of himself, to the end of his own strength. He couldn't return to Laban, and going forward could mean certain death from an embittered and/ or murderous twin brother, Esau. This left Jacob in a place of hunger and desperation for God such as he had never experienced before. This emptiness, hunger, or divine discontent is the prerequisite and catalyst for encountering God face-to-face. This is not something that can be experienced by casual or religious seekers, regardless of whether or not they are legitimate prophets. Heaven responds to hunger just as *deep calls unto deep* (Matt. 5:6; Ps. 42:7). It often requires intense suffering, persecution, failure, or

rejection to bring us to this place, but until we are emptied of ourselves and driven by a deep sense of hunger, desperation, and discontent for the presence of God—in a more elevated and concentrated dimension in our lives—this type of divine face-to-face experience or encounter will continue to elude us.

2. *The Principle of Separation.* It was not until Jacob performed the intentional act of separating himself from everything—including his family and possessions—so that he was completely *alone* that God chose to invade his mortal context. Jacob intentionally sent everything and everyone away so that he could be alone with God. The principle here is that there must be a separation or internal disconnect from everything we treasure, value, or ascribe importance to in this life if we are going to see and encounter God face-to-face. The primary emphasis and importance here should be placed on the internal aspect of separation since the aspect of reduced physical proximity becomes inconsequential when our hearts and minds are still preoccupied or distracted by these issues. In other words, this separation is more of a heart issue than anything else. This is why Jesus said, "Blessed are the pure in heart, for they shall *see* God" (Matt. 5:8). Our hearts need to be clean and untainted from worldly pleasures, fleshly desires, and idolatrous distractions if we are going to see God's face. God refused to meet with Jacob until he was alone, and He will refuse to meet with us until we have intentionally made room for Him by separating and purging ourselves of every competing or distracting element that has been residing within our hearts. This includes even God-given or God-ordained blessings. For Jacob, it was his wives, children, servants, and wealth that God Himself had given and empowered Jacob to accumulate. For us, it may be our families, our businesses, our churches or ministries, our property, possessions or wealth, but the principle remains the same. When we came *from* God, we

came with nothing; and when we come *to* Him, we must come in a similar manner.

3. *The Principle of Waiting.* As mentioned earlier, scripture is extremely silent regarding the exact time of night that this divine encounter and wrestling match occurred. This omission was not accidental; it was intended to communicate a profound spiritual principle. Jacob may have been seeking God and waiting on Him for many hours or even half the night or more. We don't know, and God doesn't want us to know. He wants us to wait. As a matter of fact, He takes delight in our waiting. He doesn't seem to care very much about our earthly schedules, itineraries, appointments, comfort, or deadlines. Had Jacob set out to dedicate only a set or allotted time to seeking God, like maybe an hour or two, he may never have encountered Him. But Jacob was willing to wait all night if he had to. Older folks who were alive and participated in the Pentecostal movement called this "tarrying." It is what Jesus had commanded His disciples to do after His resurrection in anticipation of receiving the *Promise of the Father*—the Holy Spirit (Acts 1:4–5, 12–14). When we refuse to wait and try to force God to fit into our earthly schedules and programs, His manifest presence will continue to elude us, and we never truly encounter Him face-to-face. It is the same individually as in our corporate times of worship; we will never encounter God intimately until we are truly willing to wait, even it means adjusting or discarding our earthly schedules and programs.

4. *The Principle of Vulnerability (Surrender).* During the course of my biblical study and research regarding Jacob's divine encounter with God, I came across an entry from a highly-respected commentary that I initially rejected and ridiculed until the Holy Spirit prompted me to look at it again. The author, who appears to have expert knowledge of the original Hebrew, makes this statement regarding God's touching *the socket of Jacob's hip*: "Several other

texts in Genesis involve the *thigh*. Abraham had his servant place his hand under his thigh (24:2, 9; cf. 47:29), which may be instances of 'thigh' meaning genitals. Exod. 1:5 refers to the seventy offspring who came forth from 'the thigh of Jacob.' Since *kap⁻* [the socket of] has the connotation of hollowness (as in a vessel or pan, or pouch), and *yārēk* [hip or thigh] may have the meaning of genitals, it is possible that the phrase *kap⁻ yᵉrēkô* refers to the scrotum, the hollow pouch of skin holding the testicles, rather than to the hip socket."[53] Whether or not we actually believe that the Hebrew words for "the socket of his hip" should be translated in such a manner given the context is inconsequential. The fact that God chose a term that could be translated as such and "thigh" is used euphemistically in other scriptures to convey exactly what the author above is suggesting is proof that there is a deeper spiritual principle being communicated here. A man's genitals represent the most intimately guarded, covered, and protected area of a man's physical life. It is a symbol not only of man's strength but also his weakness. This means that if we expect to intimately encounter God face-to-face, we must be willing to become vulnerable and unguarded by letting God penetrate and touch the deepest and most private areas of our hearts and lives. We must be willing to come out of hiding like Adam and Eve after the fall and allow God to deal with those hidden issues and weaknesses that have separated us from Him (Gen. 3:8). As long as we remain guarded and hidden, we will never see God's face.

Moses's face-to-face encounters with God

When we study the life of Moses and his own face-to-face encounters with God, we see these same principles come into play. For example, Moses clearly demonstrated a deep hunger and desperate desire for God as one who was completely "empty" and "poured out" before Him when, despite God's promise of total victory against their enemies and the possession of their earthly inheritance in a land *flowing with milk and honey*, Moses's one single desire was to know God and experience His presence in the most elevated dimension possible (Ex. 33:1–2, 13–23). Here was God basically offering Moses everything he could possibly want in the world, yet none of that really mattered to him if the presence of God wasn't with him and he couldn't see God's face (glory). Moses was so obsessed with God that there was no room for earthly attachments or idols in his heart. He was completely "separated," and when it came time to meet with God, he was not entangled by any distractions. Not only was he willing and able to walk alone, but he was able to step out from the ordinary into the extraordinary. While all Israel was content with merely waiting for God to show up whenever He chose to come *down*, Moses was always in proactive pursuit by ascending the mountain to go *up* where God was (Ex. 19:3, 33:7–11, 34:4–5).

When it came to the principle of "waiting," Moses epitomized this principle. Scripture gives ample record and provides substantial testimony to the fact that when Moses ascended the mountain to meet with God, he was there *forty days and forty nights* (Ex. 24:18, 34:28; Deut. 9:9, 25). The number *forty* in Scripture is idiomatic of fullness or completion with regard to a specific season or period of time. In this particular context, it represents fullness of waiting. It means that Moses was never in a hurry to meet with God and then leave His presence. Moses wasn't sitting there counting down the minutes, hours, or days. He was willing to wait on/with God indefinitely, and nothing—not even his most basic and demanding physical needs—was going to distract him from doing so.

This brings us to principle number four—the principle of "vulnerability" or "surrender." Many of us are familiar with what some scholars consider to be the most difficult pericope in the book of Exodus—the account of Moses's near-death encounter with God while at his encampment and on his way to fulfill what he had just been divinely commissioned to do (Ex. 4:24–26). All of this occurred, by the way, right after Moses's initial encounter with God. While it would require far too much time and space in this writing to examine or debunk the various interpretations of this passage, suffice it to say that the parallels to Jacob's own encounter at the Jabbok are unmistakable. Whereas God had come to fight or wrestle with Jacob, He had now come to fight—with the intent to kill—Moses. If Jacob's encounter with God was mysterious, obscure, and ambiguous, Moses's is much more. Like in Jacob's encounter, we are left with more questions than answers. And once again, the human (male) genitals come into play, emphasizing once again that we cannot encounter God face-to-face without surrendering and giving Him access to the most intimately guarded and protected areas of our lives—including our strengths and weaknesses. Up until that point, Moses never allowed God access to this hidden and private area of his life, and thus he had neglected to become fully circumcised (it is believed by most scholars that, at best, Moses was only partially circumcised at the time). When Zipporah intervened vicariously and circumcised her son (she couldn't circumcise Moses because that would have incapacitated him in his journey and mission), she, in effect, transferred the effect of the rite upon Moses by touching the severed foreskin of her son to his own genitals (euphemistically translated as feet).[54] If, like some Bible teachers and commentators, you believe that God was after Moses on account of his uncircumcised son, it still does not negate the principle. As a matter of fact, it only amplifies it. The only thing intimately protected and guarded by a parent more than their own genitals is that of their own child. Either way, Moses demonstrated vulnerability and surrender by allowing his wife, Zipporah, to perform this rite. And it was only then that God released His stranglehold upon Moses and *let him go*, which conjures up thoughts of a present-day wrestling match where the defeated opponent has to tap out in surrender in order to be released from a deadly chokehold.

Examining the evidence

When a man or woman of God attains such an elevated dimension of divine interface and intimate face-to-face communion with God, the results are profound. But not only are they profound, they are profoundly evident. You can't fake it, but neither can you really hide it. Every dimension of our earthly being is impacted by heaven's divine influence, and so much so that the hidden things of the spirit become manifest in the natural. For Jacob, it was a profound limp, indicating a God-encounter that had touched him in the most intimate and vulnerable place possible (Gen. 32:31). Jacob would never walk like everyone else again because he had been distinguished by heaven. For Moses, it was the glory of God and heavenly effulgence emanating from his earthly countenance (Ex. 34:29–30). Even though Moses tried to veil or cover his face, all Israel knew that he had seen God's glory and had spoken with Him face to face (Ex. 34:33–35).

An important interjection needs to be made at this point regarding Moses's behavior. Moses never went around trying to boastfully parade the evidence that he had seen or been with God. On the contrary, he tried to cover or hide it. Most preachers and self-proclaimed "prophets" today would have attempted to have this effulgent display captured on video and displayed for the world to see on every available platform and media outlet. The masses love to flock to phenomenon such as this, and it the quickest way to build a following or ministry. It is for this same reason that these ministers often boast about their alleged encounters with God. But when someone has truly seen or experienced God intimately, there is no longer any desire for boasting or publicity (2 Cor. 12:1–6). As a matter of fact, anyone can claim that they have seen or encountered God, but the evidence of an authentic and genuine God-encounter speaks for itself (as described above) and needs no vocal announcement. In other words, when someone has truly been with God, you'll know it without them having to tell you. And the evidence is not by their boastful testimony—which itself is a sure disqualifier—but by the deposit of heaven that is left behind and becomes manifested in their humanity.

Another profound result of this elevated dimension of spiritual sight we have described as face-to-face is the increased and elevated spiritual authority it imparts. You will remember that at the beginning of this chapter, we briefly examined Numbers 12:6–8 where Moses is identified as having greater rank and authority than the other prophets due to his elevated dimension of spiritual sight and face-to-face intimacy with God. We see this same principle in Jacob's encounter where he is given a name-change from *Jacob* ("Supplanter" or "One who seizes, supersedes or overthrows") to *Israel* ("Prince with God" or "He who strives with God"), indicating greater spiritual rank and authority. Jacob received a powerful spiritual upgrade after his encounter. As *Jacob,* he only had authority to prevail with men; but as *Israel,* he had authority to prevail with both man *and* God (Gen. 32:28).

The more elevated the dimension of our spiritual sight, the more elevated the dimension of spiritual rank and authority we will possess. This is why the third prophetic dimension will be characterized by face-to-face prophets who have ascended above the mediocrity of dreams and beyond the normalcy of visions to encounter and commune with God in the most intimate way possible. Their prophetic ministry will be infused with the spiritual rank and authority of heaven, thus enabling them to usher in Christ's return. Like the two prophetic witnesses in Revelation 11, it will be virtually impossible to determine whether or not their prophetic declarations or judgments are initiated by heaven or by the prophets themselves. Their ministry and authority, as it pertains to heaven, will be seamless and complete.

But what if God only chooses to speak with me through dreams or even visions? Wasn't it God who initiated both face-to-face encounters with Jacob and Moses? And if so, doesn't that prove that God communicates with us based upon His choosing and not ours? Not exactly! Somewhere in our earthly and human existence, we came to believe the religious lie that it is God alone who chooses or determines how we interact with Him (and vice versa). But the truth of the matter is that God loves *all* His people equally, and He has given us all equal access to His presence. This means that we must recognize the biblical tension between God's sovereignty and human responsibility.

Even though it is God who initiates this divine meeting or communication—it is God who pursued us long before we pursued Him—it is man who ultimately determines the spiritual dimension or degree of divine interface based upon his internal spiritual position and posture. In other words, God can only meet us on the level at which we are capable of interacting with Him, or according to the degree of our proximity. It is impossible for God to communicate with an unbeliever by a spiritual vision because they have no capacity to interface on that dimension since they are spiritually dead and estranged from God. The moment they become spiritually alive— born again—a new spiritual dimension is opened up to them that affords greater proximity to heaven, but that doesn't necessarily mean they will fully access it. Nothing in the Kingdom of God is automatic. You have to appropriate it by faith and pursue it with diligence. Jesus said, *"Blessed are those who hunger and thirst for righteousness, for they shall be filled"* (Matt. 5:6). The principle here, as alluded to before, is that we receive from God based upon our degree of hunger or internal dissatisfaction. It is hunger that drives pursuit. Therefore, if, as a believer, you regularly receive dreams as your most frequent form of divine communication and you have become satisfied (filled) or complacent with such an inferior dimension, that is what you will continue to receive. But if you are hungry, desperate, and deeply-dissatisfied with inferiority or mediocrity and desire to encounter or commune with God on the most elevated and intimate level through intentional, determined, and diligent pursuit, then heaven has promised to satisfy your hunger. Our hunger is never determined by God; it is determined by our heart condition. God only promised to "fill" or meet us at our point of desire. Therefore, it is man who ultimately determines the outcome through his hunger and pursuit.

Prophetic Restoration

Everything experienced and lost by Adam in the garden because of sin has been, is being, and will be progressively and prophetically restored to Christ's Covenant Kingdom Community through the obedience and sacrifice of the *last Adam* (1 Cor. 15:20–23, 45–49; Acts 3:20–21). Man was created to live, function, and thrive in an environment and dimension of close intimate communion with God and heaven as demonstrated by Adam before the fall. Heaven is actively engaged in restoring God's original order, and His third-dimension prophets are the primary human agents of this restoration. They are the forerunners. But before we go any further in explaining this principle, let's take another look at the three dimensions of spiritual sight and compare them side by side.

DREAMS	VISIONS	FACE TO FACE
• Images received while asleep	• To see or perceive while awake	• To communicate on the most intimate level
• Generally unclear	• Sometimes unclear	• Always clear
• God will speak (Num. 12:6)	• God will make Himself known (Num. 12:6)	• God will reveal His form (Num. 12:8)
• Impersonal	• Personal	• Intimate
• Common to all	• Common to some	• Common to few
• Old wineskin	• New wineskin	• Eternal wineskin
• Good	• Better	• Best
• Weak	• Strong	• Powerful
• Little authority	• More authority	• Greatest authority
• Pagan	• Covenant Community	• Kingdom
• Outer court	• Inner court	• Holy of Holies
• One-Dimensional (soul)	• Two-Dimensional (soul & spirit)	• Three-Dimensional (spirit, soul & body)

Notice the progression and increase in clarity, intimacy, and authority as one moves from dreams, to visions, then face-to-face. You will remember that when we first began this chapter, we discussed the natural degradation and deterioration of man's spiritual intimacy and divine communication with God as a result of the fall. We tracked this deterioration in stages as man's proximity to God and heaven became less and less, moving from face-to-face communication with God through the portal of heaven in Eden to visions and then dreams. By the time the prophet Malachi completes his ministry more than sixty-five generations after Adam, there is no open revelation and the voice of God is presumably silent, that is, until both Jesus and John enter the picture more than 400 years after Malachi.

As soon as the appointed time arrives for Jesus to make His earthly appearance, all of heaven begins to stir with a buzz. Suddenly heaven's silence is broken, and man begins to interface with God again. The New Testament begins, admittedly not necessarily chrono-logically, with dreams as the primary form of revelation (Matt. 1:20; 2:12, 13, 19, 22). But soon after these initial experiences by Joseph and the magi, dreams disappear almost entirely from the biblical record and is never mentioned again in the context of divine com-munication among God's Covenant Kingdom people. Instead, it is now visions that have become the primary method of divine inter-face (Matt. 17:9; Luke 1:22, 24:23; Acts 2:17, 9:10, 12, 10:3, 17, 19, 11:5, 12:9, 16:9, 10, 18:9, 26:19; 2 Cor. 12:1; Rev. 9:17).

Are you following the progression? Just as the first Adam's sin sent man into a downward spiral away from God and into lower and lower forms of divine communication, the last Adam's sacrifice has reversed that declension and is restoring what Adam lost. And the key earthly instrument in this restoration is the third prophetic dimension. Remember, John the Baptist represents the third pro-phetic dimension, and Jesus represents that same dimension, but in its fullness. It was not until that dimension was activated and released from heaven that the voice of God was heard in the earth again.

Both John's and Jesus's births were prophetically foretold through angelic visitations, indicating a powerful convergence was imminent between heaven and earth and these were going to be the two pri-mary participants (Luke 1:11–17; 26–33). God knew that before he could get a multitude of people to ascend in His presence—the place Adam had fallen from—He would need a forerunner(s) who had first experienced this kind of intimacy himself (themselves). This is what the third prophetic dimension brings, activates, and imparts until *we all, with unveiled face, beholding as in a mirror the glory of the Lord,* then see Him *face-to-face* (1 Cor. 13:12; 2 Cor. 3:18). It is our ulti-mate destination as Kingdom citizens to commune with God face-to-face, but it must begin and progress now if we are to ever arrive at the culmination (Rev. 21:2–3, 22:1–5).

Notes

1   Robert G. Paul, *The Technology of Prayer*, CreateSpace Independent Publishing Platform 1st Edition (November 18, 2013), 234–236.

2   Ibid.

3   Gordon J. Wenham, *Genesis 1–15*, vol. 1, Word Biblical Commentary (Dallas: Word, Incorporated, 1998), 108.

4   Samuel J. Schultz and Gary V. Smith, *Exploring the Old Testament* (Wheaton, IL: Crossway Books, 2001), 109.

5   Ronald F. Youngblood, F. F. Bruce, and R. K. Harrison, Thomas Nelson Publishers, eds., *Nelson's New Illustrated Bible Dictionary* (Nashville, TN: Thomas Nelson, Inc., 1995).

6   Walter A. Elwell and Barry J. Beitzel, *Baker Encyclopedia of the Bible* (Grand Rapids, MI: Baker Book House, 1988), 642.

7   J. G. S. S. Thomson and J. S. Wright, "Dream," ed. D. R. W. Wood et al., *New Bible Dictionary* (Leicester, England; Downers Grove, IL: InterVarsity Press, 1996), 281–282.

8   Walter A. Elwell and Barry J. Beitzel, *Baker Encyclopedia of the Bible* (Grand Rapids, MI: Baker Book House, 1988), 642.

9   Ibid.

10 Walter G. Clippinger, "Dream, Dreamer," ed. James Orr et al., *The International Standard Bible Encyclopaedia* (Chicago: The Howard-Severance Company, 1915), 875.

11 Walter A. Elwell and Barry J. Beitzel, *Baker Encyclopedia of the Bible* (Grand Rapids, MI: Baker Book House, 1988), 642.

12 Ronald D. Roberts, "Dream," ed. John D. Barry et al., *The Lexham Bible Dictionary* (Bellingham, WA: Lexham Press, 2012, 2013, 2014, 2015).

13 Daniel L. Smith-Christopher, "Dreams," ed. David Noel Freedman, Allen C. Myers, and Astrid B. Beck, *Eerdmans Dictionary of the Bible* (Grand Rapids, MI: W.B. Eerdmans, 2000), 356–357.

14 *International Standard Bible Encyclopedia*, revised edition, Copyright © 1979 by Wm. B. Eerdmans Publishing Co. [Biblesoft].

[15] Albert F. Bean, "Dreams," ed. Chad Brand et al., *Holman Illustrated Bible Dictionary* (Nashville, TN: Holman Bible Publishers, 2003), 442.

[16] Ronald D. Roberts, "Dream," ed. John D. Barry et al., *The Lexham Bible Dictionary* (Bellingham, WA: Lexham Press, 2012, 2013, 2014, 2015).

[17] Ibid.

[18] Walter A. Elwell and Barry J. Beitzel, *Baker Encyclopedia of the Bible* (Grand Rapids, MI: Baker Book House, 1988), 642.

[19] A good example of this principle of dream symbols being unique to the individual dreamer can be found in the biblical account regarding Gideon in Judges 7:13–15. In the dream related by the Midianite/Amalekite soldier to his companion, a *loaf of barley bread* and *tent* are identified in the interpretation as being symbolic of Gideon and the entire Midianite camp respectively. No dream book or dictionary of symbolism could have provided such an accurate interpretation when the symbolism was clearly unique and specific to the dreamer.

[20] Walter G. Clippinger, "Dream, Dreamer," ed. James Orr et al., *The International Standard Bible Encyclopaedia* (Chicago: The Howard-Severance Company, 1915), 875.

[21] Note that Saul (Paul) and Cornelius, though not born again according to Kingdom standards, received visions directly from God (as opposed to dreams) due to their fear of God and righteous adherence to His precepts (Acts 9:1–7 with Phil. 3:5–6; Acts 10:1–8). This placed them in closer proximity to receive visions.

[22] Walter G. Clippinger, "Dream, Dreamer," ed. James Orr et al., *The International Standard Bible Encyclopaedia* (Chicago: The Howard-Severance Company, 1915), 875.

[23] Daniel L. Smith-Christopher, "Dreams," ed. David Noel Freedman, Allen C. Myers, and Astrid B. Beck, *Eerdmans Dictionary of the Bible* (Grand Rapids, MI: W.B. Eerdmans, 2000), 357.

[24] Leland Ryken, Jim Wilhoit, et al., *Dictionary of Biblical Imagery* (Downers Grove, IL: InterVarsity Press, 2000), 605.

25   Note that it is not the old man or person you are called to reject, which is itself a violation of scriptural command, but the *old* principle of blindness, weakness, and impotence usually present in religion.

26   It is obvious that a literal interpretation of *young* and *old* does not apply in the text since the reception of visions and dreams are never determined or influenced by physical age. This is proven from practical experience.

27   Samuel Macauley Jackson, ed., *The New Schaff-Herzog Encyclopedia of Religious Knowledge: Embracing Biblical, Historical, Doctrinal, and Practical Theology and Biblical, Theological, and Ecclesiastical Biography from the Earliest Times to the Present Day* (New York; London: Funk & Wagnalls, 1908–1914), 3.

28   Albert F. Bean, "Dreams," ed. Chad Brand et al., *Holman Illustrated Bible Dictionary* (Nashville, TN: Holman Bible Publishers, 2003), 443.

29   J. H. Hunt, "Dreams," *Dictionary of the Old Testament: Pentateuch* (Downers Grove, IL: InterVarsity Press, 2003), 197.

30   Walter A. Elwell and Barry J. Beitzel, *Baker Encyclopedia of the Bible* (Grand Rapids, MI: Baker Book House, 1988), 2127.

31   Ibid.

32   James Newell, "Vision," ed. Chad Brand et al., *Holman Illustrated Bible Dictionary* (Nashville, TN: Holman Bible Publishers, 2003), 1654.

33   Ronald F. Youngblood, F. F. Bruce, and R. K. Harrison, Thomas Nelson Publishers, eds., *Nelson's New Illustrated Bible Dictionary* (Nashville, TN: Thomas Nelson, Inc., 1995).

34   Ibid.

35   William Arndt, Frederick W. Danker, and Walter Bauer, *A Greek-English Lexicon of the New Testament and Other Early Christian Literature* (Chicago: University of Chicago Press, 2000), 309.

36   Ralph P. Martin and Peter H. Davids, eds., *Dictionary of the Later New Testament and Its Developments* (Downers Grove, IL: InterVarsity Press, 1997), 1194.

37   Walter A. Elwell and Barry J. Beitzel, *Baker Encyclopedia of the Bible* (Grand Rapids, MI: Baker Book House, 1988), 2127.

38 Gerhard Kittel, Geoffrey W. Bromiley, and Gerhard Friedrich, eds., *Theological Dictionary of the New Testament* (Grand Rapids, MI: Eerdmans, 1964–), 449.

39 Ralph P. Martin and Peter H. Davids, eds., *Dictionary of the Later New Testament and Its Developments* (Downers Grove, IL: InterVarsity Press, 1997), 1195.

40 Ibid.

41 Ibid.

42 Ibid.

43 Walter A. Elwell and Barry J. Beitzel, *Baker Encyclopedia of the Bible* (Grand Rapids, MI: Baker Book House, 1988), 2127.

44 Ibid.

45 Walter A. Elwell and Walter A. Elwell, *Evangelical Dictionary of Biblical Theology*, Baker Reference Library (Grand Rapids: Baker Book House, 1996).

46 As noted before, an argument could be made for Saul (Paul) and Cornelius as possible exceptions; however, neither were "unbelievers" in the full sense of the word since they both feared God and endeavored to fulfill His righteous demands. In any event, they were both heirs of salvation. See previous note [21].

47 Darlene R. Gautsch, "Face," ed. Chad Brand et al., *Holman Illustrated Bible Dictionary* (Nashville, TN: Holman Bible Publishers, 2003), 546.

48 Ibid.

49 C. L. Seow, "Face," ed. Karel van der Toorn, Bob Becking, and Pieter W. van der Horst, *Dictionary of Deities and Demons in the Bible* (Leiden; Boston; Köln; Grand Rapids, MI; Cambridge: Brill; Eerdmans, 1999), 323.

50 Merrill C. Tenney, "John," in *The Expositor's Bible Commentary: John and Acts*, ed. Frank E. Gaebelein, vol. 9 (Grand Rapids, MI: Zondervan Publishing House, 1981), 34.

51 The fact that John declares emphatically that "*no one has seen God at any time*" while listing the only begotten Son—Jesus—as the only exception strongly implies that Adam did not see God in His fullness also since Adam was also a man (John 1:18).

52 A. R. Fausset, "Jabbok," *Fausset's Bible Dictionary*, Electronic Database, Copyright © 1998, 2003, 2006. All rights reserved [PC Study Bible © 2008, Biblesoft, Inc.].

53 Victor P. Hamilton, *The Book of Genesis, Chapters 18–50*, The New International Commentary on the Old Testament (Grand Rapids, MI: Wm. B. Eerdmans Publishing Co., 1995), 331.

54 John I. Durham, *Exodus*, vol. 3, Word Biblical Commentary (Dallas: Word, Incorporated, 1998), 58.

6

KEY DEFINING ISSUES OF THE PROPHETIC DIVERGENCE

NOW THAT WE have laid the foundation and have identified some of the major defining characteristics of the third prophetic dimension that is emerging in the earth—in the context of a redefined prophetic paradigm—it is time to focus our attention on some of the key defining issues that lie at the center of the current prophetic divergence. Some of these issues may have been briefly mentioned or touched on before in the previous chapters, but the emphasis here will be on the old prophetic order and the corrupt influences, practices, and architecture that exists therein.

Divination

Divination can be defined as "the [forbidden] art or practice that seeks to foresee or foretell [prophesy] future events or discover hidden knowledge."[1] There are numerous forms and methods of divination—far too many to mention in this writing—but at their core is the fundamental principle and practice of "deciphering and interpreting signs in which the future is believed to be read."[2] The following are just a few of the more common forms of divination practiced in religious Christendom today under the guise of the prophetic:

- *Aeromancy*—the prediction of future events through the observation of weather conditions.
- *Arithmancy*—divination by the use of numbers.
- *Astrapomancy*—divination by observing and interpreting lightning.
- *Astromancy (astrology)*—divination by observing and interpreting the stars.
- *Austromancy*—the prediction of events from observation of the winds or cloud formations.
- *Brontomancy*—divination by interpreting thunder or thunderstorms.
- *Bibliomancy*—divination by means of a book, especially the Bible, that is randomly opened (or cut) to some verse or passage.
- *Cledonomancy*—divination through interpreting random remarks, statements, or events.
- *Geomancy*—divination by interpreting geographic features or markings.
- *Gematria*—divination through numerology or by interpreting the numerical value of words based on their constituent letters.
- *Kabbalah*—a syncretism of various forms of divination (arithmancy, gematria, etc.) developed by Jewish Rabbis that often includes the mystical interpretation of the letters (or glyphs) found in the Hebrew alphabet.
- *Literomancy*—divination through the interpretation of letters.
- *Oneiromancy*—divination through the interpreting of dreams.

The various forms and methods of divination are so vast that just about anything in the realm of human existence could be interpreted as a sign (omen) from God, even the holy and sanctified.

At times, this hidden knowledge would be sought through darker means, including "communication with the dead, or the use of magical powers."[3] Divination, therefore, "can be said to involve the use of illicit means to seek information or direction normally hidden" from man.[4]

Using *Star Wars* (the movie) or George Lucas's terminology, if the prophetic is the "force," think of divination as the "dark side" of the "force." It is the counterfeit, corrupt, antithesis of an accurate (authentic) prophetic dimension. It is no wonder that very early in Israel's corporate existence as a Covenant Worshipping Community that God issued dire warnings against the syncretistic contamination of this false prophetic dimension.

> *You must not eat anything with the blood; you shall not practice divination, nor shall you interpret signs.* (Lev. 19:26, LEB)

> *There shall not be found among you one who makes his son or his daughter go through the fire, or one who practices divination, or an interpreter of signs, or an augur, or sorcerer, or one who casts magic spells, or one who consults a spirit of the dead, or spiritist, or one who inquires of the dead. For everyone doing these things is detestable to Yahweh, and because of these detestable things Yahweh your God is driving them out from before you. You must be blameless before Yahweh your God. For these nations that you are about to dispossess listen to interpreters of signs and to diviners, but Yahweh your God has not allowed you to do the same.* (Deut. 18:10–14, LEB)

There are a number of interesting observations to be made from the above scriptural prohibitions against the practice of divination. Firstly, this is the prophet Moses speaking (or writing) what God has decreed in heaven—a complete and total rejection of all forms of divination. And in doing so, God—through the mouth of his prophet,

Moses—employs one of the harshest and most severe expressions of divine disapproval found in Scripture, describing those who engage in this corrupt practice as *detestable* (repulsive, disgusting, or an abomination). It's interesting that almost every time this corrupt practice of divination is identified, exposed, challenged, or condemned within the corporate community of God's covenant people in Scripture, it is accomplished through a functional and authentic prophetic and/ or apostolic dimension (Lev. 19:26; Deut. 18:10–14; Isa. 2:6; 3:2; 44:25; Jer. 14:14, 27:9, 29:8; Ezek. 12:24, 13:6–9, 23, 21:21–34, 22:28; Mic. 3:6–11; Zech. 10:2; Acts 16:16–19).

In other words, it takes a functionally accurate apostolic-prophetic dimension to identify and expose a false or counterfeit one, especially in an apostate religious culture where these false and counterfeit expressions have become largely accepted.

Israel's dark roots

Divination or manticism was such a common and widespread religious practice throughout the ancient Near East and Israel's neighbors in particular that it wasn't very long before they systemically adopted and incorporated many of these corrupt practices into their own religious culture. Remember, Israel was practically birthed as a nation and spent well over 400 years in Egypt, one of the leading nations in the practice of various forms of divination. We know for a fact that they "succumbed to the influence of mantic so that it became widespread among them" by the "strong legal, deuteronomistic, and prophetic prohibitions against its practice" in Scripture.[5] Furthermore, historical evidence proves that "early Israelite culture was particularly influenced by Egyptian, Hittite, and Mesopotamian culture"—all leaders in the mantic arts. And so much so that "several Hebrew terms related to divination are linguistically related to terms in Egyptian, Hittite, and Akkadian."[6] What this means is that divination eventually became not just rooted, but *deeply* embedded within Israel's religious culture, and this occurred quite early in their existence.

Mosaics of zodiacs that have been discovered in synagogue remains suggest that some Jews of this time accepted astrology. The Dead Sea Scrolls also attest to the acceptance of astrology (Swartz, "Dead Sea Scrolls," 192). Jews of this period also devised a divination process using the breastpiece and/or ephod of the high priest, in which colors of the stones would glow in response to questions posed to the priest. (Josephus *Antiquities* 3,217; *t. Yoma* 73b)

While Talmudic rabbis recognized few legitimate divination options, many Jews nevertheless practiced multiple forms of divination and allowed for signs and omens. It seems Jews considered it improper to *ask* God for information, but permissible to *discern* divine information.[7]

The cultural and religious world in which the prophets labored was saturated with divination, but Yahweh's prophets put it in a negative light. They condemned it (Is 44:25; Zech 10:2; cf. Deut 18:10), associated it with false prophecy inside Israel (Jer 27:9; 29:8; Ezek 13:6–9, 17, 23; 22:28; Mic 3:5–7, 11), essentially equated it with lies and falsehood (*šeqer* [Jer 14:14]), and contrasted its futility with the power of Yahweh's *Spirit enabling the prophet to discern justly and declare Israel's sin (Mic 3:8). However, so deeply established was the evil of divination within God's people (2 Kings 17:17; 21:6; Is 2:6), that when the prophets pictured the collapse of society, it was specifically mentioned as part of the passing scene (Is 3:1–3; Mic 3:6). Diviners were even found in postexilic Israel (Zech 10:2).[8]

Do you see how systemic and entrenched divination became in both Israel and Judah? Even the sanctified and priestly garments given and appointed by God became items by which to divine by, sanctioned and perpetuated by the very priests. Divination become so common and normal in their religious experience that the average Jew could no longer differentiate mantic from prophetic, the same as it is today. Many believers today can easily recognize a psychic or occult practitioner because their methods are usually more distinguishable, and they generally function separate and outside of Christianity. But when similar forms of divination are dressed or paraded as Christian in traditional religious practice by leaders we have come to admire and respect, it becomes much more difficult to discern. The longer the corrupt practice continues and is accepted, the blinder we become until we begin to defend, perpetuate, or promote the practice as appointed or ordained by God. This is what happened to Israel, and it is why only a functionally accurate apostolic-prophetic dimension is capable of identifying and exposing this false counterfeit dimension after amaurosis has fully and corporately set in.

Divination versus the third prophetic dimension

Secondly, if you continue reading beyond verse 14 of Deuteronomy 18 until the end of the chapter, you will notice that the condemned practice of divination is juxtaposed and contrasted against an accurate prophetic dimension. But God doesn't stop there; He clarifies that the accurate prophetic dimension He is describing is not one that is common to their religious experience but one that is after the order of Moses (vs. 15, 18). Remember, Moses was a prophetic foreshadow of Jesus and the third prophetic dimension. In other words, this is a prophetic dimension that interfaces with God at the highest level and receives revelation (hidden knowledge, divine insight) from God face-to-face—*the third prophetic dimension!* This makes Moses's prophetic prohibition against divination even more relevant and applicable to us today. It also makes the contrast more profound. Whereas the mantic or diviner is able to access hidden knowledge independently of God through the interpretation of various signs (or other forms of divination), the prophetic dimension operates according to the foundational principles of intimacy and proximity, where revelation is a natural byproduct and is received directly from the source (God Himself).

Jesus's condemnation of seeking after signs

This is why Jesus—obviously demonstrating an awareness of the popularity of divination within the wider religious culture of His day—condemned the practice of seeking or following after signs, describing those who do so as *wicked and adulterous* (Matt 12:38–39, 16:4; Mark 8:12).[9] Some argue that Jesus was specifically referring to miraculous signs in these texts since, in other texts, He not only furnishes them with multiple signs of His second coming and the end of the age, but He also berates the Pharisees (and Sadducees) for being unable to discern the *signs of the times* (Matt. 16:2–3, 24:7, 29). This argument is baseless and invalid for at least two reasons:

1.   The request for a sign by these religious leaders was clearly not pertaining to miracles since Jesus had already performed numerous miracles in their presence (or publicly) by this time, including the miraculous multiplication of the loaves and fishes (Matt. 4:23–24, 9, 11:4–6, 12:9–14, 22–24, 14:15–21, 15:32–38). As a matter of fact, both the terminology ("sign from heaven") as well as the context make clear that what was being requested was not a miracle but a cosmic sign.[10] These blind leaders were essentially asking Jesus to predict a sign in the sky, reducing them to the level of astrologers or diviners.[11] Since the Pharisees and Sadducees represented the elite religious leadership of Israel composing the Sanhedrin, it is clear that the practice of divination was still deeply rooted and embedded within the Jewish religious culture, and its leadership in particular, when Jesus walked the earth. This is confirmed not only by their desire to see and interpret "signs in the heavens in order to determine and make known" whether Jesus was the promised Messiah and Son of God (astrology)[12]

but by their ability to predict weather patterns through the interpretation of signs in the sky—the divinatory precursor to the Western scientific method since divination in the Near East was not simply a mystical practice but "a process based upon empirical observation and cause/effect, practiced by trained specialists."[13] Thus Jesus's rebuke is not an endorsement of signs or the interpretation thereof but a sarcastic criticism of these blind sign-seekers' inability to perceive the explicit signs already before them that testified of Him.

2. There is a profound and fundamental difference between the prophetic and mantic (divination) as it pertains to signs. You may want to highlight this next statement since it is critical in distinguishing between the two. In manticism, signs are *sought* or identified in order to *interpret* (a hidden message); but in the prophetic, signs are *given* or produced in order to *confirm* (the message already proclaimed). In manticism, the sign *precedes* the message, but in the prophetic, the sign *follows* (after) the message. Thus, when Jesus prophesies His second coming and the end of the age, He identifies several clear signs *confirming* this event so that His disciples and followers would not be ignorant or unprepared. The signs were only intended to confirm Jesus's prophetic message, not to become the source of His message or something to be sought. This pattern of the prophetic message preceding the sign is consistent in all of Scripture without exception.[14] There is not a single record of a prophet seeking or identifying a sign in order to divine a message. That would be divination.

Debunking the myth of divine sanction

There are some Bible scholars and interpreters who make the unwise assertion that God permitted or sanctioned various aspects of divination, at least in Israel's early history and development, citing instances of Gideon's fleece (Judg. 6:36–40), the Urim and

Thummim (Ex. 28:30; Num. 27:21), dreams (Gen. 37:5–10), and the casting of lots (Prov. 16:33; Acts 1:26) as evidence. Some have even gone so far as "to characterize canonical prophecy as a type of divination."[15] However, in Gideon's case, he wasn't seeking a sign for knowledge or revelation but for miraculous confirmation of the already revealed will of God. He basically initiated the sign. Nevertheless, even if this was divination, we need to remember that this was a period of rank apostasy within the entire nation, Gideon included. Scripture never describes Gideon as righteous or holy like Noah or Job, only as *mighty* (Judg. 6:12). As a matter of fact, these apostate tendencies become more and more evident in Gideon's life as his story unfolds (Judg. 8:24–27).

In the case of the Urim and Thummim, these instruments were given by God to function as divine oracles (like the prophet), not instruments of divination. Contrary to the many inaccurate depictions of these devices as a pair of simple dice with yes/no answers—an obvious oversimplification and error since they provided much more than a simple yes/no answer, speaking very clear messages and providing strategic military direction when needed (2 Sam. 5:17–25), in addition to not speaking at all (impossible with a simple yes/no pair of dice) as in the case of Saul (1 Sam. 28:6)—no person alive knows for certain what these items were or exactly how they functioned. Biblical and historical records are also quite vague on the matter. And the words used to describe them are still etymologically obscure. In other words, no dice (pun intended)!

We've already discussed dreams in some detail, so no further comment is necessary. Sufficed to say that dreams only become a method of divination (oneiromancy) when the meaning or interpretation is sought through the analysis of dream symbols or when we pursue or seek to "incubate" them as a means of revelation.

There is a legitimate argument for the casting of lots to be classified as divinatory in nature; however, when one considers the fact that the practice was quite common in many of the nations of antiquity, not just as a form of divination but as a fair and impartial means of deciding important issues [e.g. dividing property (Num. 33:54, 34:13), appointing to office or function (1 Chron. 24:4–5; Acts.

1:26)] or passing fair judgment where the outcome was left totally up to God and there was no room or opportunity for human bias or error (Lev. 16:7–10; Josh. 7:14), we are left with a new outlook, especially as it pertains to how the casting of lots was used and practiced in Israel. It was no more divination than our modern-day coin toss or drawing where we pick a name out of the proverbial "hat" to select a winner. Furthermore, the fact that God not only condones but commands the practice means that it is distinct and separate from all forms of divination He has so explicitly condemned (Lev. 16:7–10; Num. 26:55–56, 33:54, 34:13, 36:2; Josh. 13:6, 14:2).

Even if we entertained the possibility of certain forms of divination being somehow permitted or sanctioned by God during the earlier stages of Israel's history—something the very theology of Scripture thoroughly contradicts—we would still have to contend with the historical context. Remember, Israel was a nation with an historical heritage—over four centuries worth—of Egyptian customs and culture, including divination (Gen. 44:5; 2 Sam. 7:23)! By the time Israel made her way out of Egypt through the miraculous deliverance of God and leadership of Moses, they were so steeped in the sinful practices of the Egyptians and estranged from God's presence that they had no capacity to hear or be led by God except through visible signs (Ex. 13:21; Ps. 78:14). But each stage of their journey toward spiritual and functional maturity, these outward signs decreased as a method of divine communication. By the time Israel crosses the Jordan River, there is no more mention of them being led or directed by a *cloud* by day or *pillar of fire* by night ever again. Their reliance upon outward signs to determine the mind of God diminishes. By the time we get to the New Testament, post Pentecost, with spiritual Israel, outward signs completely disappear in preference of the spiritual, internal guidance provided by the Holy Spirit. God will often accommodate Himself to our spiritual blindness, not because He is schizophrenic or changes His mind but because there is no other way to reach us except by communicating with us on our own (low) level. Notwithstanding, God's preference and intention is always on elevating us to His.

Divination can produce accurate information

In case you have yet to acknowledge the obvious, divination works! Scripture never argues its *inability*, only its *illegitimacy*. You will find that "the assumption in early Old Testament books is not that these means were not successful, but that they were not permissible to Israel."[16] There are a number of scriptural examples where divination was employed quite successfully. For example:

1. Balaam, who is explicitly described in scripture not as a prophet but a *soothsayer* (NKJV) or one *who practiced divination* (ESV), was quite effective in his manticism and so much so that he is credited with delivering the only messianic prophecy in the entire book of Numbers (Num. 22–24; Josh. 13:22). Not only was he able to divine accurately, but his words came to pass (Num. 22:6).

2. The Philistine priests and diviners were able to accurately divine the correct means and method for sending the ark of God back to Israel in order to avert a deadly crisis of a plague in their nation (1 Sam. 6:1–18).

3. A witch or *medium*, through the divinatory dark practice of necromancy, was able to see and communicate with the long-dead prophet Samuel and divine a very accurate message from God, even predicting the death of Saul and his sons, as well as the defeat of Israel's army at the hands of the Philistines (1 Sam. 28:7–19).

4. Magi (astrologers, diviners) were able to, through the accurate interpretation of the stars (astromancy), determine that the *King of the Jews* had been born and identify His exact location, something which none of the religious leaders in Israel who were "experts" in messianic prophecy and the scriptures were able to do (Matt. 2:1–12).

5. A slave girl during the time of Paul was quite accurate and successful in her divinatory declarations and mantic predictions. The fact that she brought her masters *much profit* indicates that she was quite effective in her craft and

that her messages were either factually true or came to pass (Acts 16:16–19).

It's worth mentioning that, at least in the case of the slave girl during the time of Paul, a *spirit of divination* is identified as the true spiritual agent or source behind the practice (Acts 16:16). All divination—regardless of how natural, innocent, or religious it may appear—is spiritual in nature. This means that even though the information may be accurate and your intent may be sincere and genuine with regard to the desire to honor and worship God (e.g. the magi), you are still engaging in spiritual adultery because there is an unclean spirit at the source.

We also need to recognize that when *false* prophecy is identified or associated with divination (the Heb root for divination, *qsm*, is never used of true prophets) in Scripture[17]—both essentially functioning within the same worldview[18]—it does not necessarily imply that the prophecy was inaccurate based on its information or details (though it often is), but that it emanated from a forbidden frequency (or source) and not the Spirit (or mouth) of God (Is. 44:25; Jer. 14:14, 27:9, 29:8; Ezek. 13:6–9, 22:28; Mic. 3:5–7, 11).

Many believers today make the mistake of believing that if a word is true, it must be God. But as we have proven above, divination can produce a "true" word just like the prophetic can. The only difference is that while divination can only produce accurate facts, the prophetic produces what no counterfeit can—an accurate spirit (truth)!

DIVINATION/MANTIC	PROPHETIC
• Prohibited	• Permitted
• Counterfeit	• Genuine
• Based upon human inquiry	• Based upon spiritual intimacy
• Seeks signs to interpret	• Produces signs to confirm
• Follow signs	• Signs follow
• Produces seekers of signs	• Produces seekers of God
• Perpetuates blindness	• Imparts sight
• Imparts knowledge (accurate facts)	• Imparts truth (accurate spirit)
• Exalts man (esp. the mantic)	• Exalts God
• Spirit of divination	• Holy Spirit

The Issachar Deception

The most common method of divination, both historically and present-day, is the practice of observing times or omens. "Omen-reading was a major occupation of the learned throughout ancient Mesopotamian civilization,"[19] and it is one of the primary reasons why nations such as Egypt and Babylon kept wise men (magicians), astrologers, and diviners in their courts as part of their political or executive council (Gen 41:8; 24; Ex 7:11, 22, 8:7, 18–19, 9:11; Dan 1:20, 2:2, 27, 4:7, 9, 5:11).

The ancient Mesopotamians believed that natural events could be read or interpreted as omens, and that all things in the cosmos were interrelated.[20] Of course, there is some truth to this belief that "terrestrial events are but shadows of the celestial realities."[21] We know there is truth because the New Testament records and connects certain earthly signs with the occurrence of certain spiritual or significant events.[22] We have examples of earthquakes occurring in conjunction with the *veil of the temple* being rent upon completion of Jesus's ultimate sacrifice (Matt. 27:51–54), when an angel from heaven descended and rolled back the stone from Jesus's tomb (Matt. 28:2), and after powerful corporate prayer and praise (Acts 4:31, 16:26). Celestial examples are the star in the heavens during Jesus's birth (Matt. 2:2) and the darkening of the heavens (solar eclipse) at midday during Jesus's crucifixion (Matt 27:45).[23] All creation operates on the fundamental principle that everything in the spiritual or invisible realm finds an outward expression in the visible or natural realm (Rom. 1:20). What this means is that natural phenomena can very often be a reflection or indicator of spiritual reality, thus making it a fairly reliable source of hidden knowledge. There's just one key issue: Seeking to access such knowledge is a forbidden and condemned practice that violates the very nature and architecture of God's Kingdom!

In the old prophetic order, this prohibition was never observed. As the religious usually do whenever there is any kind of spiritual injunction or command we are inclined to ignore, justification was sought for the continued practice in the usual way such justification is sought—scripture (usually taken out of context). Enter the doctrine of Issachar.

The doctrine of Issachar, based upon a single and obscure text, basically teaches that the biblical tribe of Issachar was a "prophetic" company that was naturally gifted by God with the ability "to understand or interpret times (or omens/signs)"—the very definition of a *soothsayer* ("observer of times") according to scripture (Deut. 18:10).[24] It is a commonly held belief in many "prophetic" circles today that this "Issachar anointing" is present and active in God's present-day "prophetic" people. Based upon this erroneous and ungodly belief, the ancient practice of interpreting times or signs should not be interpreted as divination at all but as a spiritual and godly manifestation of the "Issachar" anointing, especially when the messenger involved is a recognized and respected prophet. As such, it is now widely accepted and practiced as part of the established prophetic movement.

For example, several years ago, when I was still subscribed to certain so-called "prophetic" e-mail lists, I received an e-mail with a prophecy from one of the most recognized leaders in the prophetic movement. This leader proceeded to take the measurements of the massive earthquakes that had recently rocked both Haiti and the South American nation of Chile, apply numerological significance to the numbers, and then use it to provide the basis for the "prophetic" (or rather, mantic) proclamations that followed. I heard another key leader in the movement prophesy right after the occurrence of the unusual phenomenon of record-breaking snowfall in the US (with snowfall in all fifty states) that it was a sign (omen) from God of blessing and purification for the nation. Prophetic? Not at all! Mantic? Absolutely! And if, at this point, you are still unable to tell the difference, you need to stop right here and start over this chapter from the beginning.

Another example of soothsaying (divination) being masqueraded as an "Issachar" dimension in the prophetic movement today is the practice of taking the numbers of the calendar year—either Gregorian or Hebrew—and making "prophetic" pronouncements based upon the numerological or symbolic significance of the numbers. If there is no apparent significance in the symbolism of the numbers as they stand, then a form of math (arithmancy) is employed to break them down into smaller, more recognizably significant numbers. Thus, if the year was 2020, you would probably hear many prophecies for that year declaring it to be a year of "increased spiritual sight" or "greater discernment" or even "open visions" due to the repeated number 20 (for 20/20 vision). If it was the year 2018, some pseudo-prophets, due to the fact that there is no apparent significance in the numbers 20 or 18 as they stand, would break them down to 10x2 and 9x2 before prophesying something along the lines of it being the year of the "Holy Spirit double-portion" (9x2) and the year of "testing or judgment" (10x2). Or they may choose to ignore all but the last number and prophesy something along the lines of that number's symbolism.

I have even known some in the movement who have gone so far as to search out scriptures with the chapter and verse corresponding to the number of the new year as part of their "prophetic" message concerning what God is doing or getting ready to do in that season. Others, who ascribe more to the Hebrew or Jewish calendar, have chosen to employ Kabbalistic divinatory methods whereby the Hebrew letters, numbers, or symbols are interpreted in a mystical fashion as a means of divining knowledge for the new year. Even if we choose to ignore the fact that these practices are totally absent from the prophetic activity recorded in Scripture—prophets never prophesied based on earthly cycles, seasons or calendars (there was no "word of the Lord" for the year); neither did they prophesy by using numbers or any other inductive method, including applying any special or mystical significance to the numerical value of the calendar year—we cannot ignore the fact that these practices are closely associated with occult activity and often employed by witches, new-agers, and various other occult practitioners as a means of extracting hidden knowledge.

1 Chronicles 12:32 debunked

Let's return to the subject of Issachar for a moment and take a closer look at the scriptural text used to erroneously justify and legitimize the use of divination in the current movement.

> *Of the sons of Issachar who had understanding of the times, to know what Israel ought to do, their chiefs were two hundred; and all their brethren were at their command.* (1 Chron. 12:32)

This obscure verse occurs within the context of a key period of transition for the nation, the leadership of Saul being replaced by the leadership of David over the kingdom. Tribal warriors who were once loyal to Saul have now pledged their loyalty and support to David, enlisting in his army.

There are basically two ways that this text can be interpreted, but only one of them is correct. The first way stems from Jewish oral tradition (the Targum) and interprets the clause *had understanding of the times* to mean "observer of times" or "skilled in astrology."

> Of the 200 "heads" of the men of Issachar who came to David at Hebron, it is said that they were "men that had understanding of the times, to know what Israel ought to do" (1 Ch 12:32). According to the Tg, this meant that they knew how to ascertain the periods of the sun and

moon, the intercalation of months, the dates of
solemn feasts, and could interpret the signs of the
times.[25]

Based upon the Jewish interpretation above, these sons (men)
of Issachar were nothing more than diviners or soothsayers who were
skilled in interpreting times (including signs and omens). Considering
what we have already discovered regarding Israel's history with divination and how deeply entrenched it became as part of the nation's
identity and religious culture, including the established religious
leadership represented by the Sanhedrin during the time of Jesus, it
is easy to see how such an interpretation came about and why it was
largely accepted. Nevertheless, it is completely wrong—including the
doctrine that proceeds from it—for the following reasons:

1. The reference to the sons of Issachar being able to under-
    stand the times—whatever that may mean—is applied
    specifically (or at best) to the two hundred chiefs (lead-
    ers) and not to the entire tribe as a whole. During the
    time of David, the male warriors of the tribe are recorded
    as numbering 87,000 (1 Chron. 7:5). This means that
    the actual percentage of the tribe who demonstrated this
    understanding or discernment was less than 0.25 percent
    (or 1/400 men). Realistically, this would have been more
    like 0.001 percent (or 1/1000 Issacharites) if we took into
    account the old, women, and children. It would require a
    major stretch of one's imagination to assume that this was
    a major or defining characteristic of the tribe of Issachar.
    Quite frankly, it's ludicrous! You cannot define the many
    based on the experiences of a few.

2. There is no evidence of any inherent prophetic or even
    mantic predisposition in the tribe of Issachar, neither
    from Scripture nor historical records. You would be hard-
    pressed to name even one prophet in Scripture who was a
    member of this tribe. If this was some special spiritual gift
    or ability as some claim, members of the tribe of Issachar

would have been at the forefront of the prophetic dimension in Scripture, but they're not. Their participation is almost nonexistent. And their participation or involvement with divination was no greater than any of the other tribes. Furthermore, the spiritual gifts and graces given by God are never determined by ethnicity, genealogy, or earthly pedigree. Therefore, without the witness and confirmation of at least two or three scriptures, you cannot form a doctrine, especially not from a singular obscure text like the one being examined (2 Cor. 13:1).

3. God is not schizophrenic; He will not condemn or prohibit a practice and then turn around and contradict Himself by endorsing it. The activities described in the Targum and attributed to the sons of Issachar are unquestionably divinatory in nature. Ascertaining "the periods of the sun and moon" etc., is not astronomy, as a few Bible commentators erroneously assume. How could one's understanding of astronomy possibly be related to a political decision to transfer allegiance from Saul to David unless astrology or astromancy is being strongly implied?

The second interpretation, and by far the most accurate, deals with this controversial clause ("had understanding of the times") in a manner in which the context is allowed to determine the author's intent—as pertaining solely to the current political climate and affairs of the nation and not as an inherent characteristic or ability of the tribe. This view is held by most reputable scholars.

> The perceptive reading of the times by the Issacharites implies that there was one thing Israel should do—rally to the cause of David at Hebron. This is therefore an ideological comment, not reflecting any specific information about the tribe of Issachar. Comments about the characteristics of Issachar in other biblical contexts have no relationship to this saying.[26]

> The statement in question, therefore, affirms nothing more than that the tribe of Issachar (in deciding to raise David to the throne) followed the judgment of its princes, who rightly estimated the circumstances of the time.[27]

This means that the entire concept (doctrine) of an "Issachar" anointing is based upon a lie. It simply doesn't exist, at least not in the prophetic. The moment you attempt to align yourself with this false doctrine and practice, seeking to observe and interpret times (including signs or omens), you are no longer operating by the Spirit of God but by the spirit of divination. There are recognized and respected leaders in the current prophetic movement who may tell you otherwise, but you must let Scripture be the judge. Contrary to what these leaders claim, God never intended for man to receive hidden knowledge or revelation from the signs in the sky or from the observation of the sun, moon, or stars. And when God said, *"Let there be lights in the firmament of the heavens to divide the day from the night; and let them be for signs and seasons, and for days and years;"* He never intended for it to be interpreted in a divinatory fashion (Gen. 1:14). The *signs and seasons* these celestial light bearers were intended to convey and be understood by man are relative to his earthly existence and not God's spiritual intent. In other words, the *lights in the firmament* serve a threefold natural purpose according to scripture: "to separate between day and night, to serve as signs of the passage of time, and to illuminate the earth."[28] Any other interpretation is simply fanciful and unfounded, if not of pagan religious origin.[29]

Times and Seasons: Natural Versus Spiritual

God has never limited Himself or His dealings with man to our earthly calendars and seasons, though I would be the first to acknowledge that Israel's religious festivals often foreshadowed and intersected with a greater spiritual reality. Nevertheless, whereas we on earth may think in terms of days, weeks, months, or years, God thinks in terms much different from ours. Seasons for God consist of periods in eternity, not limited to our earthly measurements of time, wherein God has determined to fulfill a particular purpose. When we limit God to our present earthly timetables, we either totally miss God or fail to accurately position ourselves for Him. For example, entering a new calendar year does not necessarily mean that you have entered a new spiritual season. God may have nothing new to say at the beginning of a new year because He has not yet received the required obedience to His previous pronouncements necessary for transition into a new season. Even if He did receive the required obedience necessary for a spiritual transition, it is doubtful He would wait until the clock struck 12:00 a.m. on January 1 (Gregorian/Western calendar) or the beginning of Rosh Hashanah (Hebrew Calendar) to activate this new season. If He did, there would be evidence of such in Scripture, but there isn't. There is no recorded prophetic utterance after the book of Malachi for more than 400 years because despite the fact that the nation of Israel may have physically celebrated over 400 times the beginning of a new year, they had still not entered into a new spiritual season. And when that new spiritual season finally arrived, it wasn't at the start of the new year (Gregorian or Hebrew).

As prophets and prophetic people—especially those of us who are of the third prophetic dimension—we do not determine spiritual times and seasons by outward signs and manifestations or by the observation of earthly clocks and calendars or by the natural passage of time. We are supernaturally activated into this understanding through an internal time clock generated within us by the Spirit of God. We are ministers of the Spirit and not of the flesh; therefore, our wisdom is generated from an internal spiritual dimension or frequency and not through the observation or analysis of certain earthly signs or trends. This does not mean that we totally ignore them by burying our heads in the sand of our religious enclaves or by not keeping abreast of current world events. Rather, it means that we have chosen to tap into a much more elevated and refined frequency that is far more accurate and dependable, and which alone fuels our prophetic pronouncements. Otherwise, we are no better than pagans and the *foolish Galatians* who chose to *observe days and months and seasons and years,* which, according to one Bible scholar, describes

"the intricacies of calendar observation, that is, the constant preoccupation with idle questions as to what day, month, season, or year
it is, and what that has to say about what one should or should not
do" (Gal. 3:1; 4:10).[30]

Examining the Source

It has never been God's desire for man to remain ignorant, but
it has also never been His desire for man to access knowledge from
any other source than Him—directly from His mouth and not from
His creation. God is just as concerned about what you know as He
is about how you came to know it, and it matters very little whether
or not the information you received (from outside sources) is in fact
true. In other words, the point is not whether or not the observation
of times, signs, or omens is able to communicate accurate knowledge
or information, but it is about the source you used to obtain that
information.

When God made man, placed him in the garden with *the tree
of the knowledge of good and evil* in the midst of it, and then commanded him not to eat of it, He was not trying to deny Adam the
knowledge he had already been granted access to (Gen. 2:15–17).
The idea that God was intentionally trying to deny man knowledge
and insight came from satan (Gen. 3:4–5). God's prohibition against
eating from the tree was for man's own protection. Eating of it would
cause death and separation from God. The source of your knowledge
becomes the source of your life [or death] (Matt. 4:4). It's like performing spiritual intercourse or adultery.

There was nothing inherently wrong with the tree; God was
the one who created it and planted it in the garden. The knowledge
produced by eating of its fruit was also true and accurate, which
means the accuracy of the knowledge this tree produced was never
the issue. The only issue to be considered is the fact that it violated
the command of God and created an impenetrable barrier that kept
man from experiencing the fullness of God in the way He had originally intended. You may be able to gain true insight by eating of

the "forbidden fruit" (i.e., observing times, signs, or omens), but it perpetuates a system of death and separation.

One of the most poignant and thought-provoking scriptural comparisons regarding the source of revelation can be found in the sixteenth chapter of Matthew.

Then the Pharisees and Sadducees came, and testing Him asked that He would show them a sign from heaven. He answered and said to them, "When it is evening you say, 'It will be fair weather, for the sky is red'; and in the morning, 'It will be foul weather today, for the sky is red and threatening.' Hypocrites! You know how to discern the face of the sky, but you cannot discern the signs of the times. A wicked and adulterous generation seeks after a sign, and no sign shall be given to it except the sign of the prophet Jonah." And He left them and departed. (Matt. 16:1–4)

When Jesus came into the region of Caesarea Philippi, He asked His disciples, saying, "Who do men say that I, the Son of Man, am?" So they said, "Some say John the Baptist, some Elijah, and others Jeremiah or one of the prophets." He said to them, "But who do you say that I am?" Simon Peter answered and said, "You are the Christ, the Son of the living God." Jesus answered and said to him, "Blessed are you, Simon Bar-Jonah, for flesh and blood has not revealed this to you, but My Father who is in heaven." (Matt. 16:13–17)

You may recall that a bit earlier in this chapter we briefly tackled this issue of the Pharisees and Sadducees desiring a celestial sign from Jesus due to their own familiarity and involvement with the practice of divination. We won't take the time to rehash the same points or principles here except to say that Jesus uses some of His strongest and most cutting language—*wicked and adulterous*—to condemn this false religious practice of seeking after signs (v. 4).[31]

Following soon after this encounter with the Pharisees and Sadducees is the often-preached record of Peter's confession. The fundamental issue and question being asked is essentially the same as with the religious leaders (Pharisees and Sadducees) earlier and pertains to Jesus's true identity. But notice the drastic difference in Jesus's response. Instead of a scathing rebuke and condemnation, Peter is commended and *blessed* by Jesus for his response. Did Jesus's attitude and tone change so significantly on account of Peter being His close friend and disciple? Or was it on account of Jesus being in a far better mood? Neither! Peter was commended and blessed because, unlike the Pharisees and Sadducees, he received revelation and insight regarding Jesus's true identity directly from the mouth of the Father. He wasn't trusting in keen observation or the manifestation of signs. The word *heaven* in the text implies that the knowledge Peter received originated from the highest spiritual frequency—through a direct spiritual interface with the Father—as opposed to human, physical or earthly origin or agency (*flesh and blood*). The source of our revelation matters!

We must become convinced of God's desire to communicate with us intimately and directly, as discussed in the previous chapter. To believe that we cannot constantly and effortlessly interface and communicate with God in a manner or dimension similar to what Adam experienced before the fall is to dismiss Jesus's life example and diminish His redemptive work on the cross. And to postpone for tomorrow what God has given us access to today is to restrict ourselves to religious bondage. As the late Myles Munroe once wrote, "You cannot appropriate what you don't understand nor experience what you postpone."

Like the prophet Elijah, we must learn to magnify the voice of the Lord above every other voice or source of revelation. When there were great signs of wind, earthquake, and fire, he didn't allow himself to become distracted by seeking to find God in the midst of the manifestations.

Then He said, "Go out, and stand on the mountain before the Lord." And behold, the Lord passed by, and a great and strong wind tore into the mountains and broke the rocks in pieces before the Lord, **but the Lord was not in the wind;** *and after the wind an earthquake,* **but the Lord was not in the earthquake;** *and after the earthquake a fire,* **but the Lord was not in the fire;** *and after the fire a still small voice. So it was, when Elijah heard it, that he wrapped his face in his mantle and went out and stood in the entrance of the cave. Suddenly a voice came to him, and said, "What are you doing here, Elijah?"* (1 Kings 19:11–13)

Elijah refused to move until he heard God's *still small voice.* What a testimony! With all the shaking and quaking, blowing and burning, Elijah had determined that he would not be distracted by physical signs and manifestations because **the Lord was NOT in them**. Had Elijah gone after the signs, he would have totally missed God!

The third prophetic dimension is comprised of a like-minded prophetic people who have adopted a similar posture in refusing to move, act, or speak until they have heard not from a sign but from the mouth of the Lord God Himself.

Nationalism and Misplaced Loyalty

The word *nationalism* can be defined as "loyalty and devotion to a nation," especially in the sense of a national consciousness whereby one nation is exalted above all others and primary emphasis is placed on the "promotion of its culture and interests."[32] You will notice that the very first word in this definition is the word *loyalty*, which describes an unswerving commitment or allegiance to a cause, country, group, or person. This means that, at its core, nationalism is an issue of loyalty. It is also an indication of where one's true allegiance lies.

Prophets are loyal to God

Prophets of God are uncompromisingly loyal. As a matter of fact, they epitomize loyalty through their willingness to endure—often for long periods of time—intense suffering, persecution, rejection, or even death (Jam. 5:10). In case the object of their loyalty is not immediately obvious, prophets are loyal to God...period! Their loyalty is both singular as well as absolute. This means that they're not divided, double-minded, or unstable. It means that their allegiance lies solely (as well as completely) with God and that their loyalty to Him supersedes all others—including family, friends, leaders, ministry, church, network, or nation. This is a biblical concept that many religious leaders today have had difficulty understanding or accepting. They want loyal followers (including prophets) that are faithful to them and their vision. But true prophets are first and foremost *prophets of God*, not "prophets of America" or "prophets of [insert church, ministry or network name here]." Does this make them difficult to control? Absolutely! Why else do you think the prophets of old were persecuted and killed by their own countrymen—including kings and religious leaders—as political and religious rebels (Matt. 23:34, 37; Luke 11:47–49; Acts 7:52)? Any so-called "prophetic" dimension you are able to totally manipulate or control is, in fact, not prophetic but a false fatidic counterfeit.

An accurate prophetic dimension, therefore, is never nationalistic, because it is singular in its loyalty and allegiance to God. It is never blinded by personal, national, or religious interests, and it will never compromise God's truth for man's approval or applause. However, Scripture is replete with numerous examples of nationalism and misguided loyalty demonstrated by a false or counterfeit prophetic order.

Micaiah versus Chenaanah and the 400

> *Now three years passed without war between Syria*
> *and Israel. Then it came to pass, in the third year,*
> *that Jehoshaphat the king of Judah went down to*

visit the king of Israel. And the king of Israel said to his servants, "Do you know that Ramoth in Gilead is ours, but we hesitate to take it out of the hand of the king of Syria?" So he said to Jehoshaphat, "Will you go with me to fight at Ramoth Gilead?" Jehoshaphat said to the king of Israel, "I am as you are, my people as your people, my horses as your horses." Also Jehoshaphat said to the king of Israel, "Please inquire for the word of the Lord today." Then the king of Israel gathered the prophets together, about four hundred men, and said to them, "Shall I go against Ramoth Gilead to fight, or shall I refrain?" So they said, "Go up, for the Lord will deliver it into the hand of the king." And Jehoshaphat said, "Is there not still a prophet of the Lord here, that we may inquire of Him?" So the king of Israel said to Jehoshaphat, "There is still one man, Micaiah the son of Imlah, by whom we may inquire of the Lord; but I hate him, because he does not prophesy good concerning me, but evil." And Jehoshaphat said, "Let not the king say such things!" Then the king of Israel called an officer and said, "Bring Micaiah the son of Imlah quickly!" The king of Israel and Jehoshaphat the king of Judah, having put on their robes, sat each on his throne, at a threshing floor at the entrance of the gate of Samaria; and all the prophets prophesied before them. Now Zedekiah the son of Chenaanah had made horns of iron for himself; and he said, "Thus says the Lord: 'With these you shall gore the Syrians until they are destroyed.'" And all the prophets prophesied so, saying, "Go up to Ramoth Gilead and prosper, for the Lord will deliver it into the king's hand." Then the messenger who had gone to call Micaiah spoke to him, saying, "Now listen, the words of the prophets with one accord encourage the king. Please, let your word be

like the word of one of them, and speak encourage-
ment." And Micaiah said, "As the Lord lives, what-
ever the Lord says to me, that I will speak." (1 Kings
22:1–14)

In this first example, we see a clear prophetic divergence and distinction between an accurate prophetic dimension, represented by the prophet Micaiah, and a false or counterfeit prophetic order, represented by Chenaanah and the rest of the four hundred prophets. One (true) prophet is singular in his loyalty, devotion, and commitment to God, while the others (false prophets) demonstrate divided or misguided loyalties to a nation and/or its leader.

You will notice in verse 3 that Ahab's stated purpose and motivation for this military campaign against Syria appears correct, honorable, and noble. His desire was to reclaim lost territory that rightly belonged to Israel and "make the nation great again" (my paraphrase). Any Hebrew citizen who loved their country would want to rally to such a cause. And in such a context, it would be natural for an Israeli to want to prophesy success to such a military campaign. However, the prophetic dimension doesn't operate according to natural or human principles; it operates supernaturally, by more elevated and heavenly principles, through the Spirit of God. Even though it made Micaiah appear disloyal and unpatriotic, he was able to prophesy accurately because his singular loyalty to God enabled him to see beyond his own national or religious self-interests to apprehend the true mind of God for the situation. He was able to see that Israel's trajectory was one of decline (including military defeat) and not expansion, which is something the four hundred prophets were unable to do because they were blinded by their own misplaced or misguided loyalties.

It's interesting to note that even though this company of false prophets vastly outnumbered Micaiah 400:1, they were still incorrect. In an earlier account, a few chapters prior to the one we are currently examining, Elijah had issued a lone challenge to another group of false prophets numbering more than twice the amount stated here (1 Kings 18:19). It is highly probable that these four hundred prophets of Ahab were part of that very same company—the four hundred prophets of Asherah—who were apparently absent from the contest. Whatever the case may be, what we know for certain is that these were not true prophets of God. Even though the text and multiple Hebrew manuscripts (including Aramaic translations) have God's personal name, Yahweh, being invoked by these prophets, "most manuscripts read *adonay*, meaning 'lord'—a generic term that can be applied to any master, whether human or divine."[33] Also, the fact that Jehoshaphat, obviously suspicious and distrusting of these prophets' ministry, specifically requests a *prophet of the Lord [Yahweh]*, argues that these four hundred prophets were not true prophets of God (v. 7). Nevertheless, the key takeaway here is that truth is not necessarily found in the majority. As a matter of fact, it is possible for one person (or prophet) to be right or correct and everyone else to be wrong. This is evident from the text. When Micaiah boldly declared that **all** (v. 23) of the other prophets were prophesying by a lying spirit, he was, in effect, saying that he was the only true prophet (in the current context). Or, to paraphrase, "Everyone else here is deceived and in error, not me!" This statement may have caused him to appear arrogant, superior (elite), and separate (exclusive), but it represented the spirit of reformation and correctness in the midst of apostasy and error. You don't judge something (or someone) as false simply because it's unique, divergent, unpopular, or unconventional.

Nationalism is not only popular, but it is also an accepted norm. So is immorality, compromise, and sin. The point is that you cannot judge truth simply on the merit of popularity or acceptance. To do so is to encourage and perpetuate error. A false prophetic order thrives in such an environment because false prophecy is based upon self-promotion and flattery—telling people exactly what they want to hear. The desire for recognition and acceptance is what fuels a false prophet's ministry endeavors, and their loyalty usually lies in whoever (or whatever) serves their own self-interests. In the case of the four hundred, their loyalty was unquestionably to Ahab, which is why they are twice described as Ahab's prophets (vs. 22–23). As such, they were more concerned about protecting and/or maintaining their status, positions, ministry credentials, or salaries than receiving a true word from God that would possibly contradict their leader and thus reflect badly on them. But Micaiah was different. Unlike the four hundred prophets who had emerged from a place of recognition, prominence, and acceptance in the king's court, Micaiah emerged from a place of obscurity and rejection, having been imprisoned, cast aside, and overlooked by Ahab. He was only invited at Jehoshaphat's request. Yet his lack of popularity and acceptance never diminished or compromised the accuracy, authenticity, or credibility of his ministry. The temptation to speak words the king wanted to hear and join the unanimous chorus of the false prophets would have been even greater than the four hundred, yet he never succumbed. Regardless of if the ratio was 400,000:1, truth must be judged on its own merit and not on the merit of majority acceptance.

It's worth mentioning also that Micaiah was hated simply because he never seemed to prophesy anything *good* to the king (v. 8). This word translated as *good* here is the Hebrew word *ṭôb*, meaning *pleasant, desirable,* or *pleasing*.[34] It is employed at least two other times in this pericope and translated as *encourage* and *encouragement* respectively (v. 13). Whenever a particular word or phrase is used more than once in the same verse or text, it is usually a good idea to take notice because it suggests that something important is being emphasized. Ahab rejected and aggressively opposed any prophetic dimension wherein prophecy was not limited or confined to that which was "pleasant, desirable or pleasing" to the ear, and he created a religious environment where only prophets with words of "blessing" and "encouragement" were able to thrive. Sound familiar? It should since we dedicated almost an entire chapter (chapter 4) to debunking the commonly held misconceptions relative to *edification, exhortation, and comfort*; and Ahab's negative attitude toward an accurate prophetic dimension is very common, even in so-called "prophetic" circles today.

Ahab essentially created a religious culture of compromise, thus making it extremely difficult for the true and accurate voice of God to emerge. Every one of his prophets were unified in error; however, they remained blinded to this error through what they considered as noble—their unity and loyalty to king and country. Have you ever stopped to wonder just how it was that a single spirit was able to persuade and deceive an entire company of four hundred prophets? Simple, he influenced their leader, who was clearly Zedekiah, the son of Chenaanah. All of the other prophets followed his lead as a unified whole. Coupled with their unquestioning loyalty to the established leadership, it was easy to put a hook in the jaw of all four hundred prophets. Does this mean that we shouldn't be unified or loyal to leaders? Of course not! It means that both our unity and our loyalty must be submitted to God. We are only truly unified in Christ when we are fully joined and connected to the head—Christ! Any other unity, as far as the Kingdom of God is concerned, it superficial and vain. True unity is never built upon blind, unquestioning allegiance to any leader. Furthermore, the apostle Paul said *follow me **as I follow Christ*** (1 Cor. 11:1), the implication being that our first and only allegiance is to Christ. This is where our only true loyalty lies. We are not obligated to follow any corrupt leader who chooses to deviate from following Christ.

The Samuel principle

The young prophet Samuel had to learn to hear and discern the voice of God for himself while being mentored by corrupt leadership. Many emphasize the fact, and rightly so, that it was Eli who helped Samuel to recognize the voice of God—a voice that apparently sounded very similar to that of his mentor and leader, Eli. But what many fail to realize is that the whole purpose of the message given to young Samuel by God was to invalidate the ministry and leadership of Eli and his sons. God was confirming judgment upon Eli's household on account of his disobedience and deficiency in leadership (1 Sam. 3:1–14). He was basically saying to Samuel: "Eli is your mentor and leader, but he is corrupt; therefore, I have rejected him and his household (the entire system of ministry/leadership he represents). But I Am your Lord and Master. Learn to listen to My voice, for it is with Me that your loyalty and allegiance should truly lie."

Micaiah understood this principle, which is why he never faltered or capitulated under the extreme pressure created by this false religious system and counterfeit prophetic order intent on making him conform to this culture of compromise. He was able to ascend to such an elevated degree of spiritual sight that he was able to see right into the very throne-room of God and recount, word for word, what had transpired in His heavenly courts. Only an accurate prophetic dimension which has been totally cleansed of the internal defilement of nationalism and misguided loyalties is capable of ascending to such an elevated level in God (Ps. 24:3–4).

Jeremiah versus Hananiah and the false prophets

Our next example is taken from the book of Jeremiah (chapters 27–28), and it is arguably one of the most profound examples of nationalism recorded in all of Scripture. For the sake of time and space, we will refrain from quoting the entire scripture reference here, but we encourage you to pause here for a moment, mark this page, and read the entire two chapters in one sitting. When you're done, return here, and we'll pick back up where you left off.

The text begins with the prophet Jeremiah receiving the word of the Lord for several nations, including the nation of Judah. The Babylonian empire was rapidly expanding in the Middle East at that time, and the nation of Judah had already been conquered and subjugated by its might, as were other nations. In an attempt to ward off what many considered to be the greatest military threat ever faced in their territory, international coalitions were being formed. One such coalition was the occasion for several key ambassadors being sent to Judah, representing the nations of Edom, Moab, Ammon, Tyre, and Sidon. Jeremiah was commanded to intercept these ambassadors on their way to meeting with King Zedekiah in Jerusalem and command them to relay to their kings (nations) the message he had been given by God. His (God's) message: "I Am God, and it is I alone who set up rulers and mark out their territories by My own power. Nebuchadnezzar, king of Babylon, is one such ruler. He is My servant, and I have ordained that all nations—including man and beast—serve him indefinitely (until his season of dominion is fulfilled). Any nation or kingdom that chooses to violate this divine command by refusing to submit themselves to the service and welfare of the king of Babylon will be punished threefold (by sword, famine and pestilence) until they are consumed by his hand."[35] How is that for the word of the Lord?

This prophetic message, or variations of it, is repeated at least three different times: First to the foreign ambassadors (vs. 2–11), second to Zedekiah (vs. 12–15), and third to the priests (vs. 16–22). Each time the message is given, God warns against listening to the lies being disseminated through a false or counterfeit prophetic order. Clearly, there is a prophetic divergence being described, of which Jeremiah represents the scant minority. On one side stands Jeremiah, singular in his loyalty and devotion to God, declaring that it was God who was shifting the structures of power within the region and transferring the wealth and resources of the nations to Babylon. Even though this powerful nation was the epitome of evil and responsible for many atrocities, including placing multitudes in captivity, uprooting and separating families, robbing nations of their wealth and resource, destroying cities, as well as looting and desecrating God's holy temple, God wanted Judah and the other five nations to seek the interests and welfare of Babylon through servitude. To seek their own interests would bring about their destruction. This meant that Judah and the other nations would be in a state of inevitable and indefinite decline.

On the other side stood a great company of prophets and prognosticators from many nations, each true nationalists who were loyal to their country of citizenship, declaring in complete unison that it was God's will for a righteous rebellion against evil tyranny. They brought "hope" to the fainted hearts by prophesying that better days were ahead and that God was going to restore the nation to its former state, including its wealth, power, and influence. The nation of Babylon was evil; therefore, God would fight for/with them against this great evil. To surrender to this evil and serve Babylon would be to empower the evil to commit greater evil. Sound familiar? I am sure the false prophets of Judah quoted dozens of scriptures to justify their position. The problem is that even though the words sounded good—it was what everyone wanted to hear—and the argument seemed spiritual and compelling, it didn't come from God. He never *sent* or authorized any of these false prophets (v. 15).

Can you imagine how Jeremiah's message sounded against the grand symphony of what these other prophets and prognosticators were declaring? His message would have been interpreted as unpatriotic at best and treasonous or seditious at worst (Jer. 26:8–9, 11). He would have appeared as a false prophet who was supportive and endorsing of evil. And it would have required great faith and boldness to be the lone voice of dissent against the vast and unified chorus of "encouraging" words emanating from the other prophets, mantics, and fatidic prognosticators in the surrounding region.

Shortly after Jeremiah has concluded his message to the foreign ambassadors, king, and priests, he is confronted by the prophet Hananiah in the temple (ch. 28). While not a great deal is known about this prophet from Scripture or historical records, "the definite article ('the prophet from Gibeon') suggests someone well known at the time,"[36] which means that this was a recognized and established prophet in Judah. Also, the fact that he was a native of Gibeon, one of the priestly cities, suggests that Hananiah, like Jeremiah, may have also been a priest. In other words, he was a temple (church) prophet. He administered his prophetic ministry in the same way Jeremiah did. He served faithfully in the temple as a priest, and he was popular, loved, and respected by the people (conjecture). In almost every aspect of his ministry, he appeared to be the real deal. Even Jeremiah found reason to pause and seriously consider what this prophet had to say (v. 6). However, Hananiah clearly doesn't represent God or an accurate and authentic prophetic dimension. Not only is his message nationalistic in nature, but it is a direct contradiction of God's divine intent for the nation as previously expressed through the prophet Jeremiah. Blinded by nationalism, as well as his own misguided loyalties and political bias, Hananiah's message also reveals a corrupt preference for one political party over another. "Hananiah's prediction showed he favored Jeconiah over the vacillating Zedekiah" because he represented the political party that would best fulfill their religious and political agenda to "make Judah great again" through resisting Babylon.[37] No doubt the carnal desire for greater popularity and acceptance further contributed to his error, thus causing him to deliver an oracle that was "attractive in form as well as content,"[38] complete with a reasonably short and definite two-year time fame "meant to bolster the credibility of his false prophecy."[39]

I can almost hear the loud applause and shouts of amen from everyone gathered at the temple upon hearing Hananiah's ear-tickling prophecy. Heck, even the prophet Jeremiah shouted amen! But it is Jeremiah's subsequent statements that provide the profound wisdom necessary for identifying or discerning an accurate prophetic dimension in the midst of two outwardly similar, yet spiritually divergent, streams. Jeremiah establishes the principle of prophetic precedence: When God sends prophets, He usually doesn't send them to sprinkle rose petals on common paths with words of blessing. He sends them to make crooked paths straight by preaching repentance. Therefore, their messages usually consisted of *war, disaster, and pestilence*—God's divine instruments of judgment, correction, and discipline for erring people and nations. In other words, Jeremiah is establishing precedence for a prophetic dimension that establishes God's righteous judgments in the earth through a ministry that brings correction and adjustment wherever/whenever necessary. Jeremiah is not saying that true prophets only prophesy negative words of judgment, which is clearly not the case in Scripture but that their ministry is never defined by a popular or pleasing message. They are never nationalistic. Therefore, whenever there is a digression from this biblical pattern, that prophet and his message should be suspect until the time of fulfillment (v.9; Deut. 18:20–22).

Hananiah's unconditional message of blessing and breakthrough, while ignoring the sinful conditions that precipitated the current crisis, was indicative of a clear digression from prophetic precedent and principle, thus cause for suspicion. He is representative of a corrupt and lawless prophetic order where the emphasis is on blessing and breakthrough instead of true repentance. It is no accident that the name Hananiah means *The Lord has been gracious*,[40] which indicates a clear emphasis—or rather, overemphasis—on the grace, mercy, and goodness of God.[41] But any truth that is overemphasized or taken to an extreme becomes error, and there is no exception with grace (Rom. 6:1). As a matter of fact, it is precisely this type of overemphasis and deception that feeds into a nationalism mentality its unqualified expectations of blessing or favor. It is, therefore, antithetic and antagonistic to an accurate prophetic dimension. It seeks to discredit and dismantle everything the true prophet has built or is building (vs. 10–11), and by doing so weakens the nation's spiritual defenses and increases the impact and forcefulness of God's judgments (vs. 13–14).

Hananiah, and the falsehood he represented, was severely judged by God through Jeremiah and the accurate prophetic dimension he represented. Hananiah died in the space of two months after having given his false prophecy because he *taught rebellion against the Lord* (v. 16). The message is clear: Any prophetic order that is nationalistic or blessing-oriented in its emphasis is spiritually deviant and, despite its uplifting and "encouraging" words, promotes a message and culture of rebellion against God. And any corrupt or lawless prophetic order that teaches rebellion against God must be confronted and judged by an accurate apostolic-prophetic dimension.

Jezebel and the Spirit of Baal

Arguably the most infamous female character in all of Scripture, the name "Jezebel" has become synonymous with a number of different evils, the most common being witchcraft and the exercise of illegitimate control. But Jezebel's true nature and significance far exceed the limited definitions of her individual sins. Though the historical narratives regarding this evil queen are sufficient for providing the context necessary in identifying what Jezebel truly represents, it is only when we get to the end of the New Testament that this revelation is made plain.

> *Nevertheless I have a few things against you, because you allow that woman Jezebel, who calls herself a prophetess, to teach and seduce My servants to commit sexual immorality and eat things sacrificed to idols. And I gave her time to repent of her sexual*

immorality, and she did not repent. Indeed I will cast her into a sickbed, and those who commit adultery with her into great tribulation, unless they repent of their deeds. I will kill her children with death, and all the churches shall know that I am He who searches the minds and hearts. And I will give to each one of you according to your works. (Rev. 2:20–23)

In the Lord's prophetic message to Thyatira, one of the seven worshipping communities mentioned in the book of Revelation, a very clear and unmistakable reference is made to *Jezebel*, the wife of Ahab. In this reference, several key characteristics are identified that provide insight and definition to Jezebel's true symbolic significance.

1. She is a self-called, self-appointed, and self-proclaimed *prophetess*, indicating that she is neither genuine nor authentic (v. 20). Despite her popularity, recognition, and title—just like Hananiah and the false prophets in our previous discussion—she was never truly *sent* or authorized by God (Jer. 27:15, 28:15). It's interesting to note that "the feminine in Hebrew is often used *collectively* to express a multitude," as in *a company of false prophets*,[42] which may indicate that the term *prophetess* is representative of an entire prophetic order. While it is true that the ancient queen Jezebel is never specifically addressed or identified as a "prophetess" in the Old Testament narratives, she is clearly recognized and identified with a false or counterfeit prophetic order (1 Kings 18:19).

2. Her ministry and message, though beguilingly popular, attractive, and enticing, teaches and promotes a culture of rebellion against God through an idolatrous system of worship (v. 20 with Jer. 28:16; Deut. 13:1–5). Note that the Greek word translated as *sexual immorality* is used figuratively here to refer to spiritual adultery, idolatry, or unfaithfulness toward God, which is indicative of a "fundamental departure from the truth."[43] Her corrupt influence

is just as popular, powerful, and pervasive as Jezebel of old, who was able to pervert the entire northern (Israel) and, indirectly, southern (Judah) kingdoms (1 Kings 16:30–33, 21:25).

3.   She is unrepentant, which indicates a resistance or opposition to truth, correction, and/or authentic prophetic revelation. One consistent characteristic we have encountered in all of the false prophets we have examined thus far is their unrepentant resistance and opposition to truth, especially when that truth is made known through an authentic prophetic dimension. Thus, we have Zedekiah and the 400 false prophets rejecting and violently opposing the ministry and message of Micaiah (1 Kings 22:1–25), and Hananiah repeating this trend with Jeremiah (Jer. 28; see also Jer. 20:1–6). Jezebel of old is the personification of this corrupt spiritual principle, having been singularly responsible for the massacre of the true prophets of the Lord in Israel as well as being the primary adversary of the Elijah dimension (1 Kings 18:4; 19:1–2).

4.   The error and corruption represented by this Jezebelic expression is of an internal dimension or nature. The expression, *I am He who searches the minds and hearts* (v. 23), coupled with the imagery of God's eyes being *like a flame of fire* (v. 18), indicates the need for deep and penetrating spiritual discernment with regard to Jezebel and her true nature. Outwardly, she appears accurate and correct (the name Jezebel is sometimes defined as "chaste"),[44] like Hananiah who we examined earlier, but inwardly, she is corrupt and full of defilement. Her internal architecture is deficient and inconsistent with Kingdom values, but she appears as an *angel of light*, thus enabling her to deceive many (2 Cor. 11:14).

The prophetic symbolism of Jezebel, therefore, is crystal clear: She is the personification and representation of a false or counterfeit prophetic order that, though immensely popular and widely accepted, is internally corrupt and aggressively opposed to any authentic Elijah apostolic-prophetic dimension that challenges its idolatrous practice or system of worship. In other words, any false or counterfeit expression of the prophetic is a manifestation of Jezebel! But in order to fully understand and comprehend the corrupt hidden architecture of Jezebel, we must first recognize the spirit operating underneath the surface of this false system.

The root of Jezebel

The name *Jezebel* (*î zĕ būl*) is believed to have derived from a Phoenician name meaning "Baal is the prince."[45] "*Zĕ būl*, a title of Baal, was then distorted into *zebel* ('dung'; cf. 2 Kings 9:37)."[46] Jezebel was also the daughter of Ethbaal, whose name means "Baal is with him."[47] Immediately, we realize that Jezebel was closely associated and identified with someone or something named *Baal*, and this has been her identity since birth. It had become a major part of her spiritual heritage. But not only is Baal a significant aspect of Jezebel's true spiritual identity, but based on the connotation of her name ("Baal is the Prince"), it is Baal who is being actively exalted and enthroned through her life and ministry. As such, Baal represents the idolatrous spiritual principle operating within the context of Jezebel's false prophetic expression. It is this same principle or *doctrine* that our Lord describes as the *depths of satan*, indicating a profundity of insight and knowledge that appears deeply spiritual and godly but is actually antithetical to the Kingdom of God (Rev. 2:24). It becomes an open doorway to the dark side. It is not surprising, then, that Baal became the primary source of Jezebel's power and influence. This begs the question: Who or what is Baal, and how do we recognize its evil influence?

The spirit of Baal

The word *Baal* occurs 166 times in the Old Testament as a noun meaning "lord [master], owner, possessor, or husband."[48] When employed as a proper noun and "applied to a god, it occurs about

90 times"[49] and refers almost exclusively to the principal, primary, and most prominent deity in the Canaanite religious pantheon. This means that the primary and most common usage of "Baal" in Scripture pertains to the given name of a false Canaanite deity or god. This deity was worshiped and venerated as "the storm god and bringer of rain."[50] As such, "Baal was recognized as sustaining the fertility of crops, animals, and people."[51] In order to fully grasp or understand the true significance behind the power and title ascribed to Baal as the "bringer (giver, provider) of rain," one must first recognize the great importance of rain and water in an agrarian culture or society.

> The Canaanites, on the whole, maintained an agricultural economy, which was dependent on the cooperation of nature, the fertility of the field, and the welfare of the support animals needed to raise crops. They lived in a land, where drought was a much greater threat than excessive rain. Thus, its religion focused on rain, nature, and fertility.[52]

Based on this understanding of rain and what it meant to the people dwelling in Canaan, in addition to the clear typology of rain present in Scripture, we can see that rain represents blessing, prosperity, and increase (Isa. 55:10; Mal. 3:10). Without rain, the economy of Canaan came to a crashing halt and famine (lack) ensued. Therefore, when Baal is identified or described as the "bringer of rain," it means that he was worshiped and exalted for his power or ability to provide blessing and prosperity to his people. In other words, Baal is the god of blessing and breakthrough (2 Sam. 5:20–21). It was this aspect of blessing that made this idolatrous system of worship so enticing and seductively appealing to every manner of man, including God's chosen people, and so much so that "it was the Baal cult that provided the greatest and most enduring threat to the development of exclusive Yahweh worship within ancient Israel."[53] It is no wonder that "Baal was a part of the religion of virtually every culture of the ancient Near East."[54] And as a result, this idolatrous system of worship was able to demonstrably pervade the entire area inhabited by the Canaanites.[55]

Ever since Baal's introduction into man's religious context and paradigm of worship, his influence has never waned. Even though we are thousands of years (and miles) removed from the original inhabitants of Canaan and their experiences recorded in Scripture, this distorted view of God and corrupt system of worship is still very active and common today. As a matter of fact, it is the underlying principle and driving force behind every single one of today's world religions, including Christianity. It may appear very biblical, accurate, and godly, but it is highly toxic and destructive, which is why our Lord describes this doctrine or principle as the *depths of satan* (Rev. 2:24). It looks like God because we know that our God is good and He desires to bless us. But here is the key difference: Our heavenly Father wants to bless us, but His blessings are conditioned and contingent on our obedience. The Kingdom of God is based upon the Father's will (obedience) rather than our personal needs (blessing). Therefore, obedience always precedes blessing. But with Baal, this eternal principle is corrupted and blessings are given or meted out unconditionally. There are no requirements to follow or commandments to obey. If there are, "grace" diminishes their importance or minimizes their effect. According to this model, the kingdom is based upon need (what God can do or provide for me), and as Baal is worshiped, he releases his blessings. Sound familiar? Are you beginning to recognize the subtle perversion? In essence, whenever the emphasis of our worship or God's Kingdom becomes more about us and what we want (blessing), rather than about God and what He requires (obedience), we have entered into an idolatrous system of worship and have become joined to the spirit of Baal.

This blessing, or rather, "bless me" model caters to our flesh and not only creates but also perpetuates a corrupt religious culture of self-preservation, self-gratification, and self-indulgence, which is what makes this idolatrous model so immensely popular. Worship is motivated and driven by what we can get from God, who is then viewed as our personal "sugar daddy" (religious Christianity's translation for "father") or "genie in the bottle" who we can command at will to meet our personal needs. Prayer is viewed as a means of obtaining personal blessing or breakthrough, rather than as a means for advancing the Father's will and the Kingdom of God on earth. Prophecy is viewed as an instrument for making people feel better about themselves and for imparting personal or corporate blessing, rather than as a purifying and perfecting agent for accurate building (Mal. 3:1–5). Giving is viewed as a means of obtaining more and getting "blessed," rather than an expression of selfless love. In such a self-centered religious culture, we serve in order to be recognized and promoted. We support ministries based upon the "blessing" or benefits they provide. We attend Bible schools and seminaries for ministerial credentials, titles, and degrees rather than out of a genuine and heartfelt desire to know God. If you want to know what the spirit of Baal and his idolatrous worship culture looks like, you won't need to look very far. It is rampantly practiced all around us while disguised as modern-day Christianity.

It's interesting to note that several of the titles, characteristics, and depictions of Father God (Yahweh) in the Old Testament are very reminiscent of Baal. For example, in Psalm 29, God is depicted in such a way that it is referred to by at least one scholar as "a glorious theophany in the thunderstorm" (remember, Baal is the "storm god")[56] In Psalm 68:4, God is described as He "who rides on the clouds" (see also Ps. 104:3; Nah. 1:3). And elsewhere, God is identified as the provider of rain (1 Kings 18:1; Amos 4:7). The titles of *Lord, Master,* and *husband* (the meaning of Baal) are also ascribed to both the Father and Jesus as God. There are many other examples, but the main point being emphasized here is that the spirit of Baal looks almost exactly like God. This false spirit looks, sounds, and appears so much like God that he has deceived many. Only those with deep and penetrating spiritual sight and discernment to look past the outward manifestations of this spirit, to behold its true nature and character, will be able to escape this deception. The great deception isn't coming; it's already here and has been for quite some time.

Israel's early history with Baal

Sometimes we read the scriptural narratives regarding Israel's continual struggles with Baal, including their tendency as a people to almost completely succumb to Baal's idolatrous influence, and think they must have been a bunch of gullible knuckleheads. But that's because we read the scriptures incorrectly from a disconnected place without fully recognizing, understanding, or identifying with their temptations and struggles. The children of Israel were no different from many of us today. Many of the issues that Israel had with Baal were rooted in the syncretism that occurred very early in the nation's history. Remember, the nation of Israel was not only birthed but spent over four centuries in Egypt, one of the most pagan and corrupt religious cultures in the world. "There is evidence that Baal and other Canaanite deities were worshiped in Egypt, but without becoming a serious menace to the native Egyptian religion."[57] It is difficult to pinpoint the exact period when Egypt came under Baal's influence, but some scholars believe that it was "during the period of the Middle Kingdom [2000–1700 BC], if not earlier," that the Baal cult was adopted by the Egyptians.[58] This means that by the time Jacob and his family migrated and the Israelites had multiplied in Egypt, Baal worship was already an established religious practice in the nation and surrounding region. It was not long before Baal worship became syncretized and fused with the Hebrew religion. Thus, when we get to the Exodus, the evidence of the Israelites' corruption, as well as visible signs of this syncretism, become apparent.

> *Now when the people saw that Moses delayed coming down from the mountain, the people gathered together to Aaron, and said to him, "Come, make us gods that shall go before us; for as for this Moses, the man who brought us up out of the land of Egypt, we do not know what has become of him." And Aaron said to them, "Break off the golden earrings which are in the ears of your wives, your sons, and your daughters, and bring them to me." So all the people*

> *broke off the golden earrings which were in their
> ears, and brought them to Aaron. And he received
> the gold from their hand, and he fashioned it with
> an engraving tool, and made a molded calf. Then
> they said, "This is your god, O Israel, that brought
> you out of the land of Egypt!" So when Aaron saw
> it, he built an altar before it. And Aaron made a
> proclamation and said, "Tomorrow is a feast to the
> Lord." Then they rose early on the next day, offered
> burnt offerings, and brought peace offerings; and
> the people sat down to eat and drink, and rose up to
> play.* (Exod. 32:1–6)

The children of Israel, having recently been liberated from the bondage and oppression of Egypt, are now encamped in the wilderness at the foot of Mount Sinai (Ex. 19:1–2). Moses, their esteemed leader, having been absent from the camp for an extended period ("forty days and forty nights") is somewhere on the top of the mountain communing with God and receiving His divine instructions for the nation. During Moses's absence, the people grow impatient and question if he will ever return. With Moses being a type of Christ, immediately, we see a parallel here between Israel at Mt. Sinai and God's end-time covenant people as they await Christ's return.

Aaron is then approached by the people, in a corporate assembly, demanding of him to make them *gods* (plural) to go before them. He acquiesces to their request by fashioning out of the gold they provided what the NKJV translates as a *molded calf* (v. 4). *Calf*, however, is not the best translation of the Hebrew *'ēgel*, which more accurately refers to a "young bull in his first strength."[59] Since "Baal is represented iconographically by a bull,"[60] this means that the image fashioned by Aaron is most likely to be "the bull into which Baal used to transform himself" and the image or icon in which he was most often represented."[61] But then Aaron takes it a step further by building an altar for Baal upon which "the very offerings Yahweh has specified for himself" are to be offered and proclaims a *feast to the*

Lord, except the word for *Lord* here is *Yahweh*, designating the True and the Living God (v.5).[62] In other words, idolatrous Baal is syncretistically joined and made synonymous with the True God. And it is Aaron, who represents priestly service or ecclesiastical leadership and ministry, who initiates this religious syncretism through an ungodly leadership and ministry model that caters or builds according to public or popular demand. This model has become immensely popular today in a Christian culture where the main goal and objective is to grow larger churches, attract more Facebook or Twitter followers, gain more "likes," and obtain more YouTube views. And since a Baal system of worship and ministry is always engineered or modeled after popular demand—that which people want to hear—it should come as no surprise that the material (gold) used to fashion the Baal image was taken from *the ears* of the people at the command of the presiding priest or minister (vs. 2–4).

The prophetic dimension versus the spirit of Baal

With Moses being away for the purpose of receiving the elevated or high-level commands of God and the people choosing to worship and ascribe their miraculous deliverance from Egypt to Baal, they were, in effect, rejecting the authentic apostolic-prophetic dimension of Moses—with its clear emphasis on accurate Kingdom building through obedience to the divine requirements of God—and substituting it for a licentious and counterfeit kingdom model without any binding laws or strong moral demands. They desired to worship God on *their* own terms, even though the Father had made it clear repeatedly that He would be received and worshiped only on *His* terms,[63] so they created "a god who would let them live as they wished and have a good time when they wanted to and who would not impose his covenant requirements on them,"[64] but still bless them. In such a depraved condition, the people are described later on in the text as *unrestrained*, indicating a lack of discipline or moral restraint, a clear sign of the Baal spirit (v. 25). The word is employed twice in the same verse for emphasis and is the exact Hebrew word used in Proverbs 29:18: "*Where there is no [prophetic] revelation, the people cast off restraint.* "Considering the fact that the author clearly assigns blame to Aaron for his unwillingness or inability to restrain the people, the message is clear: The spirit of Baal can only thrive in the absence of an accurate apostolic-prophetic dimension, and no other priestly (ministerial) paradigm is able to expose or eliminate (stop) it.

We see this principle come into focus again when Moses returns to the camp and finds the idolatrous display of Baal worship taking place amongst the Israelis (v. 19). His immediate reaction is to smash the two stone *tablets of the Testimony*—written by the hand of God Himself and representing the most authentic and unadulterated download of prophetic revelation given to man (v. 16)—at the foot of the mountain. By this profoundly prophetic act, not only was Moses emphasizing the breaking and utter violation of God's holy covenant by His people, but he was confirming that an elevated and authentic prophetic dimension could never co-exist with the spirit of Baal or its idolatrous system of worship. To the degree that one is elevated or magnified, the other is decreased or diminished. You will never be able to access or receive elevated and authentic prophetic revelation with a Baal spirit or model of worship. Conversely, you can never be deceived or corrupted by the spirit of Baal when you are plugged in and connected to an elevated and authentic prophetic dimension. They are mutually exclusive.

Even Joshua, who was positioned somewhere on the mountain between the camp and Moses, was almost deceived by the sound of this idolatrous worship. Scripture records that *when Joshua heard the noise of the people as they shouted*—in praise and celebration unto god (Baal being worshiped as Yahweh)—that he mistook it for the sound of *war in the camp* (v. 17). Remember, this is Israel's military general. If anyone would (or should) have known what true war sounds like, it would (or should) have been Joshua. After all, they had already been in at least one battle (Ex. 17:8–16). Nevertheless, in the ears of Joshua, it sounded like warfare shouts (of prayer or praise). It sounded like God's covenant people engaging in *spiritual* warfare. It wasn't until Joshua came into close proximity with Moses—who had just come from the presence of God and had already been divinely updated about what was happening—that Joshua was able to receive clear and accurate prophetic insight regarding what was truly occurring in the camp of Israel. That wisdom, discernment, and sightedness came as a result of Joshua's close proximity to an accurate and elevated prophetic dimension. Without it, Joshua would have been deceived also.

Baal the war god

It's interesting to note that Baal is often depicted as a warrior, with his weapons being thunder (his voice) and lightning.[65] Even Egyptian references portrayed Baal as the war god."[66] It should come as no surprise, then, that warfare prayer and/or praise would be employed in a Baal system of worship seeking mainly blessing and breakthrough. We see similar warfare-type behavior manifested later on by the false prophets of Baal in their contest with Elijah (1 Kings 18:25–29). Actions such as leaping (or dancing) about the altar (v. 26), loud shouts or war cries (v. 28), and violent armed cutting or wounding (v. 28) are representative of warfare customs, rituals, or techniques. This doesn't necessarily mean that all manifestations of "spiritual" warfare in our meetings should be ascribed to Baal, but it should at least cause us to question whether we are genuinely warring after the Lord of Hosts or after this false idolatrous spirit. True spiritual warfare is *spiritual* and not fleshly or carnal. You can shout until your voice goes out and shadow-box until you're literally dripping in sweat without ever engaging in true spiritual warfare which, according to the apostle Paul, is based upon the principles of self-discipline, self-denial, and obedience—totally foreign concepts to the Baal spirit (1 Cor. 9:26–27; 2 Cor. 10:3–6). Are you "beating the air" or are you exercising true spiritual warfare? Is your warfare motivated by personal need (or greed), blessing, or breakthrough? Then it is clearly Baal. But if it is focused and fueled by a desire to establish God's Kingdom—as our King defines it—then we are truly warring under the banner of the Most High God.

Jezebel and her company of false prophets have been able to effectively erect idolatrous altars unto Baal all over America and across the world. For many of us, these altars appear accurate and normal because they represent a system of worship and religion that is very old, popular, and familiar. Religious traditions are notoriously difficult to break, and when we factor in Baal's territorial nature—he is a territorial spirit, which is why he is often referred to in both the singular and plural, and why his name is often attached to both people and places—we realize that Baal is a major stronghold in people, families, churches, cities, nations, and even regions. But just as the emergence of Elijah during the height of Israel's apostasy in the days of Jezebel and Ahab brought a clear distinction (judgment) between the worship of Yahweh and the cult of Baal, which had previously "coexisted without any problem" after Moses,[67] even so is a new and elevated Elijah-third-prophetic-dimension emerging to expose and judge this idolatrous system *like a refiner's fire and like launderer's soap* (Mal. 3:1–3). As this new Elijah dimension emerges in the earth, a new prophetic landscape will come into view.

Notes

1 Inc Merriam-Webster, *Merriam-Webster's Collegiate Dictionary* (Springfield, MA: Merriam-Webster, Inc., 2003).

2 A. Jeffers, "Magic and Divination," ed. Bill T. Arnold and H. G. M. Williamson, *Dictionary of the Old Testament: Historical Books* (Downers Grove, IL: InterVarsity Press, 2005), 670.

3 Willem VanGemeren, ed., *New International Dictionary of Old Testament Theology & Exegesis* (Grand Rapids, MI: Zondervan Publishing House, 1997), 945.

4 C. Van Dam, "Divination, Magic," ed. Mark J. Boda and Gordon J. McConville, *Dictionary of the Old Testament: Prophets* (Downers Grove, IL; Nottingham, England: IVP Academic; Inter-Varsity Press, 2012), 159.

5 Willem VanGemeren, ed., *New International Dictionary of Old Testament Theology & Exegesis* (Grand Rapids, MI: Zondervan Publishing House, 1997), 945.

6 Lowell K. Handy, "Divination," ed. John D. Barry et al., *The Lexham Bible Dictionary* (Bellingham, WA: Lexham Press, 2016).

7 Ibid.

8 C. Van Dam, "Divination, Magic," ed. Mark J. Boda and Gordon J. McConville, *Dictionary of the Old Testament: Prophets* (Downers Grove, IL; Nottingham, England: IVP Academic; Inter-Varsity Press, 2012), 159.

9 Lowell K. Handy, "Divination," ed. John D. Barry et al., *The Lexham Bible Dictionary* (Bellingham, WA: Lexham Press, 2016).

10 Ulrich Luz, "Matthew: A Commentary," ed. Helmut Koester, *Hermeneia—a Critical and Historical Commentary on the Bible* (Minneapolis, MN: Augsburg, 2001), 348.

11 Craig S. Keener, *Matthew, vol. 1, The IVP New Testament Commentary Series* (Downers Grove, IL: InterVarsity Press, 1997), Mt 16:1.

12 Joanne K. Kuemmerlin-McLean, "Magic: Old Testament," ed. David Noel Freedman, *The Anchor Yale Bible Dictionary* (New York: Doubleday, 1992), 469.

13 Mark Anthony Phelps, "Divination," ed. David Noel Freedman, Allen C. Myers, and Astrid B. Beck, *Eerdmans Dictionary of the Bible* (Grand Rapids, MI: W.B. Eerdmans, 2000), 349.

14 Ex. 7:14–21, 8:1–6, 20–23, 9:1–6, 13–25, 10:1–15, 16:4–14; Num. 16:28–33, 17:1–11; 1 Sam. 2:34; 1 Kings 13:3–5; 2 Kings 20:9–11; Is. 7:14, 44:29–30; Acts 11:28.

15 C. Van Dam, "Divination, Magic," ed. Mark J. Boda and Gordon J. McConville, *Dictionary of the Old Testament: Prophets* (Downers Grove, IL; Nottingham, England: IVP Academic; Inter-Varsity Press, 2012), 162.

16 Samuel Macauley Jackson, ed., *The New Schaff-Herzog Encyclopedia of Religious Knowledge: Embracing Biblical, Historical, Doctrinal, and Practical Theology and Biblical, Theological, and Ecclesiastical Biography from the Earliest Times to the Present Day* (New York; London: Funk & Wagnalls, 1908–1914), 451.

17 C. Van Dam, "Divination, Magic," ed. Mark J. Boda and Gordon J. McConville, *Dictionary of the Old Testament: Prophets* (Downers Grove, IL; Nottingham, England: IVP Academic; Inter-Varsity Press, 2012), 162.

18 Lowell K. Handy, "Divination," ed. John D. Barry et al., *The Lexham Bible Dictionary* (Bellingham, WA: Lexham Press, 2016).

19 Ibid.

20 Ibid.

21 T. Witton Davies, "Divination," ed. James Orr et al., *The International Standard Bible Encyclopaedia* (Chicago: The Howard-Severance Company, 1915), 860.

22 Lowell K. Handy, "Divination," ed. John D. Barry et al., *The Lexham Bible Dictionary* (Bellingham, WA: Lexham Press, 2016).

23 Ibid.

24 Ronald F. Youngblood, F. F. Bruce, and R. K. Harrison, Thomas Nelson Publishers, eds., *Nelson's New Illustrated Bible Dictionary* (Nashville, TN: Thomas Nelson, Inc., 1995).

25 W. Ewing, "Issachar," ed. James Orr et al., *The International Standard Bible Encyclopaedia* (Chicago: The Howard-Severance Company, 1915), 1542.

26 Ralph W. Klein, "1 Chronicles: A Commentary," ed. Thomas Krüger, *Hermeneia—a Critical and Historical Commentary on the Bible* (Minneapolis, MN: Fortress Press, 2006), 324.

27 Carl Friedrich Keil and Franz Delitzsch, *Commentary on the Old Testament*, vol. 3 (Peabody, MA: Hendrickson, 1996), 500.

28 Victor P. Hamilton, *The Book of Genesis, Chapters 1–17, The New International Commentary on the Old Testament* (Grand Rapids, MI: Wm. B. Eerdmans Publishing Co., 1990), 127.

29 K. A. Mathews, *Genesis 1–11:26*, vol. 1A, *The New American Commentary* (Nashville: Broadman & Holman Publishers, 1996), 154.

30 Hans Dieter Betz, *Galatians: A Commentary on Paul's Letter to the Churches in Galatia, Hermeneia—a Critical and Historical Commentary on the Bible* (Philadelphia: Fortress Press, 1979), 218.

31 The word *adulterous* in the Greek is used metaphorically to describe a person who has been unfaithful toward God (as an adulteress is unfaithful to her husband) as well as those who have neglected God and their duty toward Him. It was also used to describe those who had forsaken God to serve false gods or idols. The word *wicked* carries the connotation of someone evil, slothful, or morally corrupt.

32 "Nationalism." *Merriam-Webster.com*, Merriam-Webster, www.merriam-webster.com/dictionary/nationalism. Accessed 2017.

33 John D. Barry et al., Faithlife Study Bible (Bellingham, WA: Lexham Press, 2012, 2016), 1 Ki 22:6.

34 Ludwig Koehler et al., The Hebrew and Aramaic Lexicon of the Old Testament (Leiden: E. J. Brill, 1994–2000), 370.

35 Author's paraphrase.

36 William Lee Holladay, "Jeremiah 2: A Commentary on the Book of the Prophet Jeremiah," Chapters 26–52, ed. Paul D. Hanson, *Hermeneia—a Critical and Historical Commentary on the Bible* (Minneapolis, MN: Fortress Press, 1989), 127.

37 Charles L. Feinberg, "Jeremiah," in *The Expositor's Bible Commentary: Isaiah, Jeremiah, Lamentations, Ezekiel*, ed. Frank

E. Gaebelein, vol. 6 (Grand Rapids, MI: Zondervan Publishing House, 1986), 548.

[38] Gerald L. Keown, *Jeremiah 26–52*, vol. 27, *Word Biblical Commentary* (Dallas: Word, Incorporated, 1998), 54.

[39] Charles L. Feinberg, "Jeremiah," in *The Expositor's Bible Commentary: Isaiah, Jeremiah, Lamentations, Ezekiel*, ed. Frank E. Gaebelein, vol. 6 (Grand Rapids, MI: Zondervan Publishing House, 1986), 548.

[40] F. B. Huey, Jeremiah, *Lamentations*, vol. 16, *The New American Commentary* (Nashville: Broadman & Holman Publishers, 1993), 246.

[41] While it is true that mercy triumphs over judgment, the prerequisite for this mercy is that one must first acknowledge and submit to God's righteous judgments (Jam. 2:13).

[42] Robert Jamieson, A. R. Fausset, and David Brown, *Commentary Critical and Explanatory on the Whole Bible,* vol. 2 (Oak Harbor, WA: Logos Research Systems, Inc., 1997), 557.

[43] Marvin Richardson Vincent, *Word Studies in the New Testament,* vol. 2 (New York: Charles Scribner's Sons, 1887), 455.

[44] Joseph Henry Thayer, *A Greek-English Lexicon of the New Testament: Being Grimm's Wilke's Clavis Novi Testamenti* (New York: Harper & Brothers., 1889), 298.

[45] Chad Brand et al., eds., "Jezebel," *Holman Illustrated Bible Dictionary* (Nashville, TN: Holman Bible Publishers, 2003), 921.

[46] Gale A. Yee, "Jezebel (Person)," ed. David Noel Freedman, *The Anchor Yale Bible Dictionary* (New York: Doubleday, 1992), 848.

[47] Chris A. Rollston, "Ethbaal," ed. David Noel Freedman, Allen C. Myers, and Astrid B. Beck, *Eerdmans Dictionary of the Bible* (Grand Rapids, MI: W.B. Eerdmans, 2000), 431.

[48] James Newell, "Baal," ed. Chad Brand et al., *Holman Illustrated Bible Dictionary* (Nashville, TN: Holman Bible Publishers, 2003), 152.

[49] W. Herrmann, "Baal," ed. Karel van der Toorn, Bob Becking, and Pieter W. van der Horst, *Dictionary of Deities and Demons in*

the Bible (Leiden; Boston; Köln; Grand Rapids, MI; Cambridge: Brill; Eerdmans, 1999), 132.

50 Winfried Corduan, "Baal," ed. John D. Barry et al., *The Lexham Bible Dictionary* (Bellingham, WA: Lexham Press, 2016).

51 Ibid.

52 Ibid.

53 John Day, "Baal (Deity)," ed. David Noel Freedman, *The Anchor Yale Bible Dictionary* (New York: Doubleday, 1992), 547.

54 Winfried Corduan, "Baal," ed. John D. Barry et al., *The Lexham Bible Dictionary* (Bellingham, WA: Lexham Press, 2016).

55 W. Herrmann, "Baal," ed. Karel van der Toorn, Bob Becking, and Pieter W. van der Horst, *Dictionary of Deities and Demons in the Bible* (Leiden; Boston; Köln; Grand Rapids, MI; Cambridge: Brill; Eerdmans, 1999), 133.

56 John Day, "Baal (Deity)," ed. David Noel Freedman, *The Anchor Yale Bible Dictionary* (New York: Doubleday, 1992), 548.

57 Moisés Silva and Merrill Chapin Tenney, *The Zondervan Encyclopedia of the Bible,* A-C (Grand Rapids, MI: The Zondervan Corporation, 2009), 464–465.

58 W. Herrmann, "Baal," ed. Karel van der Toorn, Bob Becking, and Pieter W. van der Horst, *Dictionary of Deities and Demons in the Bible* (Leiden; Boston; Köln; Grand Rapids, MI; Cambridge: Brill; Eerdmans, 1999), 133.

59 R. Alan Cole, "Exodus: An Introduction and Commentary," vol. 2, *Tyndale Old Testament Commentaries* (Downers Grove, IL: InterVarsity Press, 1973), 223.

60 Mark Anthony Phelps, "Baal," ed. David Noel Freedman, Allen C. Myers, and Astrid B. Beck, *Eerdmans Dictionary of the Bible* (Grand Rapids, MI: W.B. Eerdmans, 2000), 134.

61 R. Alan Cole, "Exodus: An Introduction and Commentary," vol. 2, *Tyndale Old Testament Commentaries* (Downers Grove, IL: InterVarsity Press, 1973), 223.

62 John I. Durham, "Exodus," vol. 3, *Word Biblical Commentary* (Dallas: Word, Incorporated, 1998), 422.

63 Ibid.

[64] Douglas K. Stuart, "Exodus," vol. 2, *The New American Commentary* (Nashville: Broadman & Holman Publishers, 2006), 669.

[65] Mark S. Smith and Simon B. Parker, "Ugaritic Narrative Poetry," vol. 9, *Writings from the Ancient World* (Atlanta, GA: Scholars Press, 1997), 247.

[66] Willem VanGemeren, ed., *New International Dictionary of Old Testament Theology & Exegesis* (Grand Rapids, MI: Zondervan Publishing House, 1997), 422.

[67] W. Herrmann, "Baal," ed. Karel van der Toorn, Bob Becking, and Pieter W. van der Horst, *Dictionary of Deities and Demons in the Bible* (Leiden; Boston; Köln; Grand Rapids, MI; Cambridge: Brill; Eerdmans, 1999), 137.

7

THE NEW PROPHETIC LANDSCAPE

THE PROPHETIC MINISTRY, as we have known and practiced it, is in a season of significant upgrade and radical revision from heaven. In the midst of this divine activity and heavenly initiative, a new (third) prophetic dimension has emerged, signaling a clear break and divergence from the old prophetic order. If you have stuck with us since we started this journey, thoughtfully, prayerfully, and patiently tracking with us through every God-inspired chapter, you now understand the key issues relative to this divergence as well as the distinguishing characteristics of the third prophetic dimension. But you also understand that there is a dangerously false and counterfeit prophetic order—represented by Jezebel and her prophets of Baal— that is actively engaged in establishing idolatrous altars of worship, in addition to being deathly opposed and antagonistic to any elevated or accurate Elijah prophetic dimension. This means that the season for compromise and/or peaceful coexistence has come to an end.

Conflicts, Contentions, and Contests

During Elijah's first prophetic reformation and encounter with the false prophetic order of Jezebel, the prophetic landscape was defined by conflicts, contentions, and contests. This translated into major persecution for the true prophets of God, who were vastly outnumbered by the false yet popular prophets of Baal in an apostate religious system that was widely accepted and established in Israel. Prophets were being slaughtered, and the remaining survivors were hiding out in caves. This made for a very stressful time to be a prophet, especially a true prophet of God. But the fire of persecution also brought its benefits, one of them being the sifting out of the glory-seekers and the insincere—those not truly called or anointed by God—who were unwilling to suffer and die to be the true voice of God in the earth.

Similarly, today, you can expect major conflicts and contentions to arise between these two divergent streams and a new sifting to occur. There will never be a peaceful coexistence between the two, and Jezebel's evil intention to destroy Elijah has not changed. If anything, it has only intensified. Jezebel may not be able to inflict physical death as in the days of old, but she is still capable of inflicting death and separation in many other ways. For example, have you ever wondered where the hundreds of *prophets of Baal* and *prophets of Asherah* came from (1 Kings 18:19)? Scripture does not exactly tell us, but in the absence of any evidence to the contrary, we have to assume that they were native Israelis who were former worshipers and/or prophets of Yahweh before they were seduced and corrupted. The remaining prophets who escaped the sword of Jezebel and her corrupting influence were hidden away in a cave and silenced. The tragedy is that when Elijah finally emerged and issued a challenge to these false prophets, none of the true prophets in hiding had the courage or boldness to emerge from their caves and stand with Elijah in solidarity. They were too terrified, thus leaving Elijah to stand alone against an entire company of false prophets without any spiritual or moral support (1 Kings 18:22). No wonder he almost suffered a spiritual burnout at the end of it. Any of us would. What good is a prophet if he has no voice? Jezebel may not have been able to take the lives of these prophets in hiding, but she was still successful in taking away their voice and ministry.

If you have been like one of those cave prophets in hiding, or even one of the *seven thousand...whose knees have not bowed to Baal* (1 Kings 19:18), you are deserving of honor for your resistance to the defilement of Jezebel and your unwillingness to compromise truth. But much more is required of you. It is not enough to just resist and stand idly by while others who are proclaiming the true mind of God—an unpopular message—are forced to stand alone. It is time to come out of hiding. It is time to emerge from your cave and be the prophetic voice that God has called you to be. It is time to join hands, come alongside of, and support the Elijahs of this new prophetic divergence. Our impact and influence is limited when we stand alone, but together, we create the synergy to become a powerful and persuasive voice. Jezebel will try to intimidate us. She will try to silence us. We will be rejected, defamed, and cast aside as worthless. We will be falsely accused, oppressed, and unjustly treated, but these are marks of an accurate prophetic dimension that has always been closely associated with suffering in Scripture (Jam. 5:10).

Executing God's judgments

Do not believe, even for one moment, that this is a totally one-sided conflict or affair, in favor of Jezebel and Baal as the sole aggressors. Remember, Jezebel represents any false or counterfeit prophetic order, and Baal represents an idolatrous or perverted system of worship with a self-indulgent emphasis on attaining personal blessing, prosperity, or breakthrough. They are two sides of the same coin. Where you find one, you will usually find the other. When we encountered this Jezebel dimension in Hananiah as he opposed the true prophetic dimension represented by Jeremiah, the divine sentence was death (Jer. 28:15–17). This divine sentence was imposed again upon other false prophets by Jeremiah (Jer. 29:21–32). And we see the same divine sentence once again issued by Moses upon the children of Israel in their worship of Baal at Mt. Sinai (Ex. 32:26–28). In this particular instance relative to Moses, a divine blessing is decreed upon the *sons of Levi* for their willingness to execute God's judgment without respect or regard for personal loyalties or human preferences [family, friends, leaders, mentors, etc.] (Ex. 32:29). This divine principle has not changed. There must be a "no tolerance" policy against Jezebel and the spirit of Baal—any prophet, prophecy, or system or worship that teaches rebellion against the Most High God. And wherever this type of spiritual rebellion is found, it must be sentenced to death without regard to any personal loyalties or human preferences. We must show it (not the people practicing it) no mercy!

When Elijah had issued a prophetic challenge or contest to the false prophets of Baal and Asherah, it was for this very purpose—to expose their defilement and falsehood in order to execute God's eternal judgments upon them.

> *Then it happened, when Ahab saw Elijah, that Ahab said to him, "Is that you, O troubler of Israel?" And he answered, "I have not troubled Israel, but you and your father's house have, in that you have forsaken the commandments of the Lord and have followed the Baals. Now therefore, send and gather all Israel to me on Mount Carmel, the four hundred and fifty prophets of Baal, and the four hundred prophets of Asherah, who eat at Jezebel's table." So Ahab sent for all the children of Israel, and gathered the prophets together on Mount Carmel. And Elijah came to all the people, and said, "How long will you falter between two opinions? If the Lord is God, follow Him; but if Baal, follow him." But the people answered him not a word. Then Elijah said to the people, "I alone am left a prophet of the Lord; but Baal's prophets are four hundred and fifty men. Therefore let them give us two bulls; and let them choose one bull for themselves, cut it in pieces, and lay it on the wood, but put no fire under it; and I will prepare the other bull, and lay it on the wood, but put no fire under it. Then you call on the name of your gods, and I will call on the name of the Lord;*

and the God who answers by fire, He is God." So all
the people answered and said, "It is well spoken." (1
Kings 18:17–24)

I have heard this passage of scripture taught or preached over
a dozen times, and every time the story is portrayed or applied in
such a way that it is Elijah—representing the true prophet—against
a clearly recognizable group of "psychics" or occult practitioners. Of
course, nothing could be further from the truth. This is not a contest against forces *outside* the religious context and community of
Israel but *within*! If the error was blatant and easily recognizable, the
entire nation would not have been deceived, and a contest would not
have been necessary. But the people were straddling the proverbial
fence between Yahweh and Baal, between Elijah and the false prophets. There was no spiritual sight or discernment to correctly judge
between the two. And with the major and most highly established
voices in the nation, i.e. Ahab, casting doubt and suspicion upon
Elijah with false accusations of being the "troubler of Israel" (v.17),
coupled with the popular and sensual appeal of Baal worship, it is
easy to see why the people were double-minded and confused. The
whole point of this contest, therefore, was not so much about *manifestation*—as in who had the superior power to call fire down from
heaven—as it was about *validation*! In Scripture, whenever there was
a supernatural manifestation of fire from heaven, it usually communicated either divine approval or divine judgment (Lev. 9:24, 10:2;
Num. 11:1, 16:35; 1 Chron. 21:26; 2 Chron. 7:1).

In this particular context, God was validating Elijah and the
accurate prophetic dimension he represented. God was officially
confirming and putting His stamp of approval upon Elijah and his
prophetic activity. At the same time, God was also invalidating, officially rejecting, and pronouncing divine judgment upon the counterfeit and corrupt prophetic order represented by the prophets of Baal.
He exposed their impotence and rejected their pseudo-prophetic
activity—including their laborious "spiritual" warfare and prolonged
prophesying (vs. 27–29). Were it not for God's divine fire of illu-
mination and judgment, the Baal company of false prophets would

have appeared the most accurate based on their actions alone. They prayed, prophesied, and warred patiently and passionately for the better part of an entire day. Imagine going to a church or meeting and finding a company of prophets engaged in similar activity so passionately. Wouldn't you be impressed? But God wasn't because He doesn't see as man sees. He looked past their outward display of passionate religious activity and saw that the spirit and internal principle by which they operated was incorrect. But when He looked at Elijah and the altar he had built (or rebuilt), He saw accurate architecture and a prophetic dimension characterized by correctness. If you read the entire story, you will realize that not only did the fire of God fall and consume the sacrifice, but it consumed the entire altar he had built unto God, including the water that had been poured upon it (vs. 30–38). In other words, God was saying that not only was Elijah's worship and ministry correct, but also, the design and architecture of his prophetic building.

Once God had pulled back the veil of darkness and provided open validation for those who were willing to see, it was time to execute His righteous judgments on the now exposed apostate order. The prophets of Baal were thus seized and executed according to the same death sentence pronounced by Moses and Jeremiah. It will require similar divine validation and judgment in our present-day prophetic divergence. And God's validation will be made evident in those He answers. For just as Elijah was able to spiritually accomplish in less than a minute what the false prophets of Baal were unable to do in the better part of a day, even so will those who have been approved by God receive answers from heaven almost effortlessly. These divine answers will be in response to their accurate faith and obedience in honoring God and hallowing His name above all else.

The false prophets of today may be passionate in their expert display of pseudo-spiritual warfare. They may be able to prophesy quite impressively (lengthy and detailed) in their ungodly pursuit of greater blessing and breakthrough, but they will receive no answers from God and will be sorely lacking in true prophetic fulfillment. In other words, God's invalidation and rejection will be made known in those whom He chooses to ignore. Once God's righteous judgments have been made known, we must then choose to exercise it immediately and thoroughly, without regard for personal loyalties or human preference. We must execute Jezebel and the false prophets of Baal, and we can practically accomplish this by refusing to support or follow these false ministers or ministries. Leave their churches. Unsubscribe from their email lists. Unfollow them on Twitter and Facebook. Refuse to buy or read their books. Death implies total separation, which is totally consistent with New Testament apostolic teaching (2 Thess. 3:6; 1 Tim. 6:3–5; 2 Tim. 3:1–5). To do otherwise is to rebel against God and *falter between two opinions* (v. 21). Why be a partaker in another man's sins (Eph. 5:6–7)?

Wisdom Versus Warfare

The prophetic movement has long been closely associated with spiritual warfare. But while there is certainly a legitimate spiritual warfare dimension to the prophetic, as evidenced by Elijah's conflict with Jezebel and the false prophets of Baal, there is a major difference in principle with how this warfare is fought or exercised. For example, in Elijah's spiritual contest with Baal and his false prophets, his spiritual warfare is exercised through internal correctness, personal obedience, and accurate building. There is absolutely nothing visibly warfare-like in his ministry or actions during this contest. Even his prayer to God was short and revealed a clear and unmistakable emphasis on God and the glory of His name. His prayer was never focused on, neither did it at any one time address, Baal. Sure, Elijah did execute all the false prophets of Baal at the end of the contest, but by this time, the real spiritual warfare was already over and he had already won. He was just executing the judgments written—post warfare!

What is usually described as "spiritual" warfare today and closely associated with the present-day old-order prophetic movement can be more accurately defined as a Baalistic expression of pseudo-spiritual warfare. This type of warfare, as evidenced by the behavior and actions of the false prophets of Baal, is focused on outward religious performance without regard for any true inner (spiritual) reality. As mentioned before, their actions of leaping about (or dancing), shouting, and violent armed assault (cutting) with swords and lances are representative of customary warfare practices we see even today. Their long, passionate, aggressive, and militant prayer and prophesying—though outwardly impressive to those so religiously inclined—were impotent and superficial because there was no internal principle of obedience (2 Cor. 10:3–6). In reality, all of their "prophetic" warfare activity was vain and amounted to nothing more than beating the air (1 Cor. 9:26–27).

The Davidic delusion

Unfortunately, it is this superficial expression of spiritual warfare that is most often ascribed to the prophetic today. This error, overemphasis, and misuse of the warfare concept has spawned other erroneous beliefs or doctrines within the movement, including what I refer to as the "Davidic delusion." According to this false teaching, David's tabernacle—the temporary tent of meeting built by David for housing the ark of the covenant and worship—was intended by God to be a prophetic model for new covenant worship and the present-day prophetic movement. It is hinged upon an inaccurate interpretation of Amos 9:11 and Acts 15:16–17, and it is incorrect for the following reasons:

1. The prophecy given by Amos and then quoted by the apostle James in the book of Acts regarding the *tabernacle of David* being rebuilt is interpreted by most scholars to refer "to the restoration of the 'house' or family of David and thus to the promised Davidic kingdom,"[1] not the physical tabernacle that David erected for the ark (1 Chron. 15:1, 16:1). This is not to say that neither context allows for any other interpretation; it just means neither context allows for this interpretation of it being the physical and temporary tent that he constructed.

2. If the temporary tent that David erected for the ark of the covenant held any prophetic significance for a present or

future model of worship or prophetic activity, why would David have expressed dissatisfaction with it (2 Sam. 7:1–2)? And why would God then command Solomon to build the temple that would far supersede the tent that David had constructed (1 Chron. 22:7–19)? This temple, by the way, was built according to the architectural blueprint and design given to David by the Spirit of God (1 Chron. 28:10–19). In other words, Solomon may have built the temple, but it was by God's intent and design given to David. The tabernacle or temporary tent erected by David had no divine architecture like the tabernacle of Moses or the temple of Solomon because he received no divine instruction or direction to build it. Thus, there could be no divine or prophetic significance in its construction.

3.   The tabernacle of David never received any divine validation from heaven, thus making it inferior. The tabernacle of Moses received divine validation because it was built and constructed according to divine architecture and design. Thus, upon its completion, the tabernacle of Moses was filled with God's glory (Ex. 40:16–35). A similar occurrence took place upon completion of the temple of Solomon, thus indicating divine validation also (2 Chron. 5; 7:1–3). But there is no such recorded occurrence for the tabernacle of David, not even close. It is, therefore, ludicrous to believe that God would seek to perpetuate what He has chosen not to validate. This doesn't necessarily mean that what David built in erecting the temporary tent was wrong; it simply means that it holds no divine or prophetic significance for us today as a model for worship or prophetic activity.

Here is why the Davidic model can never provide an accurate pattern for the prophetic:

*But God said to me, "You shall not build a house for
My name, because you have been a man of war and
have shed blood." (1 Chron. 28:3)*

David was disqualified from building a house for God because
he was a *man of war*. The principle here is that you can never effectively build anything for God while operating from a paradigm or
mentality of warfare. Put another way, whenever warfare becomes a
significant part of our spiritual identity, we are divinely disqualified
from engaging in any heavenly building initiatives. It is impossible
to build and wage war at the same time. And since an accurate prophetic dimension is always focused and engaged in building accurate
divine architecture in the earth, the Davidic model must be rejected.
Prophets who have taken on this false "warfare" identity in their lives
and ministries, constantly expending time and energy fighting battle
after battle—imaginary or otherwise—with unseen spiritual forces,
have thus disqualified themselves from entering into a true apostolic-prophetic dimension.

The priority and prerequisite of wisdom

God chose and commissioned David's son, Solomon, to build
His temple because Solomon operated from a position of rest, and
his heart was attuned to seeking after wisdom (1 Chron. 28:6; 2
Chron. 1:7–12). Building requires wisdom, which is why the apostle Paul referred to himself as a *wise master builder* (Prov. 24:3–4; 1
Cor. 3:10). Wisdom is not only the mark of the apostolic but the
prophetic as well. Furthermore, wisdom is described in Scripture as
being not only *better than strength* but also *better than weapons of war*
(Eccl. 9:16, 18). In other words, wisdom is better than warfare! It is
also described as *the principal thing*, indicating that it is of primary
importance and priority (Prov. 4:7). This explains why the kingdom
was only firmly established under the rule of Solomon and not under
the rule of David (2 Sam. 7:13–16).

As this new third prophetic dimension emerges in the earth,
the divergence between the old prophetic order will become more

apparent. One will be defined by an emphasis on warfare, with little to no results and the absence of any authentic building architecture, just like the prophets of Baal. The other will be defined by wisdom, requiring much less effort with far greater results, and accompanied by accurate and authentic building of divine architecture in the earth. This is what we saw with Elijah in his contest with the prophets of Baal. He built (or rebuilt) an altar unto the Lord in wisdom and established a correct pattern of worship and prophetic activity that heaven could not deny. It will require similar wisdom—not warfare, at least not as we have come to define it—to establish the Kingdom of God in the earth today. This does not mean that we ignore the fact that we have a spiritual enemy or pretend that he does not exist. It means that we are no longer "beating the air" in pseudo-spiritual warfare. Rather, we are establishing God's Kingdom and enforcing the enemy's defeat through the wisdom of God, personal obedience, and death to self (Rev. 12:11). Even so, it is time to make ready for our Master's return.

Notes

[1]   David G. Peterson, "The Acts of the Apostles," *The Pillar New Testament Commentary* (Grand Rapids, MI; Nottingham, England: William B. Eerdmans Publishing Company, 2009), 431.

To order books and other resources by Robert Paul or to make contact for ministry requests, please use the information provided below:

Kingdom Ambassadors International
177 Apostles Way, Box J
Santa Rosa Beach, FL 32459
1-888-NOW-4KAI (1-888-669-4524)

E-mail:
ambassadors@kaiembassy.com or
invitation@kaiembassy.com

Visit us on the web:
www.kaiembassy.com
www.facebook.com/kaiembassy
www.twitter.com/KAIEmbassy7

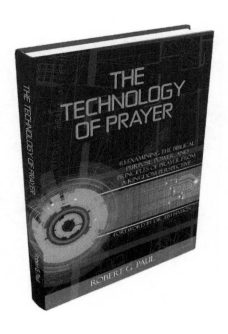

The Technology of Prayer

Prayer is by far the most common and familiar religious practice known to man. However, do we really know *how* to pray? Why did both Jesus and John the Baptist find it necessary to teach their disciples—religious Jews who were supposedly already very familiar with the concept and practice of prayer—how to pray?

In *The Technology of Prayer*, you will discover the biblical science or technology of prayer that causes it to be focused and effectual in reproducing and establishing God's Kingdom architecture here on earth.

ISBN-10: 1493511637
ISBN-13: 978-1493511631

Available from amazon.com and other online sellers.

ABOUT THE AUTHOR

ROBERT G. PAUL is the president and founder of Kingdom Ambassadors International, an embassy dedicated to the promotion and proclamation of God's Kingdom agenda in the earth, as well as the establishing of new reformation positions and patterns throughout the global community of Kingdom citizens otherwise known as the Church.

Robert is a born native of the beautiful twin island republic of Trinidad and Tobago, where he faithfully served for more than a decade as a musician, worship leader, Bible teacher, and coordinator of a successful outreach program to the public schools before migrating to the United States during the turn of the new millennium.

Robert is an avid student of the Word as well as an able minister of the Spirit, with a strong reformation mentality and Kingdom thrust. He ministers with a notable apostolic, prophetic, and teaching grace with almost three decades of diverse ministry experience and leadership development behind him. He is also a graduate of Christian International's School of Theology and has served on staff at CI—the ministry of Dr. Bill Hamon—for over fifteen years. His heart is to see the Body of Christ built up and His people matured so that they accurately demonstrate the Kingdom.

CPSIA information can be obtained
at www.ICGtesting.com
Printed in the USA
BVHW030748221121
622221BV00005B/31

9 781641 400039